BISIA & ISHAM
The Countess & the P.O.W.

Toni Reavis

Copyright © 2022 Toni Reavis

All rights reserved. No part of this book may be reproduced or transmitted in any form or by any means, electronic or mechanical, including photocopying, recording, or by any information storage and retrieval system, without permission in writing from the publisher.

Cleveland Circle Press—San Diego, Ca.
ISBN: 979-8-9871080-0-0
ISBN: 979-8-987-1080-1-7
Library of Congress Control Number: 2022920193
Title: *BISIA & ISHAM: The Countess & The P.O.W.*
Author: Toni Reavis
Digital distribution | 2022
Paperback | 2022

In Memory of Mom & Pop

"I think that, as life is action and passion, it is required of a man that he should share the passion and action of his time at peril of being judged not to have lived."

—Oliver Wendell Holmes, Jr., Memorial Day speech to U.S. Civil War veterans, Keene, N.H., 30 May 1884

Table of Contents

Preface vii
Map xi
One— Bisia... 1
Two— Lesko 16
Three— Isham 25
Four— Leaving Home 32
Five— Zagórz.. 42
Six— Visit to Lesko 53
Seven— Pearl Harbor 59
Eight— Gestapo.. 65
Nine— Besko Lure 74
Ten— Officer Material 81
Eleven— A Machine Gun, What Else? 87
Twelve— Sunday Morning in Your Heart 96
Thirteen— Skirmish 107
Fourteen— C'est La Guerre 114
Fifteen— Searching For Jas... 122
Sixteen— Escape 126
Seventeen— The Artists' Café 139
Eighteen— Old Bishop 146
Nineteen— Wedding Day 151
Twenty— Another Damn Fool Thing 158
Twenty-One— Home 161
Twenty-Two— Kraków.. 165
Twenty-Three— Gee Whiz Doesn't Work Anymore..... 172
Twenty-Four— The Green Frontier 179
Twenty-Five— Nuremberg... 188
Twenty-Six— Reunited 199
PostScript.. 212
Author's Note 216
Selected Bibliography 218
Chronology 219
Index 221
About the Author 226

Preface

On Valentine's Day 1945, two soldiers met in a small café in Lublin, Poland, both caught in the tragic and uncertain currents of a world at war. 23-year-old Countess Elżbieta (Bisia) Krasicka was a lieutenant in the Polish Home Army, fighting for her nation's doomed freedom. 33-year-old Isham Reavis was lieutenant in the U.S. Army, an escaped prisoner of war, searching for an American mission. Neither spoke the other's language. Yet 11 days later they married, beginning a life of 64 years together. These are the tales that led to their meeting in the Artists Café in Lublin, and Bisia's subsequent escape from Soviet-occupied Poland as she sought to reunite with the husband she barely knew.

As one of Bisia and Isham's three children, I grew up with remnants of their story scattered throughout my childhood, like artifacts from a perished museum. Untold stories hung behind the ribbon-strung medals framed in an upstairs hall. Details lay muted within the sepia-toned pictures sequestered in black-matted photo albums. But I also saw traces of their story in my parents' eyes, in the flashes of anger and intolerance, and heard echoes in the frustrations and recriminations that might otherwise have gone unspoken if not for the war that shaped the remainder of their lives.

Still, while known in its skeletal form, the body of their story remained inanimate, absent the sinew and breath of detail to bring it to life. Not until a post-Christmas letter arrived from Mom in 1983 did evidence of a pulse first come to life.

December 29, 1983
My very dear one,

Who writes to whom?
What about?
Why?
Words,

Whimsical thoughts,
Wisps of oneself,
Winding their way,
Whispering,
Weeping,
While life
Whirls by.

It is a shame one can't express adequately all one holds inside. Maybe, one day, we will write that book we spoke about, its title: Shadows and Silhouettes. Some events, as well as people, cast shadows on one's life, while others are etched in one's being and their outline remains clear and strong forever. There are many shadows, fewer silhouettes.

 The winter, being as harsh as it is, prevented us from going to the woods this weekend. I missed the open space and the peace nature gives with such generosity.

 All my love, happy New Year, and all the very best for your birthday.

 Mom

 P.S. In darkness, so many things seem brighter: stars, thoughts, and tears. It is night.

&

Though expressing her feelings more fervently than ever, the poignancy of the PostScript spoke in Mom's familiar accent of reticence. Thus did these stories sink back into their deep, sheltered silence, where they remained until 14 February 1985, when a random call home finally brought them fully and lastingly to light.

 "Hi, Pop."

 "Oh, hi, Tone."

 Turning from the receiver, he called out, "Bisia, Toni is on the phone."

 "I just called to see how you two are doing."

 "Hi, Anton."

 Mom joined us on an upstairs extension.

 "We were just sitting here remembering it was on this day forty years ago that we met, your father and I."

"Yes, in Lublin, Poland, in the Artist's Cafe," Pop said, speaking as so many long-married couples do to complete the thought of his partner. *"Sounds strange today, doesn't it? But things happened during the war and you just did them. You didn't analyze, you acted."*

After the many years of silence, I had stumbled upon Mom and Pop's private reminiscence of the most consequential time of their lives, and the antecedent to my own.

We spent the next several hours opening long closed portals of memory, establishing the outline and tone of a full narrative. Before hanging up, we agreed I could continue to draw out their tales as I wished, though it would require many such calls and many travels for their full story to emerge.

And so, from the secret code they devised to communicate while separated, to the forged identification papers, and the medals: his, the Silver Star for gallantry in action, her two awarded by the Polish government to a resistance fighter who was born in a castle, in the following pages we hear tales that bear witness to the indomitable Polish character and enduring American spirit, even as we take a measure of the tectonic upheavals of war itself.

***

Map

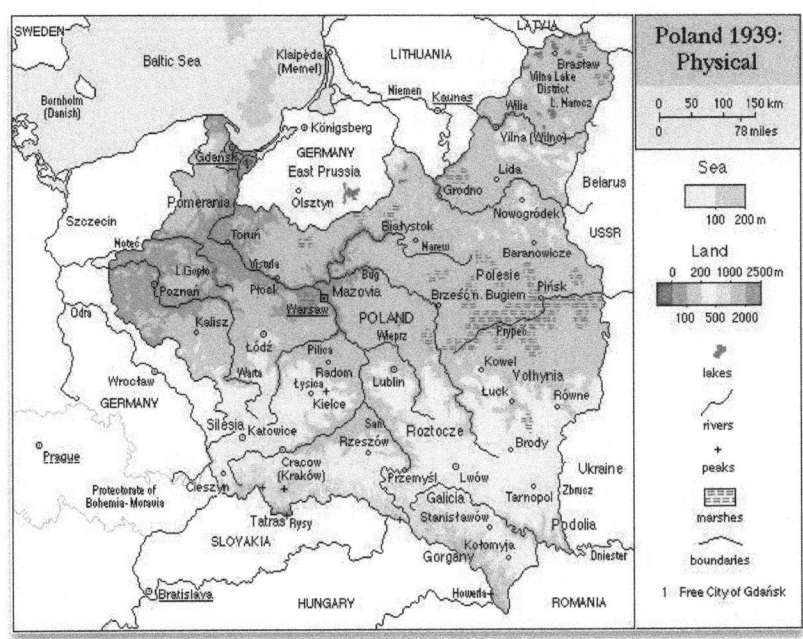

By: Mariusz Paździora

1
BISIA

~ November 4, 1945 ~

*T*oday, I am 24. By writing my memories, I want to relive once more both the good and the bad of the past years, as I live now in the world of dreams. I want to write so my children can learn what their mother loved in her youth. I will be frank and self-critical, giving facts, chronology, and real names as best I can.

There is a picture of Lesko in front of me, the home of my childhood. I look at it now with the eyes of a child.

*

One month later, on Tuesday, December 4, 1945, the same day the U.S. Senate voted 65 to 7 to approve American participation in the United Nations, Elżbieta K. Reavis stood on the deck of the *Belgian Unity*, a Liberty Class freighter bound for New York City out of Antwerp. Everything she owned she carried in a single pigskin leather bag: two dresses she bought in Nuremberg, a sweater, some underwear, one pair of shoes, and the little French-English dictionary she kept from her escape out of Kraków.

As the clean sea breeze brushed along her brow, Bisia looked back at the only world she had ever known as it slipped from view. The previous six years had shattered much of that world, so, too, many of its people. Some, like Bisia, now found themselves scattering like wind-blown seeds to faraway lands with little more than their memories and dreams to sustain them.

All I knew was there was a world out there for me to see, and I would have no second chances, no second thoughts.

Christened 13 months earlier at the South Portland Shipyard in Maine, USA, *Belgian Unity* was among hundreds of ships ferrying men and war materiel stateside following the end of the conflict in Europe. Though they had to navigate through a series of German mines still menacing the North Atlantic, their passage proceeded well enough until they reached the Azores some 1800 kilometers west of Portugal. That's when the savage storm hit, and once again peril joined Bisia as a close traveling companion.

Oh, with the horn sounding constantly, pleading like the bleat of a lost lamb for days on end. It was incredible. My stomach flew into my throat as we plunged down another sheer wall of water.

In the storm's initial onslaught, *Belgian Unity's* two sister ships had turned back. Now alone and vulnerable, the 441-foot freighter pitched like a cork atop the sea's undulant power.

Inside the wheelhouse on the bridge deck, the captain leaned into the helm, working to maintain the ship's critical angle through the towering seas. Close by, Bisia braced herself to keep from being thrown as the ship rolled hard to starboard.

"Madame!" the captain called out over the shrieking wind and battering waves. "This is the inclinometer." He nodded at a brass instrument with a dimly lit white dial on the console before him. "It shows the angle of the ship to the horizon. As you can see, we are listing over about 55 degrees. Another degree or so, and we'll be sunk. We've also lost all communication with the outside. So, let's you and I have another drink."

Bisia offered a wan smile for the captain's sardonic humor. She also wondered if this was what the fates had planned, that she should come so far, through so much, only to have it end beneath the howling black curtain of the Atlantic.

How often had her personal inclinometer tilted to its last degree over the last six years? Now, even if it were possible, there was no turning back. All she had to count on was her instinct, no matter what the world presented, be it a Gestapo officer with a pistol in hand or an angry ocean intent on swallowing her whole.

The Countess & The P.O.W.

*

Born Friday, November 4, 1921, Elżbieta Maria Karolina Teresa Siecina Krasicka (Krah-seech-kah) was the youngest of six children born to August Konstantin Krasicki and Izabela Wodzicka Krasicka, the Count and Countess of Siecin. Four brothers and a single sister preceded Bisia, the eldest of whom, brother Antoni, was 17 years her senior. They all grew up in a 16th century castle overlooking the San River in southeast Poland in the small city of Lesko.

Bisia's birth followed closely upon Poland's own return to the family of nations via the Treaty of Versailles in the aftermath of World War I. The country's resurrection ended 127 years of partitioning by Austria, Prussia, and Russia, and represented a major accomplishment for an otherwise failed peace conference, one that left both victors and vanquished dissatisfied with the outcome.

In particular, the punitive treatment of Germany by the allied nations would come to haunt the treaty's drafters. Forcing Germany to accept full blame for the war, to cede territory at home and its colonies abroad, to pay enormous reparations, and to limit the size of its army seeded, then fertilized the rise of Nazism in Germany over the next decade.

On the same day of Bisia's birth in 1921, the Nazi party held a public meeting at the Hofbräuhaus in Munich. There, 32-year-old firebrand Adolph Hitler inflamed both his followers and opponents alike. In the melee that followed, Nazi "Brownshirts" mauled the protesters. For this "breach of the peace", the German court sentenced Hitler to three months in prison, though he only remained incarcerated for little more than a month.

Two years later, inspired by Benito Mussolini's successful "March on Rome"—which brought the Fascists to power in Italy in October 1922—Hitler led a coalition in a failed "March on Berlin" on November 8-9, 1923. Thwarted by Munich police and convicted of high treason, Hitler received a five-year sentence for what came to be known as the "Beer Hall Putsch". But as in 1921, he only served a brief portion of his term. The failure of the 1923 coup, however, convinced Herr Hitler to forego further attempts at outright insurrection, and to turn instead to the ballot box.

With Hitler's xenophobic appeal to national pride, and the subsequent collapse of the German Mark, the Nazi Party continued to attract public support throughout the 1920s and early 1930s until it became the largest party in the Reichstag. When the world economy crashed in October 1929, worsening an already skyrocketing German inflation, President Paul von Hindenburg finally appointed the Nazi Party leader Chancellor of Germany on January 30, 1933.

With the imprimatur of the state now firmly in hand, it was only a matter of time before the Führer began exacting revenge upon those he blamed for his nation's beleaguered state.

Three years later, in March 1936, German forces marched into the Rhineland, the strip of German land bordering France, Belgium, and the Netherlands. This incursion directly contravened terms outlined at Versailles, which declared the area a demilitarized zone. Yet neither the French nor the British stepped in to intervene, choosing to appease rather than confront the volatile German leader.

In 1938, still undeterred, Hitler's forces entered Austria and forced a vote to bring Austria into union (Anschluss) with her northern neighbor. Though Hitler declared Austria as the last of his territorial claims, not six months later, he demanded the return of the Czech Sudetenland, an area that Versailles had stripped from Germany after WWI. He followed with the takeover of Bohemia and Moravia in the spring of 1939. Again, no nation stood up to say, halt.

As the decade of the 1930s neared its climatic end, Poland found itself ringed on three sides by the belligerent German regime. Notwithstanding her alliances with Great Britain and France, which pledged support in case of a German attack, the new Poland remained isolated.

To the east loomed the Soviet Union, which regarded its defeat at the hands of Marshal Piłsudski's Polish Legions in 1920 as a stain in need of cleansing. To the Soviets, the 1921 Treaty of Riga, pushing the Polish-Russian border eastward, was as illegitimate to their territorial claims as were the Versailles Treaty's boundaries to Hitler, to the west.

*

With Sacred Heart boarding school finally at an end in June, 17-year-old Bisia Krasicka joined her family for their summer vacation in Stratyn, one of her father's properties, some 235 kilometers east of the family's main estate in Lesko, Poland.

*

"Come on, slowpoke, let's go," said cousin Anna as she and Bisia's older sister, Zosia, had already mounted, and were eager to be off on their morning ride.

Bisia (right) with sister Zosia in Stratyn in the summer of 1939

Bisia hurried across the courtyard, taking a last drag from her cigarette. To the west, a dark band of clouds gathered, but overhead only tendrils of gray cut into the arching summer sky.

"Why don't you two go ahead," Bisia said when she got to her horse, Kuba. "I think I'll wait for Stas. He bet me I couldn't do the jumps with him this morning."

The second eldest of her brothers, Stas (called "Stosh", b. April 1, 1906) lived full time at Stratyn with his wife Jadwiga, whom they called Gusia, and their two young boys Jerzy and Andrzej (George and Andrew). Stas would inherit the property one day, but for now it remained in his father's name and control.

"You said you were going with us," Zosia said as she settled in her saddle. "Anyway, Stas is just goading you. Why do you always play into his hands?"

Being the youngest in the family, Bisia had faced challenges from her four older brothers for as long as she could remember. Stas, especially, thought she had a tendency to be frightened, and often chastised her with his maxim: "Everyone is afraid of something, but only a coward shows it."

And while it was true Bisia had been frightened by storms and lightning as a young girl, with the family's 16th-century castle yet to be wired for electricity, the place could seem dark and brooding at night. So, whenever one of her brothers would send her off to bring him cigarettes after supper, she would have to go past the colonnade to the left of the tower with only a small oil lamp in hand.

It would be pitch black just beyond the small pool of light, and with the creeping sounds and flickering shadows along the cold stone walls bringing to mind all kinds of ghost stories they had constantly heard growing up, yes, she was frightened. But at the same time, she constantly fought to prove that she could make it, both to herself and to her brothers who had forgotten, maybe, what it was like when they were young.

Just as Bisia was fitting her right boot into the stirrup, Stas walked up wearing a beige houndstooth jacket, high riding boots, and jodhpurs looking every bit the elegant country gentleman.

"So, are you ready?" he asked as his horse clopped out, led by one of the stable boys.

With Zosia's admonishment in mind, Bisia saw the chance to turn the tables on her older brother.

"You know, I think I'll take your money for jumping some other time. I promised Zosia and Anna I'd go riding with them this morning."

Brother Stas

Stas took the reins and mounted.

"Still scared, huh? I knew you wouldn't go. Anna, how about you? You want to try?"

"Go away," said Zosia. "Find somebody else to torture, and leave us alone."

"So, you are all afraid, then."

With that, Stas brought boots to his horse's flanks, and rode off at a clip. Bisia just laughed and gave Anna and Zosia a wink. Then she stuck her tongue out at her fleeing brother, knowing for once she had gotten the better of him.

As the three young women rode out into the countryside, only an occasional thatch-roofed farmhouse broke the gentle heave and roll of the land. Out in the fields, farmers stood bent beneath the sweeping arcs of their scythes as they reduced the meadows to rounded stacks of summer hay.

Zosia rode in the middle along the narrow dirt road, her face smooth and unlined, her hair held in place by two barrettes. Anna rode to her left, Bisia on the right.

Two and a half years apart in age, Bisia and Zosia were the same height, and both strong. Neither one liked playing with dolls as a young girl and instead took as their friends the family dogs and horses.

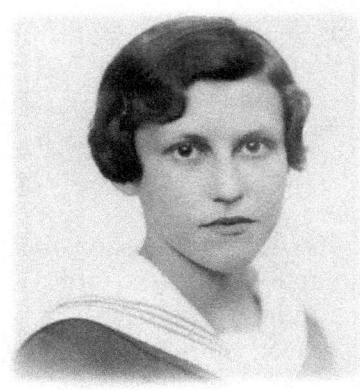
Sister Zosia

Our park and garden were also our friends, if you could call them that.

They had been out over twenty minutes when Zosia sat up in her saddle and pointed to a figure walking along the brush of the road up ahead, a long-handled scythe draped casually from his shoulder.

"Is that Pan Janek?"

Looking up, Bisia released her reins, tucked both little fingers into her mouth, and let out a piercing whistle that had the heads of both the animals and farmers turning as one.

"Pan Janek," she yelled. "Oh, Janek!"

The area farmers had worked her father's lands for as long as the girls could remember. Bisia and Zosia had known Pan Janek most of their lives.

"Dzien dobry," the girls announced as they rode up to him.

"Good morning to you," Janek said as he leaned on the long wooden handle of his tool. "Out looking for the soldiers, are you?"

"Soldiers?" asked Anna with a glance in Bisia's direction. "What soldiers?"

"There must be military maneuvers around somewhere," replied Janek, wiping the back of his sleeve beneath his large, spider-veined nose. "I saw a whole convoy pass by earlier this morning."

Bisia scanned ahead and then looked down for tracks on the unpaved road.

"Soldiers were here? Do you have any idea where they were going?"

"No. Just lots of soldiers, trucks, and horses," he said, sweeping one hand in front to illustrate the array he'd witnessed.

Bisia turned to Anna and Zosia.

"You know, we *ought* to go find them. I have some more cigarettes. Maybe we can hear something out about Jas."

Jas was the youngest of their brothers (b, May 7, 1917), and currently a cadet at the Polish Military Academy. But with the political situation as precarious as it was, he had been transferred recently, and the family had yet to hear of his whereabouts.

"We can stop for some food, too," Anna added before turning back to Pan Janek. "How long ago did you see them? They probably haven't gone too far. It shouldn't take us very long to find them, you think?"

Janek smiled, his small eyes crinkling into dots in his round, meaty face. He seemed to understand. A year younger than Bisia, Anna was at that age when boys were first becoming of interest.

"It must have been about an hour ago, maybe more." He hooked a thumb on his worn leather suspenders. "But they were moving. I wouldn't have any idea where they are now. Heading west is all. They didn't look like they were ready to stop, though."

Zosia & Bisia 1925

Pan Janek had labored many years in the fields, and carried the hard, broad body reflecting his life as a farmer. Though Count Krasicki owned much of the land in the area and carried ancient collateral rights as well, the people knew him as a good and fair man, considering the differences in social circumstances.

As the three young women conversed with Janek, their horses began nodding at their reins. Bisia patted Kuba on his withers, which quivered beneath her hand. But before she and Anna could set out in search of the soldiers, Zosia floated a gray cloud over the whole idea.

"You know what Papa would say," she said, her lips pursed beneath the line of her nose.

"What?" Bisia challenged her.

"Come on. There's no way he would let us go looking for soldiers, and you know it."

Being the first girl born after the four boys, Zosia had always been their father's favorite. And though she and Bisia were close - being the only two girls and only 2½ years apart in age - they didn't always see eye to eye.

"Well, I'd think Papa would welcome whatever news we could pick up," Bisia argued. "Besides, maybe we'll meet some soldiers who know about Jas."

"I think it would be fun to try to find them, too," said Anna tentatively. "Still, if Uncle August wouldn't want us to..."

"She's just saying that," Bisia said. "Why would he care? Let's just do it."

Zosia remained adamant.

"Papa knows more than whatever these soldiers could possibly tell us. Besides, this wouldn't be any search for information. Don't let her fool you, Anna."

"Nobody is trying to fool anybody," Bisia volleyed back. "We'll go and then tell Papa if we learn anything. Where's the harm?"

"Remember what Papa said last time when you took the car and chauffeur to the train station to meet soldiers? Who knows where these men are by now, anyway?"

Bisia took a long breath.

"We go down the road," she said in a tutorial tone, "and we find out. If they are around, fine. If not, what have we lost?"

"Bisia, really," said Zosia as she shook her head. "It's amazing how easily you manage to delude yourself."

Pan Janek had just stood there, listening.

"You young ladies shouldn't be arguing like this," he finally said. "Though, Pani Bisia, knowing your father, I *can* imagine what he would say."

Bisia (Bee-shah) was her nickname, short for Elżbieta. She had given herself the nickname after tiring of being called Djidjia (Djee-jah), the name she had been called most of her life, meaning baby. Though she was last born in the family, like most young people, she longed for the freedom and respect that attended age. For now, she hadn't finished challenging her sister, or trying to convince Pan Janek, either.

9

"How do you go through life judging everything on whether Papa and Mama would approve? Name one spontaneous thing you would ever do? Besides, Papa wasn't upset with me visiting the soldiers. It was because I took the car and the chauffeur. This is completely different. We are already out here, and we have the horses."

Try as she may, her argument fell barren to the road. Once again, she found herself alone in her conviction. Rather than splitting up, Anna and Bisia going in search of the troops, while Zosia headed back home on her own, Bisia wheeled her horse, Kuba, to the rear just as a cart piled high with hay clopped by filling the air with its heavy, damp sweetness.

"Bisia, please, don't be like this," pleaded Zosia.

"Like what? I'm only doing what you want, getting Papa's permission. That's what you need, correct?"

At Bisia's urging, Kuba raced away, throwing crescents of dirt high in the air behind obliging strides.

"Bisia!"

Zosia's voice rang out, but it barely carried to her sister before being swallowed by the hard beat of hooves.

Bisia was through with talking. Only with friends in boarding school had she felt like an equal, perhaps even a leader. At home, being by the youngest, she often got treated like she was from the following generation.

Along the way back to Stratyn, frustration fed her pace as the wind cut clean across her face and Kuba's mane danced in rhythm along her hands. They leaped two low fences in stride to shorten the route, and it made her wish she'd gone jumping with Stas, after all.

At 5'4" tall, 110 pounds, Bisia had become an excellent rider, in part due to the challenges of her brothers. Now, as she arrived back at the entrance of the main house in Stratyn, who, of all people, came walking out onto the front porch tamping tobacco into his pipe but Stas.

"I thought you were going out jumping," Bisia said, flipping her right leg over the saddle and sliding to the ground.

"It wouldn't be any fun if you didn't go. So, I just came back."

"Where are Mama and Papa?"

"In the salon, I think."

Bisia adjusted her hair and blew out a breath of air.

The Countess & The P.O.W.

"I'll tell you; those fences would not have been a problem today. Kuba and I just jumped two others on the way back."

"Sure," laughed Stas. "You say that now." He tossed the spent match to the ground and released a puff of smoke. "But I wouldn't go bothering Papa right now. He and Mama are involved in something or other. Everyone else is still in the dining room."

"I just need to ask Papa something," Bisia said, walking past him on the porch.

Stas pivoted on a rising voice.

"Before you go bother Papa, you should take care of Kuba. He's not young anymore, and it's not good for him to be left out when he's all lathered up like that. You're old enough to know better."

The lingering dew beaded on her riding boots. Lingering frustration flushed to her face. True enough, Kuba's breathing issued deep and even from his contracting flanks, while his tail swished to its own rhythms.

"What I'm old enough to know is that I don't need any advice from you," she snapped, unwilling to accept his tone. "What you *don't* know is that I only need to speak with Papa for a minute. I'll be right back."

August Count Krasicki

Just then, Zosia and Anna rode up.

"Don't worry, I'll take care of the horses," Zosia said. "Anna, you can help."

"Would you all please stop!" Bisia exclaimed. "I said I'd do it, and I will. If you just wait here for a second, I'll be right back. It won't be hard on the horses, or you, to stand here another few minutes!"

Allowing no time for rebuttal, she quickly entered the foyer, marching past the dining room where the third of their brothers, Xavier, sat with his wife Elka along with Stas's wife, Gusia, and Anna's mother, Aunt Maryncia. The household, as usual, was full in the summer. Before entering the salon, Bisia stopped at the large, gilded mirror hung along the corridor to straighten the tie she wore over a white shirt.

The previous evening her parents had been discussing whether the family should return to Lesko or remain in Stratyn, as the German problem continued to be a growing concern.

The fact that Hitler had signed a ten-year non-aggression pact with the Polish government in 1934 no longer offered any protection, according to Bisia's father. Many others in Poland, however, remained blind to the danger.

Since January, Hitler had railed about the return of the free city of Danzig to the north along the Baltic Sea. He also demanded freedom of passage through the Polish Corridor to East Prussia. Bisia's parents carried these worries and often betrayed their anxieties through their dealings with one another.

Entering the salon, Bisia saw her father standing beside the sofa where her mother sat wearing a flower-print dress, a book resting open atop her lap.

66 years of age, August Count Krasicki (b. April 19, 1873) stood six feet in height (1.83m) with silver hair combed back off his prominent forehead. He held a rolled-up magazine in his right hand, which he tapped absent-mindedly on the leg of his light summer suit. Bisia walked up and kissed her parents on both cheeks, as was customary.

"You girls back so soon?" said her mother, closing her book.

"Well, yes - but no, not really. We ran into Pan Janek while we were out riding, and he told us he had seen some soldiers. So, I came back to see- "

"Bisia, your mother and I are busy right now. You'll have to excuse us."

"I understand, Papa, but I just need to–"

"No!" he said, slapping the side of his leg with the rolled magazine. "You obviously *don't* understand. You need to *listen*. I said not now."

Bisia looked pleadingly at her mother.

"Mama, this will only take two seconds."

Her father turned to his wife.

"This constant self-involvement has to stop. Honestly, where did she learn these manners? Not in this house, that's for sure."

"Bisia, you heard your father," her mother said in an even tone. "We'll talk to you shortly. But not right now."

Bisia lowered her head and walked slowly toward the door. As she went, she shook her head, thinking, this is why you don't ask in the first place. The color on her cheeks still rose, but she had to restrain herself. She knew she would gain nothing by spouting off.

Though considered a good-hearted man, her father was not one to challenge. When his eldest son Antos studied at the University of Louvin in Belgium, he fell in love with a widow many years his senior, Baroness Lipowska von Lipowitz, known as Adija, who already had a young daughter. When Antos announced he wished to marry, his father refused to sanction the union because his son had yet to reach beyond his twenty-fourth year.

"If you finish at university first and then still wish to marry, I won't object," he offered as a compromise, assuming Antos would lose interest in time. But his son refused to reconsider. So, when he married Adjia, only his brother, Stas, attended the ceremony, as both parents felt the union to be a 'mezalianf', a wrong marriage. When they sent out notices of the marriage, they trimmed the edges in black, and disowned Antos from his inheritance as the first-born son of the castle and property in Lesko.

"Am I too late to hear Djidjia's request?"

Zosia led Anna into the room, breezing right past Bisia and using the name she knew her sister hated.

"Doesn't anyone listen to what I say anymore?" their father said, massaging his forehead with the tips of his fingers. But he also took Zosia and gently drew her to his side. He could never stay angry with her.

"Well, alright then, let's have it. Bisia, what's this all about soldiers and Pan Janek?"

Bisia had hoped to control the situation, but once again found herself on the spot.

"It's really nothing," she said, waving a hand like shooing a fly. "What I was trying to say. We came up on Pan Janek while we were riding, and he told us he had seen a convoy of soldiers earlier in the morning. Anna and I wanted to go to see where they were and maybe find out something about Jas. But Zosia said, no, that you and Mama wouldn't approve. So, I came back to ask your permission."

Bisia shrugged and showed her hands palms-up as if to underscore the innocence of her request. Then she nodded at Anna, hoping to secure an ally for her cause.

"Isn't that right, Anna? That's all I wanted to ask. And the horses are still outside."

"Actually," Zosia said, "we already took the horses to the stables. Stas thought it would be better."

Bisia knew right then there would be no going back out.

"Papa, I asked them to wait so I could speak with you first. This isn't fair."

Their father wore a moustache with its ends curled slightly upward, brushing the deep-cut lines alongside his nose. He slid a forefinger through before addressing his youngest child in French.

Izabela Wodzicka Krasicka

"Bisia, non. Ca ne ce fait pas chez nous. This is not done in our home. Young women do not go meet soldiers, especially when they are in the serious business of training. It's simply not right for either party. And I won't have it from my family. Do you understand?"

"Oh, Papa, you met Mama when you were a young soldier. We would only go to see them and ask about Jas."

"Bisia, you are missing your father's point."

Now 57, her mother (b. Izabela Wodzicka, June 26, 1882 in Kraków) set her book aside and rose. Once a young woman with a sensitive beauty, she now wore the bearing of six children and her avocation of physical labor more prominently.

"These maneuvers aren't games," she said in a manner that suggested understanding. "They are not to be disturbed. Besides, there are standards." She turned to her older daughter. "Zosu, I want you to apologize to your sister. She is no longer Djidjia, though sometimes she makes me wonder. Come on now."

"Yes, Mama. I'm sorry, Bisia."

Zosia's words obeyed, but the apology rang hollow in her sister's ears. Bisia refused to acknowledge it. Instead, she plopped into an armchair, deliberately refusing to mask her displeasure.

Tired of this minor contretemps, their father dropped his magazine atop a side table, and encouraged everyone outside as 'it is a lovely summer's day not to be wasted indoors'.

Through the tall, arching windows of the salon, Bisia could see the others from the dining room had already moved to the front garden. The men had removed their jackets and taken to the canvas-backed lawn chairs, newspapers spread out before them, their pipes curling small tails of smoke into a smudged blue sky.

As Zosia, Anna, and her father withdrew, Bisia's mother remained, resting her hands gently atop her youngest child's shoulders from behind. She waited until the others had left.

"Bisia, you may have just finished school, but you still have a lot to learn. You have many talents and advantages, in some ways more than your sister. But the world isn't here simply for your amusement. And I can assure you the self-indulgence you display and this, this petulance you give in to so freely, will only remind people how young you are. Is that what you want?"

She leaned down and kissed the top of her youngest child's head.

"Let's go outside and join the others."

Though her mother had softened it, Bisia felt her parent's reprimand like a sting. No matter what she did, it seemed wrong. Yet what everyone else proclaimed as the right thing felt so unnatural. She wondered when, or if, the time would ever come when her instincts would finally serve both her and convention as one.

Not several weeks later, the Krasickis returned to their principal estate in Lesko as the political situation grew increasingly grave.

***

2
LESKO

~ August 1939 ~

Nestled into the forested foothills of the Carpathian Mountains in the far southeastern corner of Poland, the small town of Lesko had been founded in the second half of the 15th century within the province of Krosno, 15 kilometers from the city of Sanok. Arranged atop the eastern bluff of the San River, Lesko had remained a vibrant little town of roughly 4000 people through the centuries, best known as a center for trade and craftsmanship. In 1939, sixty percent of its population was Jewish, as Sephardi Jews fleeing persecution in Spain had settled there in the 16th century.

The castle in Lesko and its 13,000-acre estate had come into the Krasicki family via marriage in 1799, the only way the estate ever changed ownership since being constructed as a fortress through the Dukla Pass in 1539 by Peter Kmita, the Great Crown Marshal of Poland.

In its rural setting, life in and around Lesko had changed little since feudal times, a social and economic construct primarily benefiting the hereditary landowners like the Krasickis.

In the last few years, the family had discussed many times whether war would come or not. What was curious was the Krasicki family always thought it would, while many others, whether in the city, schools, in houses of friends, and even in high governmental circles, were more trusting and optimistic.

There were a quite a number of people who chose to believe the whole thing was just posturing by Hitler, nothing more than idle threats. And even if war did come, they thought it would last a few weeks at best, and somehow, we'd end up occupying Berlin.

According to her father, the Polish people were very poorly informed, while a great deal of propaganda was being spread by the official press.

They seemed to think they could exorcise the devil with bravado, and somehow that could be effective as concrete acts.

"Some in the government are forced to say one thing publicly, while privately they aren't convinced at all," Count Krasicki would say. "They must walk on this narrow ledge with very little space on either side. But since we understand German, we were not so easily indoctrinated by all of these official pronouncements."

Based on what he knew of the Germans, Count Krasicki was sure of two things. First, that war would come, and second, that when it did, Poland would be in no position to suppress, much less win it. Primarily, this was because Krasicki understood Germany's real strength, the potential of its economy. The Germans had more than double the population of Poland, 80 million to 34 million. This alone gave them an enormous military capability.

Krasicki used to tell the following story when asked if there was still hope for peace.

The previous year, their cousin, Kazimierz 'Kasik' Krasicki, served as secretary to the Polish Foreign Minister Colonel Józef Beck. Kasik and Colonel Beck were on a steamship crossing the Baltic to Scandinavia in 1938 when a telegram arrived from the foreign office announcing that Hitler had occupied Prague. Kasik brought it to the deck where Beck was sitting. After reading it, Kasik said, 'Excellency, this means that the war is coming'. And Beck replied very quietly, 'Well, of course it does. And Poland will be burned, not once, but three times, and half the world with it'.

Though Colonel Beck had once thought Poland safe from Hitler's intentions, and even entertained the idea that she might be on the cusp of becoming a first-rate power, Poland's allies, the count knew, could not attenuate either the raw power or the deceitful web that Hitler had been spinning to his advantage.

*

With civil defense leaders coming to discuss war preparations, Count Krasicki streamlined all basic protocols throughout the estate. If someone needed firewood from the forest, for instance, they would no longer require a permit. Every reasonable request was to be accommodated. Also, the family had to begin packing while there was still time.

Krasicki siblings circa 1936 (l-r): Zosia, Xavier, Stas, Jas, Antos, Bisia

"Your mother and I will make the final choices," said the count as the family gathered in the castle library, "but I want you to collect anything you think might be important and set it aside."

As each family member began searching the 6000-volume library for their favorite works, the phone rang in the anteroom. After a few moments, Józef, the head butler, came to the door.

"It is for Count Jas," said Józef, nodding toward the family's youngest son, a light artillery cadet at the Polish Military Academy. Jas was home on leave for a short visit. He sat at the far side of the library at a table with a stack of books he had collected.

"You mean *Cadet* Jas?" Bisia's father said as Jas got up to take the call. "I'm the only count here."

The Krasicki family lived a privileged life. At the time of the third and final partition of Poland in 1795, only eight families carried the foreign title of Count, including the Krasickis. Though the King of Poland granted the original Krasicki properties in 1504, most Polish nobility received their titles from foreign governments. Emperor Ferdinand II granted the hereditary title, Count of the Holy Roman Empire, to Jerzy Krasicki in 1631. Besides the castle and estate in Lesko, and the property in Stratyn, the family also owned an apartment building in Kraków.

Throughout her childhood, Bisia never heard the townspeople ever address her parents by their first names, only as Count and Countess. Yet despite the gulf between the classes, no one held themselves as better than anyone else. The family lived in a manner that reflected what 19th-century Polish writer Adam Mickiewicz described in his book *Pan Tadeusz* as "hospitality without ostentation, ceremony without condescension, wholesome appetite without greed."

"Who was it?" asked his father when Jas returned.

"My regimental commander. I have to return to duty tomorrow."

His father nodded, expecting the answer.

An avid painter, genealogist, botanist, and writer of military history, August Count Krasicki fought in the Austrian cavalry with the Polish Legions during WWI, while Poland remained under partition. In the 1920 Russo-Polish War, he served as adjutant to the commander at the Polish army headquarters on the Northeast Front, where he received a promotion to the rank cavalry captain with seniority.

During the interwar years, the count served on many local and regional governmental organizations, including as councilor of the Town Council in Lesko, beginning in 1934. The thought of what lay ahead weighed heavily on him.

Though Poland had regained national sovereignty at Versailles, the vast majority of her people still had no say in the outcome of their lives. And with over a century and a quarter of partition just behind, Poles didn't view government as a tailor suited to their interests. Citizenship, therefore, made for an ill-fitted suit to the Polish frame, and two decades of interwar freedom was far too short a time to make the proper alterations.

Besides external factors, there were problems Poland had long faced internally. Through five long generations, the partitioning powers had done nothing to build the national capacity of Poland as a coherent state. Instead, they used her resources to service their own needs. This alone would have taken decades to overcome.

Then there was the matter of a divided leadership during the interwar years. On one side sat the World War I hero Marshal Józef Piłsudski (1867-1935), a long-time Polish nationalist who proclaimed Poland's independence and expanded her borders to the east after driving the Bolsheviks from Poland in the Russo-Polish War of 1920, known as the Miracle of the Vistula.

Famed pianist and composer Ignacy Paderewski (1860-1941) led the other faction, elected Premier in January 1919 even as Piłsudski remained Chief of State. It was Paderewski who signed the Treaty of Versailles, though he would resign in December to take on the role as Polish ambassador to the League of Nations. In 1922, he returned to his music and touring. Piłsudski retired a year later, only to re-enter the political arena in 1926, leading a coup d'état that secured for him a virtual dictatorship until his death in 1935.

As had historically been the case, a matched set of vulnerabilities faced Poland in 1939; not just the temerity of her allies and brutishness of her neighbors, but the fragility of her own internal fault-lines.

Though she had long ago been a continental power, Poland's heroic self-image as the last outpost of the Holy Roman Empire and shield of Christianity standing guard against Soviet atheism did not align with her true status as a fledgling nation wedged between two major powers. To attain full national maturity would have required not only a term of internal stability, but the economic and political support of an understanding international community. Neither was in the offing.

*

In late August 1939, the area's civil defense officials came to the castle in Lesko to meet with Count Krasicki. The hope that war would pass had succumbed to the hard-headed practicality of what to do when it finally arrived.

The count and his eldest son, Antoni, received the local civil defense officials in the castle office. Bisia's mother, her aunt, sister Zosia, and her cousin Anna went out to the gardens. Bisia, however, remained, innocently taking a chair beside the office entrance.

Atop the table beside her chair, Bisia found her father's two-volume memoirs of World War I published two years earlier. She picked up the first volume, opened the cover, and read the dedication:

"To my dear Lisia (a special nickname her father had given his second daughter), I hope the romance of war you will only learn from this book."

While she pretended to read, Bisia listened intently as town officials asked her father to allow anti-aircraft trenches to be dug and guns to be placed in the park next to the castle. The park, she knew, contained trees and animals her father loved, like children. Both would surely come under attack if they set gun emplacements there.

The silver-haired count held nature in high regard, a belief enhanced through his post-graduate studies at the Academy of Forestry in Tharandt, Saxony. His botanical research led to the development of a new variety of pine tree later named in his honor

(Picea Krasiciana). Whenever a child would pull too hard on a limb or hit a tree in passing with a stick, he would chastise them. "They feel it as much as you do, but can't tell you."

"We could be at war in a matter of weeks," Bisia heard her father say to the civil defense officials. "If we ask for Soviet help, they will most likely exact payment by demanding military bases in Lwow, Best, Bitok, and Wilno. And those concessions would amount to the loss of Polish independence. We can only hope the West wakes up before it is too late, for its own sake as well as ours."

The men from civil defense requested the family tape all the windows in the castle to protect against the bombing they expected to begin soon. They also suggested removing the fountain and lovely flower gardens fronting the castle, as from the air both would serve as geographical landmarks and bombing targets.

As Bisia leaned in to hear more of the conversation in the office, she didn't notice the family's head butler, Józef, coming down the hallway.

"Pani, you shouldn't be here," he said. "You should be outside with your mother and sister."

Bisia looked up and flushed. Sitting back, she tried to pretend Józef hadn't caught her eavesdropping. Fearing her father may have overheard Józef's reproach, Bisia returned the book to the table and departed, though she shot a disapproving glance at Józef as she walked away.

*

The last chance for Poland to stave off war vanished on August 23rd when Germany and the Soviet Union signed the Molotov-Ribbentrop Pact, a secret protocol dividing Poland into spheres of influence. The pact proved to be another brilliant strategic maneuver by the German chancellor, who harbored fears of another Triple Entente between Britain, France, and the Soviet Union that formed the spine of Anglo-French cooperation in World War I. In its place, the Molotov-Ribbentrop Pact left Germany free to mass its entire force against Poland before pivoting to Western Europe without fear of a second front opening to the east.

Allying with Stalin had not been Hitler's first choice, however. Since 1935 he had tried to lure Poland into his Anti-Comintern Pact against the Soviets, which Japan signed in 1936, and Italy in 1937. But the agreement would've required Poland to concede lands in the north for vague promises of post-war gains taken from Belarus and Ukraine to the east. As a practical matter, any concessions to the north would block Poland's access to the Baltic Sea, meaning the nation's entire economy would become dependent on Germany.

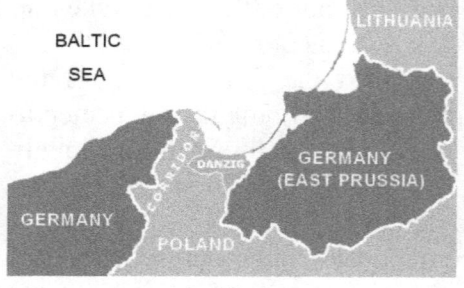

Image by Space Cadet at English Wikipedia

After British Prime Minister Neville Chamberlain signed the infamous "Peace in our time" Munich Agreement on 30 September 1938, ceding the Czech Sudetenland to Germany, Poland joined in the dispossession by annexing disputed land along the Czech-Polish border in Cieszyn Silesia, where many ethnic Poles lived. Hungary chewed off even more Czech territory in Slovakia and Carpathian Ruthenia to the south and east, which were heavily populated by Hungarians.

These small partnerships in carving up Czechoslovakia allowed Hitler to spread the blame for his wolven ways, while allaying the fear many Poles had of him. Yet he fervently believed wherever German culture was predominant, people should have the right to self-determination, meaning to join the Fatherland. Since a significant German-speaking population lived in Poland, and the German province of East Prussia remained separated from Germany proper by the Versailles Treaty-created Polish Corridor, Hitler envisioned a Greater Germany at the expense of Polish territory.

Since he made similar calculations without constraint during the Anschluss in Austria and while annexing Czech lands, why, he wagered, would the West object if he chewed off a piece of Poland, too, especially a part that was predominantly German in makeup? Besides, both of Poland's western allies, Britain and France, were hegemonic powers themselves. Surely, they must understand Germany's affront. Not that their understanding mattered in the least.

In his thuggish brinksmanship, the German chancellor found compliant opposition as the carnage from World War I still haunted the people and leaders of Europe.

Though it had a standing army of five million, the largest on the continent, France suffered more than a million dead in the Great War. Devastated by its losses, and fearful of a new conflict, the French public turned inward, while their government focused purely on defensive measures in the face of the growing German threat. Throughout the 1930s, the country erected the massive Maginot Line series of fortifications along its central border with Germany rather than confronting Hitler directly while it still held a military advantage.

Years earlier, just two months after Hitler took office as chancellor in 1933, Poland's Marshal Józef Piłsudski urged France to join him in a preemptive war as he feared the speed of German rearmament. After French Prime Minister Édouard Daladier, who had fought on the Western Front in WWI, declined, rather than advancing alone, Piłsudski signed a ten-year non-aggression pact with Germany on 26 January 1934. It would prove another empty promise, as Hitler renounced the pact in March 1939, laying the foundation for his invasion on September 1st.

On August 31st, 1939, German SS troops dressed in Polish uniforms staged a false-flag attack on a German radio tower in Gleiwitz, Poland, meant to portray Poles as the aggressors. Though it was a thin tissue easily seen through, the raid gave Germany just enough political cover to launch "Operation Weiss" the following day. On that fateful Friday, over 60 German infantry and panzer divisions supported by 1200 Luftwaffe aircraft poured into Poland, setting off the greatest conflict in world history.

The next day, Bisia's brother Antos received a letter from his friend, Lt. Colonel Stefan Szlaszewski, commanding officer of the Polish 2nd Podhale Rifles Regiment in Sanok, the largest city in the region. He was with his troops going to the field after having been at the Krasicki home for a last dinner. He wrote:

"In the day after the proclamation of the general mobilization, and the day we are leaving the Sanok garrison, we are very grateful to say farewell to our friends during the dinner offered by Mr. Antoni Krasicki. And to remember well all the nice and charming hours we (he and wife Mimi) spent always together, for maybe it will be the last time we are ever to see each other."

Despite the prewar confidence of the Polish people following the 1920 Miracle of the Vistula, when Piłsudski repelled the advancing Bolsheviks, the Polish cavalry units, with their flashing sabers and flags fluttering from raised lances, proved no match for the mechanized German Wehrmacht and dominant Luftwaffe overhead.

Poland fielded 39 infantry divisions to defend herself, thinly spread out along the full length of the German and Slovak borders. But numbers along every conceivable metric stood in Germany's favor, and it used them all with devastating effect.

Though the Treaty of Versailles had relaunched the Polish ship of state, the Second Polish Republic (1918-1939) now found itself confronted by an iron tide rolling in from the west, engulfing both paternity and pride. Bisia's vacation was at its end. The storm was quickly rising.

***

3
ISHAM

~ September 1939 ~

Even as the drumbeat for war grew louder each day from Europe, it didn't penetrate Isham Reavis's consciousness in the least in St. Louis, Missouri. He wasn't interested in politics, only in his own little world; the war news didn't touch that.

One month shy of his twenty-eighth birthday in September 1939, Isham Reavis lived with his 60-year-old widowed mother, Lena, and his 25-year-old brother, Burton, in a small one-bedroom apartment at 5514 Pershing Avenue in the Debaliviere Place neighborhood of St. Louis. For the last three years, he had worked nearby at the Gatesworth Hotel at 245 Union Boulevard, first as a clerk, then head of promotions, and finally as assistant manager. He worked seven days a week on a split shift: 7 a.m. till noon and 6 to 11 p.m. one day, then just noon till six the next.

While Isham burrowed into his work, American politics of the time pivoted along an interventionist-isolationist axis.

Combined with the economic crisis brought about by the Great Depression, the lingering memories of 116,000 American dead in World War I supported a strong anti-war movement rooted in George Washington's farewell address to Congress warning against foreign entanglements, especially in Europe. Many Americans, notably in places like St. Louis with its large German immigrant population, didn't see how the war in Europe was any of their concern. But politics, alone, wasn't the only factor for America's hesitance.

Toni Reavis

When Germany invaded Poland with over 60 divisions in September 1939, the U.S. Army totaled just 175,000 men and officers, making it the 16th largest army in the world, smaller than its counterparts in Poland, Czechoslovakia, and Spain, to name just three. Many of its divisions also stood at half-strength or poorly supplied with antiquated equipment.

All we had were a few old guns and some broomsticks.

*

A native of Falls City, Nebraska, Isham had moved to St. Louis with his mother and younger brother after his father died suddenly of a heart attack on February 3, 1932, at age 56. Amidst the Great Depression, the family didn't have money enough to pay rent on their house in Omaha.

After working two years to save for college, within five weeks of his dad's death, Isham had to drop out of the University of Nebraska in Lincoln and move with his mom and brother into his grandmother's apartment at 5305 Delmar in the Visitation Park neighborhood of St. Louis. The brothers had to share the same bed.

"That first year in St. Louis I didn't do anything, didn't go anywhere, and didn't know anyone."

The Great Depression exerted its tightest squeeze on the U.S. economy in the early 1930s. Almost a quarter of the American workforce, 24.9%, was out on the street in December 1933, according to the U.S. Department of Labor, Bureau of Labor Statistics. It marked the highest unemployment year of the 20th century. Not a good time for young men with no connections in a strange new city to be out looking for work.

How often had Isham experienced a door closing behind him, with the words "Nothing open as yet, but we'll keep you in mind," ushering him out?

Same old story, same old line.

At least Isham was single. How many married men with families had to wait outside an open gate every day until some foreman stepped out and said, 'I only need seven today; I'll take you, you, and you, and you four'? Then, cut every other hope with a curt, 'That's all,' without the slightest concern how the others would have to shuffle back home without another day's wages to help their families live.

Whenever he got down, though, Isham's thoughts would drift toward home. Not Omaha, that was just a city where they used to live. No, home always meant Falls City, Nebraska, to Isham. His older sister, Mary Keller, lived there with her husband, Fred Keller. And though he once thought of it as just a dull little Midwestern town of a few thousand people, he no longer looked at it that way at all.

After every disappointing job interview, Isham would walk back to his grandmother Mary Kilgore's apartment reminiscing about that beautiful old house on Chase Street in Falls City. Built in 1898 by his paternal grandfather and namesake, Judge Isham Reavis, the place acted as a hub around which the Reavis and Dorrington families revolved. And a smile would come to his lips.

Yes, Falls City always had that effect on Isham. And when he arrived at his grandmother apartment across from the Westminster Presbyterian Church on Delmar and Union, he'd run upstairs, knowing he'd go out looking for work again the next day.

Judge Isham Reavis

*

Isham's frustration with not finding work was not unique. He shared that anxiety with his brother and millions more, just like them. What was singular, however, was his first name, Isham, though people mispronounced both of his names upon seeing them for the first time, usually as IH-shum REE-viss. The correct pronunciation was EYE-shum REH-viss, and it carried a long family tradition, long by U.S. standards, at least.

Toni Reavis

The first Isham Reavis was born on September 19, 1748, in Northampton, North Carolina to Edward Reavis, Jr. and Mary Isham, of Virginia. His name combined both family's surnames. His grandfather, Edward, Sr., had come to the U.S. from England in the late 1600s. From North Carolina, this branch of the Reavis family came into Tennessee via the Cumberland Gap, then to Illinois. After passing the bar in Illinois, 22-year-old Isham Reavis (January 28, 1836—May 8, 1914), arrived in Falls City, Nebraska, on May 8, 1858, less than a year after the city's founding.

Judge Isham Reavis had been a true pioneer, referred to in the History of Nebraska as "a jurist of exceptional ability and renown, a lawyer of profound learning, a pleader of exceptional force, and a strong man who sliced and carved out a career during an age when strong sturdy characters were necessary to create a state."

He argued many times before the U.S. Supreme Court; served as an Associate Justice of the Arizona Territorial Supreme Court (August 1869—December 1872) appointed by President Ulysses S. Grant; and in his time, was the most famous lawyer in Nebraska.

His request, at age 19, to study law with a Springfield, Illinois family friend, produced a response that would become a standard reference of instruction for all future members of the Reavis family.

Springfield (Ill.), Nov. 5, 1855

Isham Reavis, Esq.

My dear Sir:

I have just reached home, and found your letter of the 23rd. I am from home too much of my time for a young man to read law with me advantageously. If you are resolutely determined to make a lawyer of yourself, the thing is more than half done already. It is but a small matter whether you read with anybody or not. I did not read with anyone. Get the books and read and study them till you understand them in their principal features; and that is the main thing. It is of no consequence to be in a large town while you are reading. I read at New Salem, which never had three hundred people living in it. The books and your capacity for understanding them are just the same in all places. Mr. Dummer is a very clever man and an excellent lawyer (much better than I in law-learning); and I have no doubt he will cheerfully tell you what books to read and also loan you the books.

Always bear in mind that your own resolution to succeed is more important than any other one thing.

Very truly your friend,

A. Lincoln

*

The judge's grandson, my father, arrived in this world on October 11, 1911 in Falls City, as the first boy and second of three children to Burton Isham Reavis and Lena Katherine Reavis (nee Stites) of St. Louis.

Burton & Isham, June 1922

In some ways, Bisia and Isham had grown up in similar circumstances. Lesko, Poland, was a small, rural town of approximately 4000 people, as was Falls City, Nebraska. In Lesko, Bisia's father, the count, was the leading citizen and jobs producer. In Falls City, Judge Reavis and fourteen Reavis/Dorrington family households owned about everything worth owning:

the bank, the electric company, the hardware store, the furniture store, the granary.

Though his folks moved to Omaha following his grandfather's death in 1914, Isham, his older sister Mary Keller, and younger brother Burton returned to Falls City each summer to live with their paternal grandmother, Annie Dorrington Reavis, in her beautiful old Victorian house at 1421 Chase Street, with its wide rooms, fourteen-foot ceilings, and shaded wraparound porch.

For us, it was a wonderfully uncomplicated life. Nobody locked their doors. Why would they? Everyone knew everybody, and it was rare to see someone in the neighborhood you didn't recognize.

*

Their second year in St. Louis, Isham, his mom, and brother found an apartment of their own at 5514 Pershing Avenue, a few blocks north of Forest Park. They paid $40/month for the spare, one-bedroom unit on the third floor.

With the Great Depression easing due to FDR's New Deal legislation, Isham landed his first steady job in 1936 as a desk clerk at the Gatesworth Hotel, a five-minute walk from the apartment. During his first years at the hotel, he found he enjoyed the rhythm of the hotel business.

The Gatesworth Hotel, St. Louis, Mo.

There was always something going on, people all around and parties every night.

*

With the war boiling over in Europe, in May 1940, First Lord of the British Admiralty Winston Churchill replaced Neville Chamberlain at

No.10 Downing Street as British Prime Minister. He immediately began to lobby U.S. President Franklin Roosevelt to bring America's industrial strength into the fight.

Despite his personal fondness for Churchill, FDR downplayed any inclination he might have had to bring America into the war throughout the 1940 presidential campaign against Republican candidate Wendell Willkie. Yet he quietly assisted Churchill, too, trading 50 navy destroyers for 99-year leases on British bases in the Caribbean and Newfoundland.

Opposing FDR on this and other creeping involvements was the strong isolationist movement. After visiting England and Germany before the war, aviation icon Charles Lindbergh publicly announced, "I have been forced to the conclusion that we cannot win this war for England, regardless of how much assistance we send." Novelist Ernest Hemingway also forewarned against being "sucked in" to another European conflict.

But after Poland, Belgium, Holland, Norway, Luxembourg, and France all fell, and a German air campaign commenced over England, Congress passed the Selective Service Act in September 1940. The law required all able-bodied men ages 21 to 45 to register for the first peacetime draft in U.S. history.

***

4
LEAVING HOME

~ September 1939 ~

In his general mobilization order, Polish President Ignacy Mościcki (1926-1939) decreed that all the young people not already involved in the war effort should evacuate to the east away from the front.

Notwithstanding this order, August and Izabela Krasicki refused to leave Lesko. Bisia's older sister, Zosia, remained, as well, devoted as she was to her father.

"I have never taken to the idea of running away when invaders try to overrun us," the count said as the rest of his family prepared to depart. "Someone has to stay behind and protect our friends and property. I'm older and the Germans will be less likely to trample the lands of a former Austrian cavalry officer."

As the rest of the family began their long journey east, Bisia's oldest brother Antos spoke what many dared not.

"It is an old and fading idea that the benevolent count can somehow protect his land and its people."

*

The family departed Lesko on Sunday, September 10th, the same day that Canada joined Britain and France by declaring war against Germany. The Krasickis rode out of Lesko in three horse-drawn wagons, heading toward their summer property in Stratyn some 235 kilometers to the east.

Their little convoy comprised 12 to 15 people, led by Bisia's oldest brother, Antos. They were not alone in their flight. The strength and speed of the German invasion displaced thousands who now sought safety to the east, choking the road with both servicemen and refugees.

On the wider political front, Polish President Mościcki and his cabinet fled to neighboring Romania, with whom they shared an alliance. However, rather than finding a haven, the Polish leaders were arrested, as the Romanian government feared Nazi reprisals. With its head of state in foreign hands, Polish officials worried the government would lose its legitimacy.

To offset this concern, Mościcki resigned, and Marshal Władysław Raczkiewicz took the presidential oath of office. Soon, the Government of the Republic of Poland in exile formed in Paris under the premiership of General Władysław Sikorski, later moving to London. Though only legal devices, these transfers of power effectively gained the government-in-exile recognition from the western allies, while authorizing it to coordinate and fund a resistance movement back home.

The first leg of the Krasicki's journey to Stratyn took them 80 kilometers north of Lekso to Tuligłowy, where they planned to stop at the estate of their friends Stanislaw and Maria Bal, another of the ancestral landowners in the region.

Count Krasicki with sons (l to r) Jas, Antos, Stas, and Xavier

As their wagons rolled over the hard-packed dirt road, Bisia recalled visitors and family friends coming from all over Europe to hunt wild boar and stags in the forests in the area. The family crest, Rogala—the crest of horns—reflected this hunting heritage, depicting the horn of a stag upon a field of white beside one of a bison on a field of red, with the shield topped by a nine-pointed crown.

On their second day out, the drone of airplanes approaching from the west silenced the roll of the wagon wheels on the unpaved road as the family scanned the sky. Cousin Anna sat alongside Bisia on the third of the family's three wagons. At age 16, Anna Michałówska was a year younger than Bisia, and still a student at the Sacred Heart boarding school in Tarnów where Bisia graduated in June.

As the planes neared, the family's two dachshunds nesting on Bisia and Anna's laps jumped to their feet and began barking, their tales stiff to the heavens. With a ferocity Bisia had never experienced before, German Stukas swarmed overhead before diving with a terrible scream. The horses strained at their equipment, stamping, and whinnying as the German planes began strafing the small convoy.

"Jump!" said Antos. "Run to the forest! Hurry!"

It was Bisia's first taste of war, yet rather than fear, excitement rushed through her body. After being closely regulated throughout life, whether by governesses, boarding school nuns, or older siblings, Bisia sensed the rules being stripped away in one savage moment, horrible as the cause may have been.

After the planes flew off, Antos regathered the family. His wife, Adija, had been grazed on the arm as the small party dashed for cover. Bisia bandaged her wound before they left, grateful for the first-aid classes she had received at school.

"Bisia, take your wagon up front and keep a good pace," said Antos. "We need to make as much distance as we can before dark. Anna, make sure the dogs stay in back from now on."

All around, other people along the road tended to their wounded and regathered belongings they abandoned in their flight. The family continued under the cover of night, uncertain whether the Germans would return. Their earlier mood of adventure now turned to one of apprehension.

Behind them, the entire horizon to the west blazed beneath German fire. Perishing, too, were the hopes and dreams of a cherished but fragile way of life.

We worried about the fate of Lesko, but inside, I had to admit; I experienced only curiosity and excitement. This feeling would change quickly.

Winter often arrived early in southeast Poland, but in the fall of 1939, the weather remained clement, as the summer had been one of the warmest and driest in memory. With no immediate forecast for rain, the wide Polish plains to the west offered excellent ground for the Germans to drive their mechanized armored units. It was another tragic happenstance of that fateful year.

After the initial German air attack, the family restricted its travel to nighttime while resting in the forests during the day. On the fourth morning out, however, Antos's wife made the case they should move during the day, as time was their most important ally. The farther from the front they rode, she argued, the safer they would be.

Bisia's brother Antos was a lightly built man in his mid-thirties with dark eyes. He stood 5'10 ½" (1.79m) tall, but because he suffered from asthma since boyhood, he never excelled in sports or served in the military. Yet, as the leader of their small group, the family trusted his judgment implicitly.

As they prepared the wagons for travel, Antos reenforced his wife's plan to leave the cover of the woods.

"If there aren't many travelers on the road, the only other place people could be is in the forests. The Germans will be less likely to bother with one small group."

Brother Antos

A few fellow evacuees followed their lead, but none of the soldiers who had also sought cover in the forest with them. Their journey remained uneventful for a while before the unmistakable drone of approaching warplanes rose again in the distance.

We never abandoned the hope that the British and the French would live up to their promises, but as the number of German sorties increased, the less likely it became that they would ever come to our rescue.

Dark columns of smoke billowed skyward as the forest they left came under intense bombing. Open countryside and harvested fields spread along both sides of the road they were on as the planes soon zoomed overhead. There was no obvious place to hide.

Not waiting for instructions, Bisia took off running as the planes dove with a terrible wail.

I thought if I ran fast enough, I could hide in the gathered cornstalks in the middle of the field. But I felt exposed, too, like they could see me from kilometers away.

The excitement of war ended beneath the fury of German Stukas. The planes dived at a frightening speed. Fear became Bisia's companion, one she would come to know well in the following years.

I was running with our dog, Bozo, in my arms. Anna stayed behind, crawling beneath the wagon with Jolly. I feared the horses would pull away and it would expose me on the open road.

Running proved difficult over the uneven ground. Bisia didn't make it far before she tripped, sending Bozo flying. He rolled over several times before shaking the dirt from his coat and barking defiantly at the planes circled above.

As Bisia tumbled, she tried to fall face down, so she could avoid seeing what was coming. Instead, she ended up flat on her back as rows of bullets ripped into the surrounding ground.

I was afraid to move. The Stukas buzzed so low I could see the eyes of the pilots through the cockpit windows. I held my breath and prayed.

A few others from the road also made a run for it. To Bisia's left, a young girl ran with her arms pinwheeling for balance. Bisia peered through slatted eyes so the whites wouldn't give her away.

Another Stuka swooped in like a bird of prey. Its wings cut at an angle, placing its guns along the girl's escape path. At first, Bisia felt relief not to be its target. But when bullets began to spit from its wings, she realized, "I might be next."

The young girl was hit as she ran 30 meters from where Bisia was lying. The force of the bullet spun her around and carried her forward with its momentum. Bisia's hand jerked to her mouth. The girl thumped to the ground, her face speckled with dirt, her hair askew across her forehead. Bozo spun around, barking at the retreating plane while another young girl ran to the side of the fallen girl. Bisia wondered if they were sisters. In tears, the girl took her friend or sister in her arms and rocked back and forth, hoping the force of her embrace might undo the terrible damage.

Less than a minute later, the planes flew off, leaving only silence and destruction. The family reassembled. After checking the safety of their party, the number one concern was the horses. Bewildered by the attack, they stood wide-eyed in place, still blinkered and hitched to the wagons, awaiting their fate.

Later in the day, the Krasicki party approached the Bal estate, which stood off the road like a plantation house from the American South. But instead of finding refuge, the Krasickis discovered German soldiers from the Fourteenth Army Corps already settled there.

The German Blitzkrieg engulfed thirty miles of territory per day, and the antiquated cavalry-based Polish military offered little resistance. Intercession from the British and French never arrived, yet

Bisia and her family refused to acknowledge the news, thinking it was more German propaganda.

That night at dinner, a group of German officers joined them. Their commanding general addressed the table.

"I have no obligation to do so, but as an officer and gentleman, let me warn you. The Russians will come to this area soon, and I doubt as estate owners you will want to stay."

"Why would the Russians be coming here?" inquired Maria Bal, the wife of the estate owner.

"Because our government has signed a pact with them and this area will come under their control."

The thought of Germany and Russia as allies defied comprehension. Throughout the run-up to war, many Poles believed their nation's saving grace lie in her position as the buffer between Fascist Germany and Communist Russia. The so-called "Bavarian theory" also supported this belief under the assumption the German high command - Hitler, Goering, Hess, and Goebbels - did not come from Prussia, where the historic animus with Poland was at its greatest.

Two years before signing its non-aggression pact with Germany in '34, Poland had penned one with Russia, too, fearful of losing all she had gained through the twenty-year interwar period. From such a hazardous position, she played both sides from the middle. Now they were being told their enemies had eliminated the middle ground.

For years, Jewish-Bolshevism sat atop Hitler's list of enemies. In a 1936 address to 50,000 Hitler Youth, he said: "There is another country full of cruelty, murder, and arson, destruction, and upheaval, filled not with life but with horror, despair, complaint, and misery."

Joseph Goebbels, Hitler's minister of propaganda, echoed the Führer's sentiments, calling Jews and Bolsheviks "indistinguishable". Now the Krasickis and the Bals learned a secret pact aligned the two opposites, with Poland caught between. It seemed unimaginable.

Despite all the German aggression to date, Poles still viewed their neighbors to the west with more lenience than the Russians. The Soviets were another breed altogether.

"No pact with Stalin is acceptable in a civilized world," Mrs. Bal said to the German general.

An intelligent person full of humor, Maria "Kinia" Bal was a revered figure in Polish artistic circles and served as the model for famed artist Jacek Malczewski's best-known works. She was also renowned as a charming, outspoken hostess.

Her husband, Stanislaw, nine years her senior, was very much her opposite, a sedate, courteous, gentlemanly squire of a beautiful country estate. His family received its title and land in the region even before the Krasickis.

"You must forgive my wife," he said. "Sometimes she speaks before thinking."

Kinia threw her husband a hard glare.

"That's nonsense! Landowners make the laws on their own property. It's the same in Germany. Communists kill landowners and confiscate property. You can't trust anything Stalin says."

"Take it for what you will," said the German. "I am simply informing you of the current political order. We will return west in a few more days."

While conversations around the table often centered on politics, discussions mostly involved speculation. Now, the talk carried real consequences. Regardless of Mrs. Bal's attitude, nobody had the luxury of dismissing the German general's warning.

After traveling under attack to reach what they thought would be safety, the news of the Molotov-Ribbentrop Pact forced the Krasicki party to turn around and retrace their steps to Lesko toward an unknown fire. They also feared for the safety of their brother Stas and his family, who remained in Stratyn still unaware of the Russian-German agreement.

It was an unsettled night at the Bal estate. Bisia and Cousin Anna shared a room but awoke before dawn to begin their long return home.

While their journey east came under German attack from the air, the return found the Krasickis sharing the road with an endless convoy of German soldiers, tanks, motorcycles, and trucks, all streaming east. The evacuees walked opposite or rode in wagons, a silent procession of fear and anxiety. Bisia walked with Anna when a young German soldier held out a pack of cigarettes.

"Fraulein, would you like a cigarette?"

Under her breath, Anna said, "Bisia, no," with an anxious look toward her cousin.

The only men Bisia and Anna had met to this point had been friends of her brothers and sons of neighboring land owners. And because of the disparity in age between her and her brothers, these men had always been much older than she.

"Where are you going?" Bisia asked the German soldier while accepting the cigarette.

"Toward Lwow. And you?"

Bisia understood Anna's concern. The only attitude to adopt with invaders was cold dismissal. But she also realized they might gather information by striking up a conversation.

We tried not to believe what they were telling us about the lack of support from the west. And we could tell the Germans didn't take us as any kind of threat. Their arrogance in sharing information was another German vanity we played upon.

Speaking fluent German and being young came with its pluses, as did her gender. Bisia would depend on each in the years ahead.

Upon their return to Lesko, the sight of German tanks lining the front of the castle horrified the family. They soon learned German officers had moved into the residence, taking the castle as their regional headquarters. The Germans permitted Bisia's parents to continue living there, as the count still had to manage the property. But everyday life around the castle grounds was no longer normal.

*

For generations, the owner of the castle in Lesko represented his own law and order on his family's land, while the people of the town and neighboring villages worked on the estate as their fathers had before them. It was into this world the German force intruded.

The day following Bisia's arrival home, the adjutant to the German general approached Count Krasicki in his office.

"Mien general would like to meet with you," the officer said, after bowing in deference to the count's position.

The count remained seated at his desk.

"You can tell your general I am not disposed to meeting with anyone who imposes himself on my land.

"Mien general's intention is as a courtesy call only."

"Courtesy would be not taking my home."

Count August Krasicki

"Very well."

The German clicked his heels, bowed, and left. Later, in the afternoon, he returned. Again, the count refused to talk. Finally, the general, himself, came to the office.

Count Krasicki served as an Austrian cavalry officer during World War I, and this seemed to influence the general.

"My dear Reichsgraf," he said, using the German word for Imperial Count. "I apologize for the intrusion. I hope we won't upset your routines too much. However, I wanted to warn you. One of the demarcation lines between the German and Russian zones is here along the San River. The Russians will arrive within several days, and we will leave. As you're aware, the frontier over the San is closed, but I wanted to give you an opportunity to leave with your family."

With the estate spanning both sides of the river, everything west of the San would come under German occupation, everything east, including the city and the castle, would fall to Soviet control.

"This property has been in our family for nearly 150 years. I won't abandon it or its people no matter who you have a pact with."

"Reichsgraf, the Russians will deport any members of the aristocracy they find. What good would you be to your family or peasants, then? You can take whatever time you need. I'll make sure you have transportation. But you'll have to sign a memorandum stating you will deposit the artwork from the castle in the regional museum in Sanok and not dispose of it without permission of the German government."

"I won't do anything of the sort. These things belong to me, and no one will tell me what to do with them."

Salon in Lesko Castle

"My God, man, don't be so romantic. I have a duty to perform, and I'll do it with or without your consent."

Not waiting for a response, he clicked his heels and departed.

Notwithstanding the count's objections, family honor bowed to necessity, and the Krasicki family abandoned Lesko. The Germans confiscated everything not considered of value to their war economy.

Before they departed, the count addressed his family at their last dinner at the castle.

"When we leave here, we leave as refugees. And as refugees, if we cannot take our people, we cannot take our dogs, either."

Their father's words stunned Bisia and Zosia.

It was three in the afternoon on Tuesday, October 3rd, 1939. I'll never forget it. I remember leaving the dogs behind after saying goodbye to our staff and entering the trucks. This would be the last time I saw Lesko as my home. Our sense of dislocation was acute. With three trucks loaded, German soldiers drove us away to Zagórz.

As their small convoy trundled over the loose lumber forming the bed of the bridge crossing the San River to the village of Huzele, Bisia looked up to the castle sitting atop the bluff. It would be two long years before she would see it up close again.

***

5

ZAGÓRZ

~ October 1939 ~

Since learning the Molotov-Ribbentrop Pact would place the family castle in Soviet hands, Bisia's father sent his butler Józef ahead to find suitable accommodations for the family and staff. Ten kilometers northwest across the San River, tucked into the forest below the road to Zagórz, stood a lovely little Italian-style castle owned by Baron Adam Gubrynowicz, a family friend who lived abroad. The Krasickis received permission from the baron's administrator to live in his place as a refuge from the Russian occupation of Lesko.

The Gubrynowicz lodge in Zagórz became home to Bisia, her sister Zosia, their parents, brother Antos and his family, along with Aunt Maryncia and her children Anna and Zygmund. Six servants also quartered downstairs, making for a full household.

The Germans had confiscated all radios, but Bisia found an old crank-style record player in a closet the evening they arrived. She also found several records, including one called *La Poloma*.

While the song played, the family gathered around the chalet-style wood-burning stove on the first floor. Bisia's mother told them about the song's connection to her father, who spent 1864 to 1867 in Mexico under the command of Austrian Archduke Ferdinand Maximilian, Emperor of Mexico.

"While he was in Mexico, he fell in love with a young woman named Emelie. Years later, he requested they play La Poloma at his funeral, in memory of his time in Mexico."

Let your sorrow take wings,
Let your heart ever sing love,
As you cherish the memory of our love,
That a dove may bring.

The ambiance in the lodge suited their reminiscences. Like at the castle in Lesko, the lodge was lit by paraffin-fueled lamps, which only seemed to intensify the darkness at the edges of their amber halos.

Grandfather:Count Stanislaw Wodzicki circa 1867, age 24

The next morning, as the family gathered for breakfast, Bisia saw a red German car approaching along the outer frontage road. But before the car looped back around to reach the front of the lodge, it stopped. The passenger-side door swung open and the family's dogs came running out. A German soldier got out, saluted, then turned the car around and drove away.

Since Count Krasicki remained an influential landowner, the lodge quickly became a hub for men and information moving through the frontier to the West to join Allied forces. And since Zagórz was only 70 kilometers from the Hungarian border and surrounded by dense forests, it made for an ideal hiding and transport place. Hungarians also offered invaluable help to escaping Polish troops trying to avoid capture.

Though Count Krasicki still managed the estate day-to-day, the German administration in the area appointed a Nazi overseer who demanded the Krasicki estate deliver a quota of farm produce, livestock, and timber to support the German war effort. Failure to comply would mean arrest and deportation to a concentration camp and confiscation of all properties.

While Germany concentrated its forces to the west after subduing Poland, the Soviet Union's Red Army moved from its invasion of

Poland in mid-September 1939 to regions of Finland before annexing Estonia, Latvia, Lithuania, and parts of Romania.

It took the family a few months to settle into their new environment and to become accustomed to German movements. Bisia's youngest brother Jas was in active service, a cadet in the Light Artillery trained in Przemyśl. From there, they sent him to the western front as a warrant officer, at which time the family lost track of his whereabouts. Third-born Xavier Krasicki and his wife Elka were expecting their first child, Magdalena, at any minute. Their whereabouts were unknown to the family, although they later received word they were in Warsaw.

Brother Stas served with the 12th Mounted Rifles, part of the 1st Polish Armored Division. His wife, Yadwiga, known as Gusia, and their two sons, Jerzy and Andrzej, remained in Stratyn. Later, they escaped to her family's home in Lwow after the Russians invaded. Finally, in the spring of 1940, Gusia and the boys joined the family in Zagórz, having lived through their own harrowing escape from Russian forces.

*

Before the government-in-exile officially formed the Polish Home Army, Armia Krajowa (abbreviated AK), in February 1942, a resistance movement arose automatically in reaction to the occupation. The Count retained his uniformed forest rangers, and instructed them to guide refugees to the Hungarian border, including many Jews who escaped from already established German camps. These actions fit with the Krasicki family motto: Amor Patriae Nostra Lex: Love of Country is Our Law. When called to fight for Poland, nobody hesitated. God and country came first, with family third.

The Blitzkrieg proved swift and decisive. The Polish Campaign lasted only five weeks, ending on 6 October. Afterward, the Germans could re-deploy to counter the Allied offensive the following spring.

Because people could move through their place in relative safety, the Krasicki lodge in Zagórz became the legal transfer point for official messengers, and the Count silently controlled who moved through his property to protect the ones carrying important information.

As the landowner, Papa still issued passes for people to buy lumber or firewood from his properties. This gave a semi-legal status for people to be in the area. These men would go to the forest to collect wood and disappear.

In the end, they reserved the exodus for movement runners going west to report to the government-in-exile.

There were only a few mountain passes linking Poland and Hungary. These men traveled on foot through the snows with little more than the clothing they wore. They were authentic heroes.

During this early period of occupation, three Polish officers hid at the lodge before attempting their escape through the mountains. One afternoon, an automobile drove down the road from above the lodge.

Zosia peered out the front windows to confirm what they suspected: an unannounced German visit.

The countess clapped her hands to alert their three guests.

"Quick, go outside to the shed and begin chopping wood. I will talk with the Germans."

The Krasicki family understood the Gestapo threat all too well. During the Anschluss of Austria in 1938, Nazi Germany arrested Austrian Chancellor Kurt von Schuschnigg after he banned the Nazi Party and arrested its members.

One of the weekly magazines the family subscribed to, *French Illustration*, always arrived wrapped in brown paper. Bisia recalled seeing her father opening the magazine one day as she stood beside his chair in the salon. After he put it down, she saw the picture on the cover of Chancellor von Schuschnigg being led in handcuffs by Gestapo officers. Her father quietly remarked, "This is the beginning of the end for us, too." Now, that same menace stood at their door.

Though the Germans took notice of the men chopping wood in the yard, they never questioned their presence. Instead, they only asked the Count to contact their commander in Sanok at his convenience.

When they departed, everyone let out a sigh of relief. The danger, however, never fully went away. Later, it fell to Bisia to lead the men through the surrounding countryside and forests toward the Hungarian border.

I took them with a horse and a two-wheel buggy we called a tag. It was the first of many such excursions for me.

~ There is Comfort in this Cage ~

Already involved with the underground movement, Bisia found it easy to overhear soldiers talking about troop movements and arms shipments in area cafes without raising suspicion. Afterward, she would report to her father and other officials with the information she gleaned.

One morning, Bisia walked five kilometers to the village of Poraz from the lodge. As she walked in the frigid air, the bright sun glanced off the snow and threw long shadows from the stands of trees along the sides of the narrow road. When she passed by the public schoolhouse in Poraz, she noticed a ladder leaning up against its front. Atop it stood a German soldier, pulling down the Polish emblem from above the door.

She stopped, hands clenched inside her coat pockets, her shoulders hunched against the cold. Her face must have betrayed her feelings because the young German officer in charge came over.

"You don't have to do this," she said through a white plume of breath, nodding at the man on the ladder.

"I do as I am told."

He asked who she was, and she told him.

"May I come to warn your family one day about what can happen?"

"Who am I to stop you?"

Bisia took a cigarette from her jacket and lit it.

"Do they approve of your smoking?"

"Who?"

"Your parents."

"Why would you ask that?"

"I might say the same about this."

He gestured to the school.

"I don't think my smoking is my parents' primary concern. This, I would say, is."

"Just warn your family. The regular army will move out of the area soon, and the Gestapo will be coming. They wear the same uniform as we do, but with one slight difference, the insignia on their lapels."

"I am aware."

"Remember, the bird on the left means the regular army, bird on the right means Gestapo. It might mean the difference between life and death."

Apart from the German eagle, the Gestapo troops also displayed silver "skull and crossbones" on their cap and lapels. The macabre insignia trumpeted their trade and terrorized anyone who came into contact with them.

Like with the Polish emblem on the schoolhouse in Poraz, the Germans began systematically destroying all forms of Polish culture throughout the country, as they tried to obliterate the underpinnings of what it meant to be a Pole. With the goal of creating a Greater Germany, they sought to eliminate the educated class, dismantling top Polish universities, stripping museums, closing theaters, newspapers, and radio stations. They even removed the bronze monument to Frédéric Chopin in the Lazienki Gardens in Warsaw.

Why Chopin? Because his music was the symbol of Polish patriotism; it was the sound of the Polish soul, and they snuffed it.

As Bisia and the young German officer continued to converse, he asked, "Why are you so down? You live in a beautiful home with servants. Is life so bad?"

In speaking with the Ritmeister, (meaning master of riding) Bisia realized it would be difficult to explain her feelings. While he was correct in his assessment of her exiled living conditions, in her heart she recalled the words of her great uncle, Prince Bishop Ignacy Krasicki (1735-1801), the pre-eminent Polish writer of the 18th century and Catholic primate of Poland. He wrote fables, satires, poetry, plays, and Poland's first modern novel. One parable, in particular, was à propos to their current situation and would answer the Ritmeister's question perfectly.

A young finch asked an older one why he wept:
"There's comfort in this cage where we are kept."
"You who were born here may well think that is so,
But I knew freedom once and now weep to know."

Perhaps my feelings were unjustified. Many countrymen lost a great deal more than their homes. But one doesn't choose such emotions, merely experiences them.

My friends, my friends
Can you explain to me?
How does it feel?
How does it really feel,
To be young and free?

How does it feel,
To walk happy and gay,
To the tune of one's heart,
Without fear, without bombs,
Which are burying fast,
One's present,
Future and past?

My friends, my friends,
Can you explain to me?
Is it merely by chance,
That you can give the answer,
While I can only ask,
How does it feel,
To be young and
Happy and free?

*

Bisia lived at the hunting lodge in Zagórz from October 1939 until the fall of 1940, when her parents decided she needed a change of scenery.

"I understand your young German soldier sent you a letter," her father said one night at dinner.

The accusation caught Bisia by surprise.

"*My* young German?"

"You have been communicating with him."

"I can't help if he sends me a letter."

Her father put down his fork and took her eye.

"And what are people to think?"

Earlier in the week, a letter arrived from the German Ritmeister Bisia met at the schoolhouse in Poraz. His name was Hans Rotewald, and in his letter, he informed her about the wounds he suffered in France before returning home.

"Bisia, your mother, and I think it's best if you go back to school for a while. There is a technical business school run by nuns in Nowy Sącz. It will give you something to do."

"I already have something to do. I have a job to do here."

"Exchanging correspondence with German soldiers?"

"Not exchanging. But, yes, to a certain degree, getting information is my job. Papa, I can learn a lot about what's happening more than other people."

Bisia turned to her mother.

"Didn't he tell me about the Gestapo coming when I first met him in Poraz?"

"Bisia, we don't think it's in your best interest to stay here right now."

In the year since Bisia completed Sacred Heart boarding school in June 1939, her parents came to think her life lacked structure. The school in Nowy Sącz would provide it. Bisia was young and headstrong. With so many troops stationed in the area, the possibility she might fall in love was always a possibility.

"They're sending me off to school in Nowy Sącz," Bisia later confided to her sister as she packed. "Mama says I'm growing too wild."

*

140 kilometers west of Lesko, Nowy Sącz sat close to the Czechoslovakian border and the rugged Tatra Mountains. The Gestapo stationed a reconnaissance unit there to cut off escape routes to the border.

Nowy Sącz was a lovely place, but God, it was cold. I slept in my sheepskin coat and woolen socks, and during the day, I wore gloves in class.

Her school was only eight kilometers from the home of her cousins, the Stadnickis, and she spent much of her free time on weekends at their lovely palace with her cousin Józef. Though his sisters had attended Sacred Heart boarding school in Tarnów with Bisia, Józef soon became her closest ally.

Despite being paralyzed by childhood polio, Józef was very active in the local underground, and used his disability to his advantage. To get around, he built a combination buggy and sleigh, which held his wheelchair and allowed him to travel by horse in any weather. Many times, Bisia would go with him and gallop through the forest on weekends.

It was great fun. He was full of life and adventure.

Just as they had taken the castle in Lesko before the Russians came at the onset of the war, the German command set up their regional headquarters at the Stadnicki Palace in Nowy Sącz.

From this lovely place, Józef maintained an active presence, conducting night raids with the local underground. He frustrated the local Gestapo no end.

"You play cards with this man?" the Gestapo officer would say to the regular army troops garrisoned at the palace.

"Why not? He isn't very good and is easy to beat."

"Do not trust this guy," one particular Gestapo officer would say. "He is one of those who does all those things at night, blowing up the bridges and moving people to the border."

Józef would sit in his wheelchair playing bridge with the German officers while the Gestapo accused him of sabotage. A bemused look played across his face at the idea of their charges.

"Ah, what are you saying?" the garrison officers said as they continued the game. "The man is paralyzed. What can he do?"

But it was all true, and Józef continued playing bridge during the day and blowing up bridges during the night. And try as they might, the Germans never caught him.

~ A Proposal ~

Early in the summer of '41, when her school session ended in Nowy Sącz, Bisia returned to the family lodge in Zagórz. Along the way home, she picked up rumors the Germans were about to attack Russia.

I spoke with some German officers in a café, and they told me. I always extracted information by simply saying, "Good morning" and letting the conversation flow. Strange, because that was why Mama and Papa sent me away.

Around this time, a significant buildup of German war machinery in the area suggested something big was about to happen. Bisia overheard one German bragging in a café, 'Tonight we will be in Moscow'.

The Countess & The P.O.W.

When Bisia arrived in Zagórz, plans were already underway for the celebration of brother Jas's name day on June 24th, the Nativity of St. John the Baptist. In Poland, celebrating the day of the year associated with your baptismal name superseded your birthday in terms of importance.

On the night of the 21st, a large group of family and friends gathered atop the tower at the lodge, hoping they might see evidence of the rumored attack. They stayed up all night. At dawn, as the sky blushed with the coming day, it began as a faint murmur. But slowly the dull roar of engines increased until the full power of the German Luftwaffe appeared overhead.

And we were on the tower drinking champagne. Toast to the defeat of Germany! Toast to the defeat of Russia! Vivat! Toast to the freedom of Poland!

They drank with a reckless hope, still unwilling to accept this collapsing star of their world.

It was such an exhilarating feeling. Maybe twenty of us were up there. And boy, it came. Oh, God! There was one German Stuka after another, one warplane after another. Waves! Hundreds of planes heading east to attack Russia. They filled the skies, overwhelming any attempt to speak over the roar. At last, the historical dream was coming true, that they would kill each other, the Russians and Germans. What a joy!

They stayed up the entire night drinking and listening to records on the old hand-crank phonograph Bisia found the first night of their arrival. They carried it up from the library earlier in the evening. Among the guests was her old friend Andrzej Morawski.

Though his family didn't hold a formal title, Andrzej's family came from an old lineage in the gentry-class and owned a small piece of property in Niebieszczany, 11 kilometers southwest of Zagórz. His father was a colonel in the Polish army away on duty, but his older brother had been killed in France. His mother also passed within the last year, suffering a heart attack after a surprise search of their home by the Gestapo. Afterward, Andrzej visited Zagórz more often, and he and Bisia struck up a close friendship.

I knew Andrzej was fond of me. But since I'd been away in Nowy Sącz, I was a little unprepared when he approached me the night when the Germans attacked the Russians.

As the party continued, Andrzej walked over to where Bisia was standing at the parapet, smoking a cigarette. He had been too young to enter the military when the war began. After the German occupation, he administered his family land while his father served. It placed him in an uncomfortable position, not being in the military, like most young men.

"Wouldn't it be something if the Germans and Russians killed one another?" he said.

"We should be so lucky," Bisia said as music from a phonograph played behind her.

Life during the occupation had taken on a louche quality, as uncertainty weighted the days, and fear menaced the nights. Nothing was permanent, including liaisons. In a normal year, a young woman like Bisia fresh out of boarding school might expect to attend a round of fall galas and balls where she would meet eligible young men. But like so much else, the war upset the traditional social routines.

You lived in the moment. The world shrank to small groups of friends, relatives, and compatriots because everything beyond them wasn't to be trusted.

"I would've liked to have lived a little longer in our old world," Andrzej said as they leaned along the parapet. "And Bisia, I know I can't offer much. And I realize your parents would never allow it, but —"

She stopped him with a brush of her hand through his hair before letting it rest on his forearm. They shared a lot together, and he had lost a great deal.

"Andjey, you are one of my dearest friends," she said, "but who can make plans now? Please, let's just salute the Russian and German divorce tonight, and not talk about other things, alright?"

By addressing her parents' probable reaction and his own lack of social standing, Andjey failed to win points with Bisia. She never cared about such things. Instead of presenting the positive side of his proposal, Andjey offered only its minuses.

***

6
VISIT TO LESKO

~ 1941 ~

After the German declaration of war on the Soviet Union in June 1941, the Russians abandoned the castle in Lesko. Still, the bridge over the San River remained closed, and the family was unable to return home.

Not long after, Zosia and Bisia rode their bicycles from Zagórz back to Huzele, the small village across the San River from Lesko.

"We should go up and look around," Bisia said after they arrived at the foot of the bridge.

Looking east past Huzele to Lesko across the San River

"I don't think that's a good idea."

"Why? The Russians left; the place is probably empty."

"Probably?"

"Didn't you hear Jas say one of our old coachmen went across to visit his family by bribing the German guard? He said there was nothing to worry about.

"How can we tell if it will be the same guard?" Zosia asked. "Or that he'll be honorable?"

"Why wouldn't he be? He's only passing the day, standing alone on a small bridge. What difference is it to him if two girls go to visit their home, and he makes a small profit? Come on."

Despite Zosia's reluctance, the guard allowed the girls to pass with a quick word and exchange of money. They walked up the path through the park to the castle grounds. For the two young women, their first visit home after a two-year absence was an emotional moment.

The park was a paradise in our childhood. As a botanist, our father taught us the name of every tree, every rock, every plant. We would write the name of every tree on a little piece of paper and attach it close by. There was also a little glen where I would go after being punished to contemplate and cry about my disappointment.

Zosia with small deer in the park

Now, as their father once feared, the fluted stands of lindens and beech trees had been shelled. A bunker and gun emplacement still stood abandoned in the park, too. To see their home, once so care for, now broken and overrun with weeds, a home now homeless, hit them hard.

The castle itself sat empty and ravaged. Twice in the past, fires had scarred the castle: first in 1701 during the Deluge, the war against the Swedes; again in 1915, when Russian soldiers torched the place, retreating from Austrians during World War I. Both times, the castle had been rebuilt, so only in the rear did the castle still resemble its medieval heritage.

When Zosia and Bisia entered, they did not find the same home they left two years before. Like a once proud man bent by time, the rooms stood hollow, stripped of their furniture, books, and paintings.

The place resembled a barn, filthy, smelling of animals. It broke our hearts to find it in this state, haunted by the memories of so much joy. But it was good to be there, too, because we loved the place a great deal.

Zosia wiped debris off the mantel over the fireplace in the front salon. Next, they went upstairs to their old rooms before moving to the balcony outside. When Bisia fixed her gaze to the distance past the village of Huzele to Gruszka Mountain, it was almost possible to imagine the gardens below still in full flower, with flax, petunias, and red salvia ringing the close-cut grass inside the circular drive. Around the fountain, she recalled the agave plants her father planted with their spiny leaves. Girding the driveway stood large wooden pots holding exotic palm trees, which the gardeners returned to the hothouse each winter.

Though blocked by the canopy of the trees in the park, Bisia recalled the low rumble of horses and carts making their way across the loose wooden bed of the bridge spanning the San River to Huzele. The sound held a comforting reassurance of what once seemed a timeless way of life.

In the distance rose the forest they called Gruszka, the Pear, rising to nearly 2000 feet (ca. 610m). Gruszka was the center of the estate's timber business and also where the family skied in the wintertime. The horizon to the west rose and fell with the line of the Bieszczady Mountains, crowned at their peaks with thick stands of spruce, fir, and pine. To the south, Czulnia rose 1900 feet (ca. 579 m), with another expanse of forest curving around to the town of Hoczew, 7.5 kilometers down along the San. On the western side of the San spread the checkerboard of green and gold farmland dotted with haystacks, resembling rows of thimbles from Bisia's distant perspective.

Bisia also remembered watching the early summer sunsets over Gruszka from the cool stone veranda beneath the portico. Smears of pink and violet cradled the sun in its descent, comforting as a mother's hand.

As she viewed this vacant land where the birds no longer sang, she understood why Zosia questioned the need to return. When her gaze fell again to the castle grounds, the reality hit. The lush green ivy that once scaled the columns in front now hung ripped and sagging, like the celibate silence that had replaced the joyful sounds she once remembered.

"Bisia!"

Zosia's voice broke through Bisia's reverie. Looking out, Bisia saw two tall Germans marching up the path from the park through the colonnade of trees, one tapping his baton against his shiny black boots.

"You, up there," said the one pointing with his baton. "What are you doing here? Who are you? Are you Jews?!"

"This is our home," Bisia said as she leaned on the railing. "We are just visiting."

We had not expected company once we got past the guard at the bridge. I had never seen Zosia so afraid. I recalled seeing signs mounted on the gates saying, "Jews not allowed."

The two men waited as the young women made their way downstairs. Both men wore the eagle insignia sewn on the right lapels of their uniforms, identifying them as Gestapo officers.

"Who are you?"

"We grew up here," Zosia said. "This is our father's place, and we came back to visit after the Russians left."

"Fine, then you should be able to show us where everything is. You!" And the German on the right pointed his baton at Bisia. "Show me."

One herded me and the other took Zosia to tour the castle. I couldn't tell what they would ask, or how to respond, because Zosia and I had no chance to prepare anything.

At each doorway, the Gestapo asked what they should find inside. Not knowing how the Russians changed the place, Bisia and Zosia said only what they remembered from two years earlier. The last room they came to had been her mother's room. Bisia was told to sit. The floor lay covered with straw, only a filthy Russian table and chairs made of rough wood remained as furniture.

"I can't sit in this mess," Bisia said in protest.

On one wall, a torn poster of Stalin hung with one of its corners drooping. The Gestapo officer ripped it down and slapped it hard on one chair.

"Now sit!"

Trying to stay calm, Bisia said, "We also came to visit Madam Glixelli. She was our housekeeper. She is Italian, your ally."

Weakness, I learned, never worked with the Germans, especially the Gestapo. He kept switching moods. One moment he would seem understanding, the next bark at me like an angry dog. A tremendous amount of nervous tension coursed through the room.

"I'm telling you. Our father is Reichsgraf Krasicki. We lived here our entire lives until the Bolsheviks took it. And we were homesick. Wouldn't you be?"

Though the Germans held all the force, Bisia's pugnacious attitude along with an obvious knowledge of the place backed her claims. The Gestapo officers escorted them back to the bridge.

"This is not your place anymore. Don't let us find you here again. You understand?"

Bisia wasn't so delusional that she didn't realize how fortunate they had been in this confrontation. The Gestapo might have done anything: rape them, kill them, throw them into the San, and no one would ever be the wiser. The family didn't even realize they had gone to visit Lesko.

As they crossed back over the bridge to retrieve their bicycles, Bisia turned and scanned the view of her home, beleaguered and empty on its bluff above the river.

Strange, I would still use the word home. I was aware the reality of it had changed, but the feeling remained strong: things might still turn back, if only in the future.

Since the attack by warplanes on their journey east in the first days of the war, Bisia always held her composure. But now the tears came, like from a reservoir whose dam had given way. Zosia put her arm around her sister as they walked. As it was Bisia's nature to fight, so was it Zosia's instinct to comfort, though tears streaked her face as well. For Bisia, the experience felt like she had picked at a scab and now regretted it.

*

Around the time Bisia returned home, word circulated the Germans were deporting Jews from surrounding towns and villages west to Zasław. Jewish ghettos existed in Warsaw and Nowy Sącz, each filled with thousands of poor souls from the city and surrounding towns. At first, the adults whispered among themselves when speaking of these ghettos, while the children listened in silence.

Before the outbreak of the war, there had been a thriving Jewish social and cultural life throughout Poland. In 1939, the Polish population of Jews stood at 3.3 million, the second largest Jewish community in the world. Jews made up some 30% of the capital's 1.3 million inhabitants.

A well-developed Jewish press circulated over 30 daily newspapers and 130-plus periodicals in Polish, Hebrew, and Yiddish. Jews filled important segments of Polish society, including doctors, dentists, lawyers, academics, writers, and entrepreneurs. The military formed another career path.

Yet the Jewish population did not share in the fruits experienced by other Poles during the economic boom in the mid-to-late 1930s. Jews did not work in the civil service. Nor did many find employment with the railroads or other state-controlled industries. Further, by law, all businesses closed on Sundays, which only reduced Jewish commerce even more because their businesses closed on Saturdays for their own Sabbath. None of it mattered now.

Later, Bisia learned how most Jews from Nowy Sącz and the local area faced execution in Zasław, while the Germans transported the rest north to the Bełżec death camp, where gas chambers awaited.

In the fall of 1941, Bisia's parents again shipped her west to her cousin Stadnicki's place in Nowy Sącz, where she took instruction in agricultural production. With her cousin Józef and his sisters, Bisia sat grouped around a hidden radio in December 1941, applauding as they listened to the BBC report the entry of America into the fight after the Japanese attack on Pearl Harbor.

We were hoping so much the Americans would change the war, hoping it might be over fast, and our lives might still return to what we remembered.

***

7
PEARL HARBOR

~ 1941 ~

When Congress passed the first Selective Service Act in 1940 to spike the size of the U.S. military, the local draft board classified Isham as III-C, sole support for his mother. Over the next year, the once meager U.S. Army, though still in need of modernization, had swelled to 1.4 million.

In June 1941, Isham received a promotion to assistant manager of the Gatesworth Hotel, putting him in charge of the entire 150-person staff. His duties were to keep the hotel filled, keep it clean, sell banquets, sell parties, and manage the Walnut Room. The hotel was where he ate his meals, bought his cigarettes, drank, washed his laundry, everything.

Designed by Preston J. Bradshaw and built in 1925, the Gatesworth Hotel stood along the northern edge of Forest Park, site of the 1904 St. Louis World's Fair.

That summer, along with many others, performers from the Muny Opera lived at the hotel during their summer runs, as 30 percent of the hotel occupancy was long-term guests. The Muny was the oldest and largest outdoor amphitheater in the country, seating 11,000 for its summer musicals since 1917.

Monday nights after a show opening, the Walnut Room at the hotel filled with the cast, crew, and audience members. People stood outside looking in through the windows, because the singers in the chorus, even the lead actors, would often go up and sing and entertain. It would always be quite a show.

King Kosher, manager of Park Plaza Hotel; Bill Vickers of Lenox Hotel; all the managers and assistant managers at the Coronado, the Jefferson, Congress, and Senate Hotels would show up, and Isham would sign their tabs, same as they did for him at their bars and showrooms, as a professional courtesy.

*

Five months later, on a lazy Sunday morning in early December, Isham was at his desk going over inventory lists for the Walnut Room. His desk sat just off the lobby, behind a set of double glass doors leading to the executive offices. Three black phones rested atop his desk, one for in-house use, one for outside local calls, and the third for long-distance. A beam of sun from a nearby window slanted across his right trouser leg. After a while, Isham noticed guests mingling in the lobby, joined in animated conversation.

"What the hell is going on?" he wondered, but only with a passing interest as his mind remained focused on the mystery of the missing beer in the Walnut Room.

For several weeks, discrepancies had been showing up in both the bottle and tap beer logs. They created inventory lists every night after closing, then again before the place re-opened at three the next afternoon. The boss even put locks on the ice cabinets. Somehow, the beer still kept disappearing, and Isham pledged to find out why.

"What is all the commotion about?" Isham asked as an army colonel staying at the hotel came up to his desk to cash a check.

"You haven't heard?" the army colonel said to Isham. "The Japanese attacked Pearl Harbor this morning. The news is all over the radio."

People got all their news from the daily papers and radio in that era, but Isham had become disillusioned with the St. Louis papers after their turnaround on the Russians following the Soviet invasion of Finland in 1939.

At first, the papers portrayed the Russians as horrible, barbaric people. Then, all of a sudden, they turned into honorable warriors because of the German threat.

Isham accepted the check, and wrote the man's details on the back, including the date, December 7, 1941. He had been on duty since 7 a.m. and the hotel remained quiet with the usual light traffic to and from church services and breakfast in the restaurant. Now, the place buzzed like a hive. Isham felt a little embarrassed as he handed the money to the colonel.

"I've been so focused on this hotel. I haven't paid much attention to the news."

The colonel explained how devastating a surprise attack would be on our naval base of operations in the Pacific. Then, after receiving his money, he checked out of the hotel and headed back to his post at Fort Leonard Wood, west of St. Louis.

There was no screaming or panic, more like hearing about an accident on the railroad, like hearing a fact. But even as events unfolded, I couldn't grasp where Pearl Harbor was. Hawaii, yes, but it made little sense to me. My thoughts centered on the buildup in Europe alone. I didn't understand the Japanese involvement in the least.

Only after another guest, an Indonesian man who worked for Shell Oil, came up and read a telegram aloud, calling him back home to service, did Isham understand about the war in the Far East. That man packed up and moved out the same day, too, with his entire family.

Once the reality of the Japanese attack set in, President Roosevelt made his "A date which will live in Infamy" speech before a joint session of Congress, and the media got a hold of it with their screaming headlines, Isham, like hundreds of thousands of other patriotic young men, went down to his draft board to change his draft status to 1-A and enlist.

Here was this war, and it had to be the biggest adventure of my generation. No way was I going to miss out on it.

*

When he received his notification to report for his army physical exam on April 25, 1942, it pleased Isham a great deal. His mother did not share his enthusiasm.

"My heart fell with a thud," she wrote in her diary. *"How many, many mothers have had the same heartache? But somehow that doesn't help me at all. Please, protect my boy."*

Lena Stites Reavis, age 65

In late April 1942, Hitler and Mussolini met at the German Chancellor's mountaintop retreat in Berchtesgaden, Germany, to plan future Axis strategy in North Africa and the Mediterranean. Their principal objectives were the reduction of Malta, seizure of the Suez Canal, and capture of the rich oil fields to the east.

Saturday, May 23, 1942, was Isham's last day after 6½ years at the Gatesworth Hotel. Over that span, the hotel owner Delmar Gates had grown to like and depend on his assistant manager.

"Listen, anything you want," Gates said as he paid Isham a full salary until June 15th. "Only, come on back whenever you are ready. We will always have a place for you here."

Isham gratefully accepted Gates' largesse, but made no promises; the future was far too uncertain. But it was a patriotic time, and no one had a problem with young men signing up for the military and taking off to go fight. It just meant everyone who stayed behind would have to work a little harder.

Brother Burton tried to sign up for the service, too, but had suffered heatstroke as a boy and didn't sweat. None of the services would take him. Instead, he accepted an opportunity with D'Arcy Advertising at their home office in New York City. More than that, he wanted to leave St. Louis.

'I'm going to New York,' Isham overheard his brother say one time. 'There, I won't be Isham's younger brother.'

He didn't say it with any animosity, just a statement of fact. The move, he hoped, would free him to shine in his own light.

Brother Burton Reavis

Though Isham passed his physical exam in April, he didn't leave St. Louis for basic training until September 1942.

My papers somehow got attached to those of a man who was deceased. So, they listed me as dead for all those months, too, until somebody discovered the error.

Isham received his induction notice on September 15th and officially entered the service at Jefferson Barracks on the 24th. By October 18, 1942, he was aboard a train heading down to Camp Wolters, Texas, for thirteen weeks of basic training, the newest private in the United States Army.

*

The lightning-like successes the Germans engineered during the first years of war stalled as the theater of war expanded. In August 1942, German General Erwin Rommel's famed Africa Korps engaged with British General Bernard Montgomery's 8th Army in North Africa. On November 8th, General Dwight D. Eisenhower led an American invasion of Morocco and Algeria, forcing Rommel to take on a second front. Four days later, Montgomery re-took Tobruk. And though the Brits suffered heavy losses, they broke Rommel's 100,000-man strong Africa Korps, which took 50% casualties during * the El Alamein campaign.

British Prime Minister Winston Churchill hailed the victory as the turning point in the war, and called for church bells to be rung throughout his beleaguered country.

Isham & Jimmy Reilly at Camp Wolters

On the second day of basic training, Isham's drill sergeant named him an acting corporal, in charge of squad four, Company B-3, 59th Training Battalion. It wasn't only because he received ROTC training in school; Isham was one of the few men in the company who could read or write.

Who else were they going to put in charge?

Isham taught more men how to tie a necktie in those 13 weeks than he would have thought possible. Men raised in the hills of Tennessee would line up at his bunk, and Isham would go through the process until each man could manage a half-Windsor knot on his own.

None of these men ever wore a necktie in their lives. Probably never did again once they were out of the service. They weren't stupid, though, only uneducated. I would write their letters home, and they would polish my brass and shine my shoes. We got along great.

Before basic training ended, Isham and another of the squad leaders, fellow St. Louisan Jimmy Reilly, began planning.

"I think we should try for OCS (Officer Candidate School)," said Jimmy one night as they listened to the Falstaff Hour over KMOX radio in St. Louis. From its 50,000-watt, clear-channel location at

1120 on the AM dial, KMOX beamed out to over 40 states at night. It brought the boys closer to home whenever they dialed it in on their camp radio.

Isham slid back on his bunk, lacing his hands behind his head.

"Hell, I don't want to be a private. Besides, these clothes they issued us don't fit worth a damn. If I knew we'd be wearing these ugly pants, I wouldn't have signed up to begin with. At least as officers, we can buy our own uniforms and have them tailored."

Of course, it was much more than the quality of his clothing that motivated Isham. A sense of responsibility overrode every other consideration. Despite banging his arms, skinning his knees, cutting his hands, and pulling cactus needles from his legs, Isham wished every man could leave basic training, feeling the same fondness for the experience he did.

***

8
GESTAPO!

~ 1942 ~

Now aged 21, Bisia returned to the lodge in Zagórz in January 1942, where she became more involved with the growing underground movement.

Because of its rural setting, the road fronting the lodge remained mostly free of traffic, save for an occasional horse-drawn farmer's cart, or a passing German army truck. But one afternoon several horse-drawn sleighs and carts loaded with people huddled together against the cold stopped. Bisia's young nephew Jerzy called his mother Gusia over to see.

"Mother, where are all these people going?"

News of the deportation of the Jewish population distressed everyone in the family and led to speculation as to their fate. Sometime later, word filtered back: the Germans were holding these unfortunate people in a partially completed celluloid factory on the outskirts of Zagórz and also using the men on labor crews.

Germans used Jewish prisoners as woodcutters in the forests of the estate, and this day a gang of 20 workers stood with their guards in front of the lodge after finishing their day's work. Their breath steamed in the brittle air. Black-uniformed Ukrainian Police referred to as "Siczowcy" (Cossacks) guarded them. The officers of the guard unit entered the kitchen and demanded hot drinks.

Countess Izabela Krasicka, who her grandchildren called 'Bunia', organized the hot drinks, and, to keep the guards in good spirits, gave them some vodka, too. In the meantime, behind the guards' backs, she sent some hot soup to the Jewish men standing outside in the snow.

As the winter light faded, the Ukrainian guards exited the lodge and marched the waiting work gang back to their perilous future.

Later, four Jewish workers who remained hidden behind a snowdrift along the edge of the forest approached the lodge and asked the family for help.

We led them inside and gave them comfortable accommodations in the cellars, where they stayed for several days, gaining their strength. After supplying them with provisions, Papa's forest rangers escorted them through the forests to the nearby Hungarian border, which they crossed to safety.

After two years of ad hoc resistance to the German occupation, Armia Krajowa (The Home Army) formally organized in February 1942. Known by its initials, AK, The Home Army merged the vast Polish underground forces loyal to the government-in-exile in London. Over time, the resistance grew to 400,000 members, making it the largest official resistance force in occupied Europe.

AK's primary operations focused on gathering information and sabotaging German transports headed to the Eastern Front in the Soviet Union. Bisia took her oath to join the Home Army around this time.

Native to the area, fluent in German, and with a taste for adventure, Bisia proved a willing recruit. Though Zosia became involved in activities by her presence in Zagórz, she did not officially enter the service. She believed that a woman's job wasn't to engage in war, but to create life and raise children. Bisia realized these were not normal times. She didn't think she had any choice in the matter.

Since opening the second front with Russia in June 1941, German supply routes through Poland increased significantly. Disruption of these supply lines occupied some underground activity, but the gathering of information, and preparation for the eventual return of their government-in-exile, remained their primary duty.

Bisia's swearing-in took place in the town of Lubla, 40 kilometers northwest of Zagorz at the home of Jan Dzianott (b. 1915), a member of the AK shield who everyone called Kanty. Married with one child, Kanty often visited the lodge in Zagórz as a friend of the family. Bisia met him and they flirted. She also went to his place where they danced and drank a lot, as usual.

I think his wife was interested in somebody else, too. Kanty was the first man you might say I fell in love with.

Rudus Romer conducted Bisia's swearing ceremony. He was a patriotic Pole of German descent, and a leader of the resistance in the region. The Germans enforced a police-hour curfew, sometimes seven o'clock, sometimes nine, which restricted travel at night.

That evening, a small group of ten assembled in Kanty's living room. They all dressed in simple clothing. Romer's daughter, Ida, also took her oath that night. She attended Sacred Heart boarding school one year behind Bisia.

By the soft light of the table lamps and the glow from the stone fireplace, the two young women stood, and individually, with one hand upon a cross and the other raised, they recited the pledge following Romer's lead.

"Before God Almighty and Mary the Blessed Virgin, Queen of the Polish Crown, I pledge allegiance to my motherland, the Republic of Poland. I pledge to guard her honor steadfastly, and to fight for her liberation with all my strength, to the extent of sacrificing my own life, if that is needed. I pledge unconditional obedience to the President of Poland, the Commander-in-Chief of the Republic of Poland, and the Home Army Commander, who will be appointed. I pledge to keep secret whatever may happen to me. So help me God!"

"You are now enrolled in the ranks of the Polish Home Army," said Rudus. "Your duty is to serve. Your only compensation will be Poland's freedom. Any treason is punishable by death."

Afterward, they drank, half in business, half in friendship. It was not a party atmosphere like the night the Germans attacked Russia, and everyone cheered and drank in celebration atop the lodge in Zagórz. Instead, the moment represented a time of great meaning and high purpose.

~ Adam ~

The Sanok District Command, code-named "San," was subordinate to the Kraków District Inspectorate and Jasło Inspectorate of the Home Army. Command headquarters for the Sanok District had first been in Poraz, 5 km south-west of Zagórz, 8 km south of Sanok. But in mid-February 1943, a new commander for the South Home Army Group moved to the Gubrynowicz lodge in Zagórz by order of the AK command after consultation with Count Krasicki.

A career army officer from Lwow, Captain Adam Winogrodzki took part in the September '39 campaign at the start of the war. Taken prisoner by the Germans, he escaped from a P.O.W. camp in Kraków in December and returned to Przemyśl, a town 70 kilometers north of Lesko.

AK officials asked Count Krasicki if he would appoint Winogrodzki as his secretary and estate administrator as a cover job for his role as commander of all AK units in the South Home Army Group. The count agreed, and though it would place the entire household in constant danger, it was a danger everyone patriotically assumed.

If the Germans discovered Winogrodzki's identity as the AK commander, everyone in the house would be in jeopardy. The household, therefore, saw men coming and going from abroad constantly, but always with an eye out for German intrusion.

Adam Winogrodzki

Winogrodzki carried two underground names, Korwin and Ordon, as AK gave everyone in the movement false names to protect their fellow partisans in case of capture and torture. Some people Bisia knew only as 'Raven', 'Satan', or 'Lightning'. Her own nom de geurre was 'Barbara', though whenever she worked in her home district, she used her actual name.

*

Bisia was still away when Adam arrived at Zagórz. Upon her return to the lodge, they met when he was coming down the steps as she was going up.

"Gen dobre, Pani," he said as they met along the staircase. "People told me a lot about you."

In his early forties (b. 25 May 1901), Adam was tall, with a strong profile. He wore his light-brown hair combed straight back. His hair and small mustache showed flecks of gray. He wore high riding boots, riding pants, a blue coat, a simple white shirt, and a tightly knotted red tie. Bisia recognized him, but what to say? So, with a smile and a slight nod, she continued on her way.

Adam was a charismatic man, and I soon came under his immediate command, serving both as a courier and for reconnaissance. I also had a crush on him. Most of the women did.

For Poles, fighting was a patriotic duty. But for Bisia, a sense of daring contributed to the movement, too, like riding or driving fast. Bisia, and others like her, fell into this war because it was their generation's fight. But Adam served because he enlisted as a professional soldier. He chose to fight, and it added to their admiration for him.

Many husbands were away fighting abroad, including Bisia's second brother Stas. His wife, Gusia, arrived in Zagórz from Stratyn with her two sons, George and Andrew in 1940. Three years later, she began flirting with newly arrived Captain Winogrodzki.

In part because of their 16-year age difference, Bisia always looked up to and admired Gusia, whom she perceived as more worldly and sophisticated. Born in a titled family from Lwow and married in 1930, Gusia traveled between homes with her own servants and children. Bisia recently left a convent school, unworldly. Gusia had lived.

Count August Krasicki also developed a satisfactory personal relationship with the German authorities in Sanok, the region's largest city with a population of 30,000. Though they were never invited as guests to Zagórz, this cordial relationship with the authorities further covered the underground activity in and around the Krasicki lodge. It was important for the Germans, too, to maintain a social relationship with the Polish count, an ex-Austrian cavalry officer. This relationship, however, did not eliminate danger for the Krasickis.

During the German occupation, the tyranny of fear pervaded everything. In September 1941, Hitler issued a decree entitled The Night and Fog Decree (Nacht und Nebel). Any person suspected of resistance risked being seized and taken into the night, never to be seen again.

~ Gestapo! ~

One Sunday morning in the winter of 1942, Jas, Zosia, and Bisia were alone in the lodge, testing one of the three radios the family concealed as part of their underground activities. Through these radios, they monitored transmissions from the BBC in London.

They stored the radios in a bunker deep in the cellars beneath the foundation of the lodge. These cellars contained the kitchens and storerooms for the household. Hidden at the rear of the cellars in the area where they stacked all the wood used for the stoves and fireplaces, Adam Winogrodzki kept a specially constructed hidden bunker. In it, he operated his AK command. It could also be an emergency hide-away if a sudden raid took place. Sentries stood posted two kilometers away who could notify Winogrodzki by radio if a raiding party approached.

Many rows of logs needed to be removed before anyone gained entrance to the bunker through a narrow tunnel. Inside, Adam set up a fully equipped command post with radios, maps, ammunition, storage, and telephones. Everyone was aware of the grave consequences if the Germans discovered this bunker.

Brother Jas returned home from the front in early 1940 after the Russians overran the Polish defenses. After he returned to Zagórz, he began working with the underground. Before becoming the unit's quartermaster in 1943, his duties included monitoring radio transmissions from abroad.

That Sunday morning, the Krasickis took one radio from the bunker and brought it to the front hallway, searching for a clear frequency. As they fiddled with the dial, the crunch of tire chains coming along the snow-covered road above the lodge alerted them to an unannounced arrival.

Not bothering to see who it might be, Jas gathered the cumbersome radio receiver in his arms.

"There's no time to get it back to the bunker," he said, as he labored to carry it upstairs. "Do what you can. I'll be down as fast as I can."

People stored many things in the attic and cellars of the lodge. Not only what the Krasicki family brought from the castle in Lesko but also things belonging to the owners and others who were abroad.

Shortly, a loud banging on the front door announced their unwanted visitors.

"Aufmachen! Aufmachen!" ("Open up! Open up!")

Jas hurried downstairs, straightening his sweater as Zosia and Bisia went to the door. They opened it slowly, like for a visiting neighbor.

Sweeping into the open foyer marched three Gestapo officers with weapons in hand, along with a Ukrainian who denounced the family to them.

"This is the house with the radio," he said, clutching his hat in his hands. "They hide Polish officers here, too. I've seen them."

Though Poland and Ukraine shared common enemies in Germany and the Soviet Union, long-standing territorial disputes between the two nations also harbored ill feelings and mutual distrust. Ukrainians in the area often collaborated with the Germans occupiers against the partisan Poles.

"Who lives here?" asked the ranking German as his eyes darted across the room.

"We do," Jas said in German. "This is the home of Reichsgraf Krasicki. We are his family."

"Well, where is he, then?"

"Our parents are at church."

"I'm telling you, this is the right place," the Ukrainian said.

"All right, keep quiet."

The Gestapo officer moved farther into the foyer before turning back to Jas with his pistol leveled.

"We are making a search. We hear you are hiding Polish officers and have a radio as well."

"It's a lie," Jas told him as he walked to the fireplace. "Search all you want. Your man there is a fool."

One German herded Zosia and Bisia to the library with a wave of his gun. The other two and the Ukrainian forced Jas to take them through the house while they searched. Of course, Jas, Zosia, and Bisia knew they secured two other radios in the cellar. Bisia wondered how well Jas could hide the last one.

Though cold outside, a beam of sun gathered warmth through the south-facing window in the library. Immediately, Bisia came on the defensive, speaking to the Gestapo officer guarding them.

"Why do you listen to that man? He's wasting your time. We don't own a radio. They were all confiscated years ago."

"There will be no discussion. Sit down and be quiet."

"You don't understand. We have a phonograph right here. We play it every day. And because we listen to music, this idiot Ukrainian thinks he hears a radio? You don't believe it? We play many German songs, too. Why do you listen to this peasant?"

Instead of sitting, Bisia went over to the phonograph where she selected a popular German record, Einem Kleinen Café in Hernault. She placed it on the turntable and turned the crank several times on the side of the chest-high oak cabinet. Once the record began spinning, she lowered the arm until the needle swayed along the perimeter of the record, before moving inward, pulling the voice from between the grooves.

"You see? This is why he says there is a radio. It's a mistake, that's all."

Bisia shrugged, suggesting a simple misunderstanding explained everything. She joined Zosia on the couch, where she picked up a silver cigarette case sitting on the coffee table.

Perhaps my talking was too full of protest. And that would be a giveaway, too. But at least in talking, I channeled my fear. But I didn't make eye contact, either, afraid if he caught my eye, he would catch the truth in them.

While Bisia played her charade, Zosia avoided contact with the intruders. Bisia took out a cigarette, tapped it against the case. On the front was the family crest, Rogala, while inside were the engraved signatures of all the officers in her father's World War 1 cavalry unit. She held the case open to the German. He declined with a wave of his weapon. But her argument seemed to loosen him a little, though he still didn't talk, and kept his machine gun at hip level and pointed in their general direction as he stood inside the doorway.

Jas and the others searched the rooms upstairs for what seemed an eternity. Bisia changed the record once, chatted with Zosia, all to keep calm amidst the tension churning inside.

We didn't know what they might find upstairs, and I fought with the idea of what I would do if shots rang out. I didn't have a weapon. My only thought was to throw Papa's cigarette case at the German as hard as I could and rush him if he ducked. It wasn't much of a plan, but it at least gave me something positive to hold on to.

The clump of boots on the stairs alerted Bisia of the return of Jas, the Germans, and the Ukrainian. She stubbed out her cigarette and stood. Jas looked rather pale, but otherwise in good shape, as he shot his sisters a glance of relief.

Alongside Jas, the Gestapo officer took to bawling out the Ukrainian as he signaled for the man holding Bisia and Zosia to come with them.

"The next time you denounce someone, you better show proof, because we won't waste time bothering these people again."

And with nothing more, they all walked out the front door.

"But I'm telling you, they've been harboring Polish soldiers," the Ukrainian said in a pleading tone. "I know what I heard."

"Enough," said the head German officer, cuffing the man on the side of the head as he and his men walked to their car and drove away.

When the Germans left, Jas explained how lucky he had been during the search.

"When we came to the room where I hid the radio, I told them it was my room. For whatever reason, he said, 'Count, we will not ask to invade this privacy'. I couldn't believe it. But since I knew it was the most dangerous place, as long as he didn't ask to go to the cellars, the rest of the search would be safe."

Some days later, Gestapo summoned their father to Gestapo headquarters in Sanok to answer questions. This put the entire family into a high state of apprehension. People ordered to such meetings often failed to return. The count received a relatively civil hearing, though, considering his hosts.

Again, his fluency in the German language helped, but it also suggested to the Germans a potential alliance. They told him he should cooperate with them and inform on Polish "bandits" who lurked in the area. Every nation had its collaborators. But August maintained he would never cooperate with his country's invaders.

Faced with this curt refusal, the Gestapo man leaned across the table.

"I hope you remember where you are, Herr Graf."

But with only this reprimand, they let him go.

It was a scary time, and not the only one like it, either. But that is how we lived, always on an edge, pretending to be calm when in reality our innocence was a charade.

It became second nature to hide people and get involved in underground activity. Bisia already performed courier duties transporting information from headquarters to units in the region. Since they hid the AK headquarters at the family's residence, and the commanding officer lived with them as manager of their estate, the household hoarded ammunition, grenades, and automatic rifles in the cellar. With arms and people hidden everywhere, remaining undiscovered required a certain amount of luck they never took for granted.

* * *

9
BESKO LURE

~ Summer 1942 ~

After three years of war, Bisia had changed from a girl searching for personal freedom and excitement to a woman devoted to the service of her nation.

In the summer of 1942, she attended a secret training school in Baranowka, 230 kilometers west of Zagórz, above Kraków. There she learned the basics of topography, unit recognition, and German troop movements. Afterward, she returned home. To remain in the area, however, she needed a job the Germans recognized as necessary for the war economy. To meet this requirement, she accepted the position as governess for a local Austrian business owner named Oskar Schmidt, who lived in Besko, 25 kilometers northwest of Zagórz, past Sanok.

Once again, her parents expressed displeasure with their youngest daughter's choice. Someone from her social status would never take a job as a governess for someone else's children. But these were not normal times, and Bisia wanted to remain close to home rather than return to Nowy Sącz.

Before she departed for Besko, her father came down with a bout of pneumonia and underwent an operation to drain one of his lungs. He experienced a similar procedure in 1929 when Bisia was eight years old.

Though not as difficult as the first procedure, when doctors had to remove a rib before inserting a drain, the second operation in 1942 remained an anxious time for everyone. Count Krasicki was approaching 70 years of age. But again, as in 1929, Zosia proved invaluable in attending to her father, changing his dressing every day and nursing him back to health.

The count lost considerable weight after the procedure, but that amounted to just one more thing in a long list of losses. Yet he remained philosophical. Whenever anyone suggested he sell his property while he still could, he would say, "I didn't buy it. I didn't work for it. I inherited it."

Bisia's father expressed an almost mystical approach to the Lesko estate. Like Job in the bible, he believed God could both give and take away. After rebuilding the castle following World War I, to see it stolen and abused again drained much of his spirit. The burden of it weighed on his every thought and decision.

After her father recovered sufficiently from his illness, Bisia left for Besko to begin work for Oskar Schmidt. She set off by bicycle in mid-morning. Soon, rain began falling, driven by winds coming down over the hills.

As she pedaled, the rain slanted into her face and soaked her clothing. The chill seeped into her bones. She came off the saddle, stamping the pedals with each stroke to generate warmth. But after a while, she grew tired and stopped. She buttoned her jacket tight to the collar and stood by the side of the road, hoping to hitch a ride.

Not much traffic passed, but eventually, a German convoy came rattling along. The lead truck stopped. The passenger's window rolled down, and an officer leaned out.

"Fraulein, do you need a ride?"

"Jawohl, Danke."

She tossed her bike in the back and climbed into the cab with the driver and German officer.

The engine droned, the windshield wipers slapped in rhythmic precision, the gears meshed: a German truck.

"Where are you heading?" the officer beside her said.

"Up to Besko."

"And what do you do there?"

I was not being interrogated. He was only passing the time. Though I didn't think I should ignore him, either.

"I take care of the children for a man whose wife took sick and is in hospital."

Maybe I was naïve, but never in all my dealings with Germans did I sense they might rape me.

The drive only took ten minutes. They restricted their conversation to mundane things like the weather and road conditions, for which Bisia was grateful.

"Thank you again," she said, retrieving her bicycle once they reached Besko. The intensity of the rain had subsided but still fell in a constant patter. The Germans saluted and waved goodbye.

Oskar Schmidt was an Austrian émigré of Jewish descent who fled to Poland before the war because of the persecution of Jews back home. He built a big synthetic rubber factory at the edge of the city of Sanok and made a substantial sum of money through this enterprise.

People of our social order did not mix with manufacturers, even if they were wealthy. It was another of the unwritten, but strictly observed, social mores of our world. But I had always made friends with people who weren't in aristocratic circles, and Oskar was a decent guy.

Oskar had called Bisia in Zagórz and said in his despicable Polish - because he was Austrian - "My wife is in hospital. I cannot handle my six children alone. Would you be able to help run my house?"

Bisia's parents didn't believe he dared even ask.

But Bisia said, "Of course I will help," and so she came to manage his servants, children, and household. This job gave her papers and a suitable cover from which to operate for her AK duties.

One spring day, a fellow member of the resistance, who also worked on the farm as an agricultural supervisor, approached Bisia at her desk. Jas Poźniak, a thin man with a deeply lined face and careful, blue eyes, said, "We must go ahead with the orders."

A Ukrainian deserter from the Russian army had been hanging around the village during the spring, and they suspected him of collaborating with Gestapo by reporting people. Why else would he walk free and not be in a camp?

Besko was not a large place. It had a population similar to Lesko, around 4,000, and everyone was familiar with the man. The underground leaders became suspicious because, since his arrival, the Gestapo singled out several of their people. Suspicion alone would not suffice, however.

The AK did not arbitrarily eliminate suspected collaborators. That would make them no better than the enemy. Underground military courts existed in the shadows. Only after prosecutors provided sufficient evidence was a sentence handed down.

"How will we do it?" Bisia asked as they stood by the office door.

"You invite him for a drink somehow."

"And then?"

"We will manage the rest."
She understood.
"When do we do this?"
"Tomorrow."
"Tomorrow? Can't it wait?"
"No. We planned everything. Waiting only increases the danger. Tomorrow is the day."

Life and death questions remained for others to consider. This man's own actions sentenced his fate. Bisia knew the Ukrainian in the sense they both frequently visited the village. It would not be difficult to run into him and make their encounter appear innocent.

The next day, Bisia walked into town where, as expected, she bumped into the Ukrainian. In his late thirties, perhaps early forties, he was tall and tucked his pants into his boots, a man proud of how he appeared. Vanity would be Bisia's approach.

"Well, hello," she said with a small wave as they walked toward one another in the fading light of the evening.

"Where are you going?" he asked as they stopped to chat.

"Back to Oskar's for some vodka. Are you in the mood for a quick drink?"

Bisia began walking again, making it appear the invitation was available only for a short time.

"Sure, why not?" he said, turning to join her.

Word was he liked to drink. Such an invitation would be the easiest way to entice him. No sexual suggestion attended this deception. Even a collaborator would never approach a woman from another class in that way. The invitation to drink was enough.

Oskar Schmidt's was a typical country compound. Bisia and the Ukrainian walked past gardens and stables. The house was already lit inside, though pink and orange bands of sunset remained along the horizon to the west. The office and barn were to their right as they headed toward the outer building where they stored petrol, feed, seed, and such things. The fresh smells of spring filled the air. Oskar also stocked a supply of beer and vodka he manufactured at his distillery on the property.

Jas Poźniak and another underground member waited inside the barn with their backs pressed against the wall behind the door. They prepared the place days before by digging a grave beneath the floorboards and relaying the wood to make it appear untouched in case anyone would venture in.

"Oskar keeps his vodka in the back," Bisia said, opening the door and walking in to lure the man deeper inside. "This has become the most popular building on the farm."

She laughed, suggesting the whole thing was quite casual and normal.

I sensed my compatriots' presence. It raised the hairs on my neck and I prayed my anxiety wouldn't give away the trap. I didn't want to witness what they would do, but I feared the Ukrainian would sense the danger, escape, and report us to the Germans.

After the Ukrainian had entered a few steps, Jas sprang from behind the door, and wheeling his club, struck a blow to the back of the man's head. The man crumpled to the ground. Jas and the other man continued beating and stabbing him until he lay lifeless on the floor.

A little shaken by the brutality of the attack, Bisia exited, her breath coming in short bursts, her heart racing. The Germans didn't garrison troops in the village since it was so small, but they might arrive without warning. She waited nervously outside.

"Bisia!"

Jas called to her in a hard whisper from inside the doorway.

"Come back in here."

When she entered, she didn't see the Ukrainian, only the blood staining the floor.

"We need to clean up quickly," Jas said, and handed her a bucket with a brush.

On hands and knees, they began scrubbing the area to remove any signs of the blood and struggle.

"Where is he?" Bisia asked.

"Under the floor. We put lye and kerosene on the body to cover the smell and confuse the German dogs so they won't be able to find him."

They scoured the floor for what seemed a long time. Then they spread more dirt to make everything appear normal.

Bisia had a hard time relaxing the next few days. She was certain someone would notice the man was missing.

"Go on about your duties like normal," Jas told her. "Stay with the children. That should keep your mind occupied."

The Gestapo appeared not too many days later. The timing couldn't be worse. Inside Bisia's bedroom, a meeting of the district AK commanders was taking place, which included Adam Winogrodzki. Her bedroom was next to the office.

"Have there been any inquiries about the Ukrainian?" asked Adam.

"None I'm aware of," Bisia said. "But I've done what Jas suggested, and stayed close to the compound, working with the kids."

"A few more days and we should be clear. The Germans have enough to concern them rather than bother with the disappearance of one Ukrainian."

Her room only contained two windows. Steel bars braced the one facing the rear. The one in front had no security. Then the German car drove up.

The men had no time to exit, nowhere to hide. Only a bed, washstand, and armoire stood in Bisia's room.

"You go talk to them," Adam told her. "We'll stay here."

"What should I say?"

"Nothing. Let them talk. Find out what they want. If they suspected we were here, they wouldn't come like this. This could just be happenstance."

"What if it's not?"

"Don't worry about that now. Just go see what they want."

Bisia went to the office and closed the door to her room. The Gestapo men knocked while the underground leaders sat still.

"Guten tag," she said after opening the door.

"You work here?"

"I do."

"Do you have any fresh vegetables on the property?" asked the lead man as he scanned the room. The Germans were well aware of the organized resistance and always reacted with skepticism toward outward appearances.

"We do, in the hothouse. That is where we keep them."

She turned and waited for them to leave before shutting the door behind them, happy she managed to lead them away from her trapped friends.

"And what are you doing here?" said the Gestapo officer as they walked.

"I work here."

"Doing what?"

"Herr Schmidt asked me to help with his children because his wife is in hospital. But I work all around the place."

As they spoke, several crows flew by overhead. From behind, two other Gestapo men lifted their rifles and began shooting at the birds for sport. She couldn't imagine what her friends might think, hearing this. Please, she thought, stay where you are. But after she showed the Germans the vegetables, which they took, she walked them back to their car, and they left. Luckily, they did not bring dogs to the building to search for the man they killed, nor did the Gestapo return to ask about his whereabouts.

***

10
OFFICER MATERIAL

~ 1943 ~

When the war began for the U.S. in December 1941, the army couldn't churn officers out fast enough. But by 1943, there was an abundance of second lieutenants, so only the best survived Officer Candidates School (OCS).

Isham and Jimmy Reilly completed basic training at Camp Wolters, Texas, on February 1, 1943. Next, they applied for Officer Candidate School at Fort Benning, Georgia as part of the 26th Company, Third Student Training Regiment.

Lieutenants Reilly & Reavis

Though the strictures and demands of officer school were exacting, nothing but classes and study and exercise through a steady stream of 16 to 18-hour days, Isham and Jimmy did well in their three months at OCS and graduated with 152 other new second lieutenants on May 20, 1943.

The day before graduation, Isham's tactical officer handed him an efficiency report listing each candidate's marks on physical activity, bearing, appearance, gentlemanly conduct, attention to duty, cooperation, initiative, intelligence, force, judgment, leadership, voice, and command. And for each one, Isham received marks of "superior".

"They use that word sparingly around here," the tactical officer told him. "And to receive all of them is quite an achievement."

Isham was rather proud of being an infantry officer. The crossed-rifles insignia of the infantry made quite a hit with him, as he wrote home to his family.

In the infantry, we never need to explain ourselves to anyone. We plain fight the war with our hands, guns, clubs, or whatever is handy; nothing glamorous about us, as we have work to do. And I have earned the right to my gold bars, as they came from having lain in the mud, crawled through thorns, and walked miles and helped others. No one has yet to carry me on anything.

In fact, both Isham and Jimmy performed so well at OCS the army kept them on as infantry school instructors.

*

Taxes and rationing became heavy burdens on the country as the war dragged on. Congress approved withholding taxes on wages for the first time. Out in Hollywood, Humphrey Bogart and Ingrid Bergman starred in the classic wartime movie *Casablanca*. Many of the biggest stars in baseball, including Ted Williams and Joe DiMaggio, enlisted, and the Major League Baseball season started two weeks later than usual as teams called up prospects from the minor leagues to fill out their rosters.

Isham's first assignment as a new lieutenant was as platoon leader to a group of college men who were being groomed for work in geopolitics after the war. His 60-man platoon had three All-American football players, and all the boys scored over 120 on their IQ tests to qualify for this program.

I'm tickled silly by my new job, Isham wrote home. *It is much tougher than OCS even, but these kids are so confoundedly good men. I bubble with enthusiasm. I'm darn near in love with the brats. They are so earnest, so willing and bright; I know somewhat the feeling of a parent. As I write you from my room, their glee club is practicing in a building 100 yards (ca. 91 m) to my right. It is Saturday night, and they are in glee club rehearsal, not busy boozing up in some dirty tavern in town.*

Most of the men were graduates of Dartmouth, Yale, and Princeton — all the finer universities back east. While Isham trained them, there was always a congressional representative or an army general hanging around, inspecting his platoon. The assignment proved helpful for

Isham, too, because it forced him to study hard for those thirteen weeks to prepare to teach those boys. Most nights he'd stay awake until 3:00 a.m. studying for the next day's classes.

After several weeks, however, he received word from regimental headquarters that he was pressing too hard.

"You demand too much," his battalion commander told him. "Stop requiring perfection. Ease off some."

This reprimand teed Isham off. He was only trying to make soldiers of them.

Rather than barking orders the next morning as he normally did and drilling the men at a fast cadence, say 140 steps per minute where 180 is a run, Isham took a passive-aggressive approach. Every command he gave, he pronounced as casually as could be. He showed no spirit whatsoever. He continued in that vein for an entire week until he couldn't take it anymore. Then he got mad again.

He marched the platoon out into the woods one morning before bringing them to a halt in the stifling heat.

"For one week, they told me I can't say anything hard to you. They told me I have to treat you like a bunch of lollipops. Well, maybe that's what you all are."

He took off his shirt and threw it to the side.

"But here I am with my shirt off, and any of you who want can come to take a swing at me. Come on! I hope you do."

They all looked at one another; I made no sense to them. None of them stepped forward, of course. They stood looking uncomfortable and avoiding my stare. I was mad, alright. But not at them, only at the system that silenced me. I reamed them out as hard as I could for another ten minutes.

"Now get your dirty asses back up and fall in," I said, and they jumped to it. I called them every name imaginable.

Following inspection later that afternoon, Isham sat in his room, upset at himself for having flown off the handle. A knock at the door drew his attention.

"Come in."

Isham turned in his chair. Four of his boys stood in the doorway.

"Shit," he thought. "Here's the delegation."

He got up and walked over.

"Lieutenant," began one man, "we came by to say thanks for talking to us like you did today. We thought we'd done something wrong, and you didn't care about us anymore. We're all glad you're back and we are friends again."

The men stood close, framed by the door. Isham did not expect their reaction, but it was the lesson he needed.

"Listen, I have always been interested," Isham said, chastised by their presence. "I was having trouble handling the situation myself, that's all. We're all new at this and I guess I was being a little too hard on you fellas. I appreciate you coming over."

"We just wanted you to be aware we are glad you're our lieutenant, and we wanted to thank you for everything you're doing for us."

Isham felt embarrassed but thankful for their visit.

"Alright, get back to your work now, so I can stay on top of mine."

Everything they did afterward became tight and sharp as they responded to Isham's training. What he didn't figure was how he was being trained, too. In the last analysis, how well the boys under his command performed in battle would be the measure of his own ability to lead men effectively in combat. The army's system specifically challenged its young officers. They wanted to find out who would crack under pressure and who would hold his head up and learn.

Anglo-American Forces had landed on the Italian mainland in September 1943, after which former colleagues in the Fascist Italian government overthrew and imprisoned Mussolini. Italy then signed an armistice with the Allies, while German Field Marshal Albert Kesselring convinced Hitler to engage the Allies in Italy as far from German soil as possible.

By the end of October '43, the British 8th Army had reached Brindisi in the south east, while the American Fifth Army took control of Naples.

*

When promotions came out on Christmas Eve 1943, Isham was not one of the four who made First Lieutenant. He was disappointed, of course, but knew his company commander and the battalion commander had both included his name in their recommendations to regimental command.

Reavis remained at Ft. Benning until early February 1944, when he received an assignment with the 86th division, 343rd Infantry at Camp

Livingston, Louisiana. By now, he wanted to go overseas. Instead, when summer rolled around, he remained stuck in a reserve officers' pool, preparing other men for war.

*

They listed the names of the men assigned overseas duty on a sheet tacked to the bulletin board at battalion headquarters. Isham stood in a knot of men scanning the list. Failing to find his name, he edged out of the group and marched down the hall to his company commander's office.

"Excuse me, sir?"

Reavis knocked on the frame of the open door. The captain sat without a word, leafing through some papers atop his desk.

"They put up the latest overseas list, and my name isn't on it, again."

The captain leaned back and took Reavis's eye, setting his cigarette down in the small black ashtray along the right side of his desk.

"I half expected you'd be dropping by," he said, motioning Reavis to come in. "But I wouldn't worry if I were you. There will be plenty of fighting left by the time you go over."

"Yes, but when?"

A small oscillating fan in the corner did its best to offset the heavy Louisiana humidity, but all it did was wash a worthless current through the room.

"Believe me, I'm not saying this to hear myself talk. You think this is some kind of punishment or waste of your time or mine? You don't think I'd like to be somewhere other than this, too?"

The captain stood, walked behind his chair to the window. There, he opened the blinds to the busy road out front. The call of cadence cut through the rumble of trucks and jeeps passing by.

"You evidently don't look at this way, but you are deeper into the war right here than two-thirds of the men you envy so much in Europe and Asia. What we are doing here is important. What everyone is doing here is important. When it is time for you to be somewhere else, you'll be told."

"That's not what I meant. I'm qualified on every weapon in this army, and what has it got me? You've trained me to go to war, and I want to go. Let's go!"

I wasn't the kind to complain, but there were battles being fought, and I was not a part of them. That's what I signed up to do.

"Did it ever occur to you that you're here because of your qualifications? Training other men on how to use these weapons is a critical job."

"I know, but when is someone else qualified going to do it for a while and let me go?"

The captain turned and sat on the corner of his desk. He picked up the cigarette still burning in the ashtray.

"Where do you think all these men would be without this training? Besides, I can't do anything about it. I've already recommended you twice. You think I make these decisions?"

He continued to assure Reavis of his importance and the likelihood his overseas posting would eventually come up. But Isham carried his distress back to the barracks, throwing his cap hard onto his footlocker as he walked in, waking up his roommate, Jimmy Reilly, who was lying on his bunk.

"What do they want?" Isham said, pacing back and forth. "Hell, I'm going to screw up, if that's what it takes. Jesus Christ, what are we doing wrong, being too good?"

"Same bullshit, huh?" asked Jimmy. "This damn thing will be over and we'll be stuck in Louisiana. There's your war record."

***

11
"A MACHINE GUN, WHAT ELSE?"

~ Spring 1943 ~

Bisia was returning to Besko on horseback one spring evening from a resistance meeting at the house of Kanty Dzianott in Lubla when a commotion up ahead drew her attention. From behind, a lowering sun cast its light on three German soldiers as they dragged an old man from a farmhouse up the road. They chained the man to a boy of about 12 or 13, who resisted while the soldiers tried to load the two into a van. The old man didn't put up a fight but did not help, either, only going limp. As Bisia rode up alongside, the old man looked at her while the boy struggled, looking frantically for help.

"Don't judge them," the man said. "Try to forgive. Don't hate. Love instead."

The German officer in charge glared at Bisia as his men shoved the old man and boy into the van.

"Move along, if you don't want to join them."

Bisia rode away, more resolved than ever to return Poland to its rightful owners. Later, she would put her experience to words.

... I saw them,
and never shall I forget!
A man chained to a boy,
A mere child, not grown up as yet.
They dragged them out.
The old man kept saying something.
The sky was red, all aglow.
And as I passed, I heard
The words that were said:
"Don't judge them. Try to forgive.
Don't hate—but love instead."
I heard them, and I saw them.

Toni Reavis

> *This old man chained to a child…*
> *And time has passed, and bitter years*
> *Have chained me—to my life.*
> *Now, in the evening firelight,*
> *When skies turn red above,*
> *I still hear a voice repeating:*
> *"Don't hate, forgive, and love instead."*

While the Polish government-in-exile directed the resistance from London, the Germans controlled day-to-day life for millions of Poles. Yet beneath the occupation, a clandestine state existed, made up of the resistance army, underground schools, businesses, newspapers, publishers, political parties, even courts of law. Underground theaters rehearsed and staged performances at people's homes. Any 'normal' aspect of life maintained itself beneath the shadow of the German fist.

Estimates from the Historical Institute of the Polish Academy of Sciences in Warsaw reported one million students took instruction from over 19,000 teachers when Polish schools were illegal. To maintain the illusion of normalcy, parents paid school fees, and teachers drew salaries. Even underground universities thrived, though students had to sign a pledge swearing the strictest secrecy before being admitted.

Three previous partitions had erased Poland from the world atlas for five generations. This time, its people swore to maintain their country, no matter how the Germans tried to erase its past and prevent its future.

*

After Bisia returned to Besko, she began hearing whispered accounts reporting the discovery of mass graves of Polish army officers found in the Katyn Forest in Russia. They found thousands of prisoners shot in the back of the head before being dumped into open pits. It was the method of execution that revealed the guilty party.

Whenever Germans committed mass executions, they machine gunned people from the front as they stood at the edge of the graves they had dug for themselves. The Soviets, however, shot their victims once to the back of the head. When Germans discovered the massacre in Katyn, they contacted the International Red Cross in Geneva, asking them to come to Katyn to investigate.

Once officials verified the killings, the newspaper published by the German General Gouvernment in Poland, *Kurjer Warczawski (Warsaw Courier)* — which the Poles referred to it as 'czmata', 'the rag' — came out with a black border and the list the names of the executed men on the front page.

The Russians denied the killings, but they buried the men with all their documents and correspondence still on them. When the Red Cross checked the dates on the letters, they determined the Germans couldn't have committed the crime. Germany didn't move against the Russians until June 1941, and the evidence uncovered by the Red Cross dated the killings to 1940 — though they did not discover the massacre until '43. The Soviet secret police (NKVD) had executed almost half the Polish officer corps.

Horror, tragedy, and disbelief mingled in our hearts. And beneath it, the underlying recognition of what savages our neighbors were. It devastated our region, for many of the men had family there. It was on our minds constantly. You die in war, yes, but to massacre people because they are not communists...

After Bisia joined the Home Army, her assignments involved mostly reconnaissance. Sometimes she received messages word-of-mouth when someone would stop by on one pretext, before delivering orders in a quick, private exchange. More often, orders would come through a brief call. Since Bisia worked in the farm's office, she had access to a telephone.

One summer day in 1943, she received a call telling her to go to a smith shop in Sanok with a horse and wagon. Her contact also instructed her to bring a pistol.

They only told you to bring a weapon if you would have to use it, if only to avoid capture. I realized right away this wouldn't be an ordinary assignment.

Lying 20 kilometers east of Besko along the road to Zagórz, Sanok was the largest city in the area with a population of 30,000. The man Bisia was to meet was a patriotic Pole referred to only as "Oak", a fitting name for a man who worked the bellows. His face was broad and his eyes dark, and alongside his leather apron hung arms the size of boughs, made to appear broader by the blackened soot of the fire.

He constructed metal rims for wheels and carriages, also runners for sleds, hoes, plowshares, and axes.

Upon her arrival at his shop, Bisia and the smith exchanged simple pleasantries and identifying words. He told her she was to deliver a captured German machine gun to their AK unit in the forest.

"We will pile straw in the back of the wagon," he said while wrapping the machine gun in a blanket. "That is the best we can do to conceal it."

The blacksmith had dismantled the gun earlier, cleaned and reassembled it. Bisia's job was to transport it.

She wore a light windbreaker for the ride, and inside her left breast pocket, she carried her identification papers and the pistol. Since she was operating in her home territory, she understood if they caught her, the rest of her family would be in danger because in your home region you used your actual name. Only when operating outside the region did you employ your false identification. Bisia's underground name was Barbara (or Basia). This, again, protected the movement. If the enemy captured you, they couldn't force you to reveal the names of your compatriots.

Many members of the aristocracy fought in the underground movement, and Bisia knew many from before the war. But there were others she met only as "Kruczek", for instance, "the Crow". Other noms de guerre came from Polish literature.

Her brother Jas's nom de guerre was Jan Kowalski ("Average Joe"). The Gestapo had recently arrested another man in his cell, and AK leaders feared the Gestapo would search for Jas next. As a precaution, they transferred him to Jasło before Bisia could say goodbye.

By the time she set off from the blacksmith shop in Sanok, it was later than she would have liked. But the machine gun needed to be transported, and the longer it stayed in the city, the greater the chance for discovery.

As she headed for the countryside, she passed Oskar Schmidt's rubber factory with its red brick archways and a large clock mounted on the office tower. Police hour was approaching, so by early evening, everyone was near home. The Germans were quick to action and short on listening whenever they discovered anyone out of place.

Bisia hugged the right shoulder of the narrow country road as she rolled out of Sanok. Before too long, the clip-clop of the hooves lulled her into thinking this assignment would pass as easily as the older woman with a long switch tending her two cows on their slow walk home.

The Germans employed a system where they would first close a road and conduct inspections and then keep the same road open for weeks at a time. Of course, you never could tell when it would be open or closed.

As she crested a small rise, Bisia's heart began to race. Up ahead, she saw a German guard post manned by three soldiers. Roadblock!

She still had a way to go before she reached the forest. Open fields lined both sides of the road. If she tried to turn around, it would alert the Germans.

This is the reason they wanted me to bring a pistol, she thought. As she approached, she spun through the various possibilities. If they found the machine gun, she faced arrest, if not a firing squad. In either case, her family would be in jeopardy. But she also thought it would stretch her luck to try shooting first. A chill ran up her arms as she got closer. She took many deep breaths, trying to remain calm as she reined in her horse.

"What are you doing out here at this hour?" said the German on her left. "Show me your papers."

Bisia kept her identification papers in the same left inside breast pocket where she had her pistol. The other two Germans stood on the right with their rifles at port arms.

I tied the reins to the brake pole, patted the right side of my chest, pretending to search for my papers. The German peered under the cart, then back at me.

He extended his hand.

"Come on. Come on."

She reached her right hand across into her breast pocket and brushed against the butt of the pistol. Praying it didn't bulge, she drew out her kennkarte, the Third Reich's basic civilian identity document.

She handed down her papers before re-zipping her jacket halfway, wanting access to the gun if needed.

The soldier on the left paged through her papers while another on the right walked around to the back of the wagon.

"There can't be much traffic this time of the evening," she said, making idle conversation to calm her nerves.

The man inspecting her papers looked up without moving his head. In back, the soldier bent down to search beneath the cart before rising. He jabbed at the straw with his weapon and asked, "And what do you have under here?"

If I had any advantage, it was because I thought the Germans were predictable. I grew up speaking German and worked around them for the last few years, gathering information. I was always more frightened dealing with Russians. But if I ever needed an advantage, now was the time.

"What's under here?" he asked again, jabbing his rifle into it.

Bisia laughed.

"Surely, a machine gun, what else?"

The three Germans exchanged a glance. Then the soldier holding her kennkarte began laughed, too, but with derision.

"Oh, the young countess has a machine gun. We'd better be careful."

Bisia laughed with them and threw her palms up with a shrug.

"Well, you asked me, and I am telling you."

She played up the joke. But her stomach remained trapped halfway to her throat. Only when the soldier in back lowered his rifle and walked back to the front, still laughing, did Bisia relax a bit.

The soldier with her kennkarte handed it back and asked if she would like a drink.

"Jawohl."

She stepped down. This was the bluff, and she had no other choice but to carry it out.

They gave me some kind of horrible booze from their canteen, and we drank.

"Do you want a cigarette?"

"Jawohl."

As we smoked, we talked a while longer, typical stupid small talk, turning into one of those semi-flirting situations, keeping everything light, acting as casually as I could. But I was also afraid I might give myself away with a false moment.

"All right, I have to get going now because police hour is coming and I have to be home or you will arrest me again."

After promising she would visit them again, they lifted the roadblock and off she went. Her fear, the energy of it, turned to exhilaration. She had them. They never thought beyond the fact she was young and attractive and they welcomed the break in their boredom.

I felt almost giddy, but the soldiers took it as a compliment to their company. And I rode off to the forest to deliver my machine gun. I was nervous until the very end, but I knew I tricked them.

For this action, Bisia received the Polish Cross of Valor. The citation read: "For unusual bravery in action during the years of the Hitler terror in Poland, for your service to your homeland."

~ Partisans ~ Spring 1944 ~

The autumn rains that never fell in 1939, rains which might have turned the roads into a soupy mess and slowed the German invasion, came instead during the springtime five years later. When the AK partisans arrived from Warsaw, they strode into Bisia's office in Besko like they were delivering an order of vegetables from the market. They walked in with their muddy boots and plopped their grenades and plastic explosives on her desk in a pile.

"What are you doing?" Bisia said as she went to check no one else was nearby. "Put those away. Where do you think you are? There are Ukrainians around who will denounce us in a heartbeat. This isn't Warsaw."

It upset me they would put our safety at risk with this display of bravado. This operation was not specific to our region, and therefore not worth losing people for the sake of youthful machismo.

"What are you worrying about?" said their leader, a young tousled-hair blond. "You are so frightened out here. Back home, we walk with our weapons openly. So what line are we supposed to blow up here?"

Every regional AK unit throughout the country had received orders from London. On a specific date, operatives were to blow up all the German lines of communication to the front, from Lithuania in the north to Hungary and Czechoslovakia in the south. Code-named "Tempest", the operation represented an attempt to coordinate underground action with the expected Anglo-American invasion of the continent. But it was also to prove to the allied nations that the underground movement in Poland could organize across the entire country.

"The bridge is near Bazanowka, about 10 kilometers west," she said. "Isolated, out in the countryside, nothing more than a crossing for trains over a small creek."

"Well, the location itself doesn't present any difficulty," said the leader to one of his compatriots. "The operation should be simple enough. I'm a little worried about the rain, though. I'm not sure the explosives will hold to the train tracks in these conditions."

As they discussed the plan in further detail, the men from Warsaw took on a more professional demeanor, which allayed Bisia's initial fears of working with them.

"What we can do is sew the charge into a small canvas satchel," said one man. "That way when we tie it to the track, it will be protected from the rain."

The bridge itself was only important as a potential route for transferring German troops from the eastern front to the west in case of an allied invasion.

From the very start, the Home Army prepared for a national armed uprising as the war front moved from east to west. The plan was to cooperate with the Soviet Red Army at the first, while laying the foundation for Poland's eventual return to sovereignty by seizing arms and controlling the cities. Such an outcome required a military and political tight-wire walk, replacing one occupation without falling into another one.

Polish inquiries about the Katyn Massacre caused Stalin to break off diplomatic relations with the government-in-exile in April of '43, while Western Allies were still making little headway against the Germans on the continent.

In November 1943, the government-in-exile issued orders to the Home Army. If their leaders had not re-established diplomatic relations with the Soviets by the time the Red Army crossed into Polish territory, the AK units should remain underground until further notification.

On the night of their assignment, Bisia led the Warsaw partisans along the road toward their mission target. The going was slow because of the constant rain, endless mud, and the general lack of light, but the partisans couldn't risk taking out lamps to light the way.

It was only my sense of the place we could use as a guide. Though there were only sporadic clusters of farmhouses in the area, one could never be too cautious. It was in moments of hubris accidents occurred.

Once they arrived at the bridge, they waited to make sure they were the only ones around. But since they were far out in the countryside and the bridge traversed a creek running through the fields, the danger was not great.

The rain had swelled the creek, and the current ran stronger than normal. The men from Warsaw placed the satchel and connected the wires. When the time came for the mission, they turned into a tight, ordered unit, good men all. After securing the explosives, they backed away, running the detonating wire to its maximum length.

The young leader kneeled at Bisia's side.

"Ready?"

She nodded. He touched the wire to the terminal, and the bridge blew up in a dazzling arc of light. The blast shattered the night stillness, turning fields white, orange, and yellow as the explosion destroyed the tracks and bridge.

As quickly as possible, they slunk away. The following day, the men returned to Warsaw.

***

12
SUNDAY MORNING IN YOUR HEART

~ 1944 ~

After winning the North African Campaign, Allied leaders differed as to which direction to take next. Churchill and Stalin wanted to invade Italy, thereby opening the Mediterranean to Allied shipping, while diverting German forces from the Russian front. The Americans, with their greater force, lobbied for as early an invasion of France as possible. In the end, portions of each plan were adopted.

Operation Overlord, the D-Day invasion of France, would be put into operation in early June 1944, with the invasion of Italy taking a lesser priority mounted by General Mark Clark's 5th Army.

*

Isham departed for Europe on Friday, June 30, 1944. The next day, 730 delegates from all 44 allied nations met at the Mount Washington Hotel in New Hampshire for the three-week Bretton Woods Conference. There, they addressed post-war economic regulations and established new international monetary institutions like the International Monetary Fund (IMF) and the World Bank.

July 4, 1944

Somewhere on the Atlantic

Dearest,

As the heading shows, we are finally at sea, and I sort of think now I should like to have been a sailor. The sea is beautiful. I can easily see how the old mariners loved it. I have stood on the top deck late at night and stared at nothing but the sea and the sky and haven't ceased to marvel at the sight.

While I know you don't like this, it is the only thing wrong I can find with the news of our sailing. Selfishly, it pleases me very much. It is what I have wanted for some time. It sort of gives me a feeling of solidity, like a real soldier, and a chance to say thanks to this old world for all it has done for me.

I recently saw Bing Crosby's new show, Going My Way. It was splendid, a very sweet story told in a gentle manner. Bing is an accomplished actor and his cast was superb; don't miss it. In its theme song is one phrase, "Sunday morning in my heart". It made me think of you. You have always had Sunday morning in your heart.

Lena with Mary, Isham, and Burton circa 1916

All of your kids had childhoods that were the most beautiful things in the world, all because of you and Pop were free to bring us up in that enchanted land of Tom Sawyer, Peter Pan, and Winken, Blinken, and Nod. You would want me to help a little, so little (niece) Kathy, and all those like her, had the same chance.

I feel, I almost know, that deep down within your heart that has Sunday morning in it, you want me to do my part, though it is yours that is hard.

Toni Reavis

I have always known how deeply I love you and my family and yet knowing you would rather I didn't go just gives me another chance to show you how much I do love you.

> My dreams of life are much the same,
> As those, I feel you've dreamt.
> There is nothing about them very plain,
> Except in the manner in which they are spent.
>
> Here I find I am extravagant,
> For I give them all away,
> In exchange for the muse,
> Newly sent with a dream,
> To be dreamt today.
>
> And so, I grieve not,
> When off my dreams soar,
> To winds of every direction.
> I fear I might find each a bore,
> But naught for its own perfection.

All my love,

Isham

On July 10, 1944, Lieutenant Isham Reavis's troopship slid past the Isle of Capri before entering the Bay of Naples. Behind the city rose Mount Vesuvius. The sight brought to Isham's mind poet John William Burgon's description of the Jordanian city of Petra: 'a rose-red city on the side of a hill, half as old as time'.

In the port itself, engineers had constructed concrete causeways over the hulls of sunken ships, allowing the port to go back into operation after its almost complete destruction by naval and aerial bombardment.

When Mussolini's Fascist Regime collapsed after the invasion of Sicily in July 1943, the Germans still controlled northern and central Italy. Allied forces took Rome on June 4, advancing north past Florence. There, in the rugged terrain of the Apennine Mountains forming the spine of the Italian peninsula, Field Marshal Albert Kesselring arrayed the last major line of German defenses with well-fortified positions prepared to repel any attempt to breach the Gothic Line.

Assigned to the reserve officer pool with the 91st Infantry Division as part of General Mark Clark's Fifth Army, Lieutenant Isham Reavis spent his first month in Italy unattached as the Powder River Division pushed north beyond Florence.

The area southeast of the Futa Pass in the Apennines formed the most heavily defended position in the German Gothic Line. The Americans expected heavy opposition as the enemy held all the tactical advantages of prepared positions in a mountainous country ideally suited for defense.

As they moved north up along the Arno River beyond Florence, Isham finally received an assignment to the 362nd Infantry Regiment as a platoon leader on September 14th.

"The new invasion gives us another front, making four for Hitler to worry about, and he didn't want two," he wrote home on 17 August. "He's finished; it's just a matter of time. Hope the St. Louis Browns make the series this year. They deserve it."

New York Governor Thomas Dewey challenged President Roosevelt in the 1944 presidential campaign. Isham cast his absentee ballot for Dewey on August 11th because he thought his mother would prefer the Republican.

On August 16th, Hitler ordered the withdrawal of all German forces in southern France. Field Marshal Walter Model took command of German forces after Field Marshal Günther von Kluge committed suicide following the failed plot to kill Hitler on July 20th. In France, the Vichy government under Premier Pierre Laval resigned.

The Allies had their own tactical obstacles to worry about. They maintained command of the port of Naples along the ankle of the Italian boot, which allowed them to sustain activity in central and northern Italy. But Operation Overlord in France was their primary focus. That reduced available units and supplies for the Italian Campaign.

Throughout the first half of September, Isham remained in the reserve officer pool, and much like when he marched into his captain's office in Camp Livingston, Louisiana in February asking to be sent overseas, his frustration with his current lack of a meaningful assignment in Italy came out in his letters home.

"I'm no longer with Co. A, 362nd Infantry," he wrote to his brother Burton on September 9th. "I am back with the others in the 91st Division replacement pool, and we are all pissed off about it. I've been pretty damn close to the line, but never in battle with anyone committed to the fight."

Two days later, he continued his lament to his mother.

"I gave the boys quite a talk on censoring the other day. They were writing the damndest things to their wives and mothers, and it was all fiction. Such as, 'I am writing this by the flash of bursting shells.' In the first place, I don't think it can be done and in the second place, they aren't near any bursting shells. All they were doing was worrying the devil out of the people back home. I grant you a guy feels rather useless and impotent back here and just a bit foolish, as (Bill) Maudlin call us 'Garritroopers', far enough forward not to wear ties, but too far back to be shot.

"Censoring their letters, I knew they were suffering from an inferiority complex. So, I've done all I can to bolster their ego, make them feel important and that they are necessary for the war effort. Most of them want very badly to go into combat. That's just another reason I find pride in the infantry. They threaten other branches to be sent up if they don't behave. Here, they plead for the chance."

On 14 September Isham moved north again, after receiving an assignment as Company G platoon commander for the 362nd Regiment. From intelligence reports, the Americans expected the Germans to have four divisions arrayed along fortified positions dug deep into the inhospitable terrain of the Apennines. But any reinforcements would have to come overland through the Alps.

But the Germans kept pulling back and around, which meant the U.S. response had to adapt, moving slowly, hill to hill, always north.

At 0400 hours on the morning of 16 September, Isham stood with his Company G commander going over their maps. In the days before, the

Americans had occupied, but couldn't exploit their position because of the terrible mortar fire the Germans rained down from Hills 821 and 840 to the north. Those defenses would have to be thwarted before the Americans could continue north toward their primary objective, the Futa Pass.

The Americans assigned three rifle companies to make the assault on Hill 840. Reavis would lead Company G, 3rd platoon along the left flank. As they prepared to move out, the 346th Field Artillery Battalion lit up the horizon with a bombardment of 240 mm shells thundering from their M1 Black Dragon Howitzers.

Oh, the pyrotechnics we had. Fire belched from those immense guns. I had seen nothing like it in my life. They lit up the whole damn mountain like at a Friday night football game. But you don't like that because if you could see them, they could see you, too.

After the initial rolling barrage lifted, the three rifle companies started their push toward the slope of Hill 840.

The night was pitch-black except for the muzzle blasts belching from the big guns behind them. Isham moved forward, carrying a carbine rifle that held fifteen 30-caliber rounds. Around 0500 hours, the Americans ran into concentrated fire from mortars and machine gun positions. German artillery shells were also zeroing in on their position. Cries for medics came from everywhere. The best tactic, Isham realized, was to continue moving forward and up toward the fire.

"Here I am, the assistant manager of the Gatesworth Hotel, and I am taking on the entire German army," he thought to himself.

The Germans built up the Gothic Line defenses for over a year with hundreds of pillboxes and concrete bunkers so thick 105 mm rounds bounced off them like tennis balls. Barbed wire, tank guns mounted in concrete turrets, minefields, and ditches laced the area in interconnected fields of fire. Manning this bristling defense was Germany's Fourth Paratroop Division, one of Hitler's best.

The howitzers of the 346th Field Artillery didn't knock out the German fortifications. Instead, they forced the Germans to take cover, allowing the Americans to advance before the enemy could jump back out to man their weapons. The infantry took ground bit by bit in this fashion, moving close behind the creeping barrage.

As the old saying goes, no plan survives first contact with the enemy. On Hill 840, confusion reigned as small arms, grenades, mortars, and artillery joined in the fight. The shooting came from 40 to 50 feet (15 m) above. Explosions, too, every damn thing, like the apocalypse. All Reavis was aware of was he was in Italy.

When the American commanders back at headquarters witnessed the ferocity of the German counterattack, they radioed for their forces to pull back. But Reavis had become separated from his radioman and never got the orders. Instead, he kept advancing, covering ground as fast as possible in a low crouch, all the while throwing grenades when necessary to root out anyone who might be in a direct line ahead.

Splintered trees lay scattered all along the hill, the earth itself a casualty of both sides. The Americans would go up for a stretch, climbing over logs, jumping little gullies, but always returning fire.

Besides the bullets, barbed wire slowed their progress, too, catching on their fatigues as men brushed or ran by in the darkness. One time, after an enemy machine gun opened up, Reavis jumped left — *always left, because you carried your rifle in your right hand* — and banged his knee hard on one of the barbed wire support posts. It hurt like hell, but not nearly as much as a bullet would have.

The Germans were now close enough to throw hand grenades. When activated, they made a sound like PAC, P-A-C.

When you heard that sound, only seconds remained before it exploded. I was moving along, squeezing off rounds when it came.

Only the frenzied ribbons of tracer bullets cut through the darkness. They seemed to come from every direction. Reavis hit the ground to avoid getting hit, his chin scraping the ground as he crawled.

His breathing became labored but steady as he moved. He kept crawling up the hill until his helmet bumped into something solid, causing the rim to bite down on the bridge of his nose. After adjusting his helmet and massaging his nose, he reached out and felt the bark of a small tree, about six inches around. As he brought his hand back, the grenade went off. Everything turned bright orange and swimming green.

I couldn't tell if I got hit or not. My senses simply overloaded, and I lay stunned for several minutes. Time became non-existent as I let my vision clear and hearing ring out.

After a while, Isham tried to sense whether anything more serious may be wrong. But when he reached forward again to take his bearings, the tree he'd bumped into moments before toppled over.

If not for that tree, the grenade would have rolled into my chest. It was the second time a thing with no explanation saved me. But there was no time to dwell.

Isham kept moving forward while trying to clear the ringing. He worked under the premise that if he stayed where he was or tried to run, he would offer an easy target. His only choice was to move forward and try to put out the fire.

Over the next few hours, Reavis kept gradually going up toward the fire. Don't crawl away, he kept telling himself, move ahead. His training kicked in and he trusted it. He still couldn't decipher the strength of his own force or that of the enemy, but he was steadily moving up. Throughout the remainder of the night, orange anger spewed into the darkness.

When the first light of dawn finally striped the sky to his left, Reavis found he was within fifty yards of the crest of Hill 840. After a quick check, he figured about half his platoon remained with him, perhaps 20 to 30 men. They had fought all night, and now, with the dawn, the firing became sporadic. This was the first time there was enough light for him to take a measure of the battlefield.

At the top of the hill, the Americans ran into another German machine gun nest. The Germans were unaware of the Americans' presence. They must have thought they had turned back the attack.

Reavis crawled forward until he arrived at a thick hedgerow to the left of the emplacement. With great care, he nudged his rifle through the bushes. Through the small gap, he spied three Germans manning the machine gun. An officer sat cross-legged, manning the weapon itself. Another man lay in a prone position to his right, protecting him with his rifle, while the third man, also cross-legged, fed the ammunition belt from the left.

Reavis waited, knowing he would only have one chance.

I waited until they needed to reload. The top of their machine gun released automatically after they fired the last round in the belt. When the belt ran out, the latch released, making a small sound, Bing. That sound meant they were helpless.

When the gunner sat upright awaiting the next belt to be loaded, Isham was ready. He was no farther than the width of a small room away. The new day sun angled across the German officer's face. Reavis shot him in the head. Next, he took down the man in the support position before running up and covering the ammo feeder with his carbine.

We over-ran the emplacement, capturing two more Germans in the process. It happened fast. No wasted time. Everything is right now. Somebody loses real fast.

After securing their position and disabling the machine gun, Isham put the captured Germans in the same hollow. By this time, the German commanders on their side of the hill understood the Americans had made it to the top. They spent the rest of the day trying to knock them off.

Too far advanced to be reinforced, yet too isolated to withdraw, the remaining members of the 3rd platoon defended their position for the next three hours against German artillery and mortar fire.

If you ever want to understand what anger sounds like, it was in that sound. The shells would spin out of those wide-bore barrels no different from a thirty-millimeter round fired from a rifle. They made a horrible noise, an ungodly wail, building as they came like banshees. And its only purpose was to kill you. And they could place the rounds within five or ten yards of where they aimed. I mean, those sons of bitches are mad at you.

One artillery shell landed so close it threw Isham like a rag doll. The force tore his shirt to tatters and disintegrated his undershirt. When he crawled back into his hole, his chest was a mass of blood. But when he wiped the blood away to check for a wound, he didn't find one. Yet more blood oozed from his pores. The concussion and change of air pressure became so great his blood pressure alone was enough to push the blood from his body.

With the Germans attacking from all sides, one of Isham's men called out for him. Isham scrambled the short distance while dodging mortar shells.

"In the leg," the young soldier said, pressing the top of his leg like a kid awaiting a shot from the family doctor. Reavis gave him a sulfa tablet.

When he tore open the man's pants, he found the wound on the outside of his leg; the bullet coming out high on his inner thigh. No blood at all, like a pencil shoved through his leg.

"Is it bad?" the man asked.

"You got a close one, but it doesn't look too bad."

Isham cleaned the wound as best he could, but didn't have any tape to secure the field dressing in place.

"I have to anchor it to something."

There was nowhere else to do it.

"Hold still."

Isham fastened the bandage around the private's privates, his balls.

"Sorry. This is the only place."

When Reavis finished, the man tried to move. But Isham hadn't laid enough slack in the bandage. When the kid straightened his leg, the bandage pulled taut, then grabbed when he took his first step. He fell back down with a yelp.

"Thanks, anyway, lieutenant," the private said, tearing the bandage off and crawling back to his foxhole. In his own hole, Reavis overheard the private tell the other man with him, "For Christ's sake, don't get shot. The lieutenant will give you a bandage."

They laughed, Isham, too.

People talk about all these boys being lonely for their mother and father and all their dreams gone to hell, etcetera. Bullshit. Kid soldiers laugh. The harder things become, the more they laugh. Here we were in a fight for our lives, in danger of being shot dead at any second, and everybody's in hysterics up on that damn hill because I got this bandage tied to this kid's balls, and he couldn't move.

The Germans finally blew their foxholes away with mortar shells and started pumping small arms fire into the area. Reavis realized the hopelessness of their situation. The sky overhead was powder blue by now, with a few lonely clouds drifting in quiet formation, oblivious to the carnage below.

"We don't have the radio anymore to call in reinforcements," Reavis said to one man after asking for volunteers. "We have to let our people know we're here."

"Yes, sir, but," — he nodded at his compatriot — "my friend wants to go with me."

"That's fine."

If they were twenty years old, it was a stretch.

"You will have to go through the German lines," Isham said. "Pay no attention to that. And when you hear firing — because they'll be shooting at you — don't fall to the ground, either, because they own the ground. OK?"

They both nodded. One bit his lower lip, each on one knee, leaning on his rifle.

"Whatever you do, don't stop," Reavis said to reinforce his order. "You can't hide from bullets, so keep going hard, hard as you can. It will all be downhill, so just go."

They both got up. Isham reached up and brought the second boy back to a knee.

"Don't go together. We don't want them shooting at both of you at once."

Isham addressed the first man, a red-headed private.

"You go first. I'll send him down after."

He hoped the second man might confuse the Germans, giving the first boy a better chance of making it.

The first man left and soon enough spurts of machine gun fire came from below. Isham was certain they directed the fire at the first boy. He sent the second man. Next, he heard another string of fire. It was upsetting.

Let them through there, I prayed. Don't let them be hurt. I became emotionally involved, asking these young men to risk their lives.

The Germans kept coming up from the backside of the hill. Reavis kept scrunching lower and lower and lower into his foxhole. As the fire increased, the bullets kept zinging deeper and deeper. Two rounds ricocheted off his helmet. He thought, "The next one will be a little lower and that will be it."

No anxiety or fear. You accepted the fact of your death. All I thought was, "I hope to hell they take me back to Nebraska and bury me in Falls City."

They were impotent, and the Germans realized it, too. Isham's last defense was throwing rocks.

Sounds crazy, but it worked for a while.

Thinking he was tossing grenades, the Germans turned and ran until they realized what was happening. Reavis tucked his head down as far as he could, resigned to what he thought was inevitable.

***

13
SKIRMISH

~ September 1944 ~

As the Soviets pushed west, AK sent Bisia to Andrzej Morawski's property in Niebieszczany to find out what she could about the remaining strength of the German force in the area. The Germans had commandeered Andrzej's home as a base.

When Bisia pedaled up on her bicycle, she found Cesia, the Morawski's maid, out front.

"Cesia, please, say nothing," Bisia said with a finger to her lips after leaning her bicycle against the front gate. "I don't want the Germans to realize we are friends. Pretend with me."

Entering the house, Bisia met with the German general.

"With the front moving through the area, I was unsure about where I can go safely."

"Where are you coming from?" the general asked.

"Besko. I'm trying to go to my parent's place in Zagórz."

They told me the location of their troops, and where they thought the Russians were. They even gave me a horse and some cigarettes. I returned to my unit and reported. The information protected us from stumbling into the wrong place, but it could not hold off what was coming.

Since the first weeks of the war, Germans occupied Poland. Now faced with the Russian advance, Bisia's home area once again came along the front lines. Their AK unit received new orders to move into the forest for their safety.

Our unit was moving toward the forest when Germans from outside our area caught us by surprise in a skirmish near our property in Zagórz. My concern was the safety of my parents as the Germans fired from the high ground behind the lodge. They pinned us down along the road to the front. These weren't the same Germans who occupied the area or ran the camp in the plastics factory close to Zagórz, where they held Jewish prisoners. *These soldiers were retreating from the Russians and unexpectedly ran into us.*

OP-23 commander Adam Winogrodzki approached Bisia.

"We have to find out how many Germans we are up against. But we need more support, too. I want you to go into town. We'll fire a covering volley. Take Alec with you."

The incoming fire continued as Bisia and Alec stripped off their rucksacks to make their flight easier. The initial stretch would be the most dangerous. They had to cross an open field before reaching the cover of the forest.

We ran bent low, moving as fast as we could. We hadn't gone too far before the Germans spotted us and began firing like hunting rabbits.

Bisia and Alec hit the ground, hoping their unit would draw the German fire. Bisia brushed a strand of hair from her face.

"Don't move," she told Alec, who was only sixteen. He was breathing hard and looking anxious. "Stay still. Let our people try to draw their fire."

But he didn't listen. Instead, when the German firing stopped for a moment, he jumped up and ran. Moments later, a bullet zipped into the back of his right leg.

"Alec? Alec!?"

Bisia crawled to his side, tore off a piece of his shirt, and tied a tourniquet above the wound around his leg. He lay still, looking quite brave. How many of these youngsters had she seen, only thirteen or sixteen years old, their gun giving them an identity, though fear never fully gone?

Through clenched teeth, Alec asked how bad the wound was while looking far too young.

"Don't worry. I will go back for help. You'll be safe here. Just keep down. We will be back soon. Stay still and don't move."

Bisia managed her way back to the unit to report Alec's wound.

"We can't make it through on foot," she reported to Adam. "The firing is too intense."

"Okay, but I need you to try on horseback. We will help Alec. You ride to Poraz."

Our position was in the forest, across the road from our lodge. It seemed so strange to be fighting so close to home. But to get away, I still needed to ride through those same fields for several hundred meters, wide open to the German fire.

Bisia mounted the best horse she could find, put her head down alongside its neck opposite from the firing, and galloped away.

The sound of the hooves sounded like thunder, announcing her presence to the world.

Ping! Ping!

Bullets zipped by. She galloped, clinging to the horse's mane, leaning away from the fire, pulled toward the far cover of trees by fear, hope, and duty — mostly fear.

Her horse took a round in the neck, the stain of blood smearing back along from the small entry wound on his coat, but he never faltered. They got through to town, where she reported to the house where their unit met.

"Germans troops came through from the east," Bisia said to her compatriots. "They have us pinned down. Grab what you can and come with me."

The additional force Bisia brought arced around from the rear, creating a second front against the German position. With the Germans bracketed, the Poles soon took the initiative. Shortly after Bisia returned, they captured two German officers and three enlisted men as the German force split up, attempting to escape.

With nowhere else to take the prisoners, they escorted them to the Krasicki lodge.

Quartered in the forest, their unit didn't have any contingencies for prisoners. The Germans figured it out too and became frightened, thinking we would execute them.

Instead, the Poles surprised the Germans. While Adam weighed his options in another room, Bisia guarded the prisoners in the library: the same library where Gestapo officers held Zosia and her at gunpoint while searching for the hidden radio a few years before.

As Bisia held her rifle on the seated men, the butler, Józef, walked in and asked Bisia if anyone wanted coffee or tea. The Germans realized some connection existed between this woman holding them at gunpoint and the lodge. They asked her if it was true.

As prisoners, they were not to be communicated with any more than necessary. The same position the Gestapo took with Bisia during the surprise raid at the lodge.

"What will happen to us?" one man asked.

"I can't say."

They begged not to be executed, fearing more than anything being turned over to the Russians. After a long discussion in the other room, Adam Winogrodzki returned asking the Germans for their soldatin books.

Soldatin books listed each soldier's name, address, family, rank, and whether they were members of the Nazi Party — which these men weren't.

"There was a lot of talk about what to do with you," Adam said. "We have no place to hold prisoners here. Most of my people want to shoot you. But you are lucky. We have kindhearted women in our country and they have pleaded with me to let you go."

Our concern hinged on what the Germans would do if we released them. Because if we let them go, they could easily betray us, and reprisals would certainly follow.

"You are a lucky group today. We aren't like you. So here is the proposal. You wouldn't be here unless things weren't going badly to the east. And with the Americans, British, and French pressing from the West, how much longer will this war last? We won't kill you, but—"

"Anything, just don't give us to Russians," one pleaded.

"We are going to let you go, but only if you promise you will go straight to Germany, and not join up with the first division you find, or report our position and strength. Understand? Do you agree?"

At first, the Germans didn't believe it, thinking we would fire once we freed them. But our offer was honorable. And as they departed, they shook our hands and saluted. "Word of honor," they said, kissing the hand of Gusia and me. "We give you our word of honor." Perhaps it represented the last of our naivete, but such words still held value in our world.

After the Germans left, Count Krasicki came downstairs. Exhausted by the physical and emotional toll of the day, Bisia sat alone on the couch in the library, leaning with her elbows on her knees, smoking a cigarette. Her uniform was still dirty and her rifle rested beside her against the couch. Throughout the years, her father never allowed her to smoke, but this day Bisia did not try to hide it.

"You look like a corporal," her father said, standing at the doorway.

Bisia managed a wry smile as she took a drag on her cigarette.

"I'm sorry, Reichsgraf, but I am an officer, just like you."

He walked over, bent, and kissed the top of her head, dropping a small nugget of gray into her lap.

"You were shooting above my chair," he said as he walked away. "I couldn't relax."

Bisia looked. It was a bullet he had dug out of a wall in his room from upstairs.

*

As part of Operation Storm, the AK received instructions to cooperate with the advancing Red Army, though they maintained primary allegiance to the government-in-exile in London.

Out along the perimeter of the lodge near the road to Zagórz, AK sentries captured two young Ukrainians trying to get through their lines. While the AK officers questioned one man, Bisia guarded the other. After a short interrogation, they learned the two Ukrainians worked for the Germans.

Our hope always rested with the chance freedom would come. But we understood the Russians too well.

As the clashes escalated between the Soviets and Germans, mortars, artillery, machine guns, everything came into the battle. Bisia's unit returned to the field, set up on a hill between the two opposing forces.

The bullets sounded like a tight wire being whirled above our heads. There was nothing for us to do, no place to go. Finally, under a constant barrage, the Germans retreated, and we sent a reconnaissance team led by Zosia's husband, George Garapich, to inform the Russians we were here as allies.

A year earlier, Zosia fell in love and married the commander of the Lesko branch of AK unit OP-23, George Garapich. When George returned, soldiers from the Soviet 242nd Armoured Brigade arrived with him, not as allies, but adversaries. They rounded up the Poles like prisoners and marched them down from the forest with their hands raised.

Below, in the fields, the Russians gathered around camp fires. The seasons turned fast in Bieszczady and it was already cold. A Red Army colonel came to speak with the Poles. Bisia stood in a line before him, tired and hungry on a cold, ghost-gray afternoon.

"Father Stalin said we need no more partisan assistance," the Russian colonel told them, never offering either food or encouragement. "You must lie down your arms at once."

His words sounded like the last nail in our coffin. You sometimes hope with an unrealistic heart. For us, the hope was some space of freedom would open between the fascists and the communists. But in the Soviet colonel's words, the future became clear.

After learning the fate of his Home Army in Operation Storm, General Tadeusz Bór-Komorowski, head of the Home Army, sent a telegram to the Commander-in-Chief of the Polish Armed Forces in London. In it, he informed General Kazimierz Sosnkowski of the Russian tanks now visible in the Praga suburb across the Vistula River. If Poles hoped to liberate their capital before the Russians did, Bór-Komorowski argued, the time had to be now.

While Sosnkowski was anti-Soviet, militarily, he was not in favor of an immediate attempt to liberate Warsaw. Tragically, he never answered Bór-Komorowski straight out. With no reply coming from London, the head of the AK took it upon himself to start the liberation plan, anyway.

The Warsaw Uprising began at 5 o'clock in the afternoon on August 1, 1944.

The AK plan was to lead the liberation fight, but only until the Soviet Army reached the city to support them.

The first battle of the Warsaw Uprising took place near the Sobanski Palace, where Bisia's sister-in-law, Elka, wife of her brother Xavier, grew up. Early on, the Poles seized control of significant sections of Warsaw through close urban fighting. But when the Soviets reached the Praga suburb across the Vistula, rather than joining the fight, they halted in place. This betrayal, Poles believed, was Stalin's wish so his own takeover of Poland would be easier in the aftermath.

Though Polish General Zygmunt Berling ordered units of his Soviet-controlled Kosciuszko Division to cross the Vistula to support his countrymen, without Russian air cover and military help, the Polish liberation effort found itself pitted against an overwhelming German force.

The Poles' goal was to drive the German occupiers from their capital to underscore Polish sovereignty and to forestall the division of Central Europe into spheres of influence under the Allied powers.

The insurrection lasted 63 days. Over 200,000 people died, insurrectionists and civilians alike. General Bór-Komorowski surrendered on October 3rd after negotiating with the Germans to regard the surviving insurrectionists as prisoners of war rather than as terrorists.

Hitler became so enraged by the Warsaw Uprising, he ordered his troops to raze entire sections of the city, block by block. By war's end, adding the damage from the initial German invasion in 1939, and the Warsaw Ghetto Uprising in 1943, as much as 85% of the capital now lay in ruins. The people who survived moved west.

As the fate of Poland was being decided in London and Warsaw, the Russians escorted Bisia and her unit under guard to a barn where they kept them for twenty-four hours before allowing them to go home. On September 19, 1944, the Russians officially disbanded the Polish underground. But that did not mean they gained their freedom.

"The war is still on," they told us in the following days. *"You should still fight. Poles must fight for their freedom. The Germans need to be defeated, and you have combat experience and training. So we created a Polish unit for you to join."*

There would be no choice. Bisia could either go fight the Germans on the front or be sent to a labor camp in Siberia. With those as her only choices, she deemed it simpler to serve with the new regime for a limited time while she assessed her options.

***

14
C'EST LA GUERRE

~ September 1944 ~

No matter what else they might say about the Germans, they made fine soldiers. Listen to their language. Even their most intimate phrase — Ich liebe dich, I love you — is hard and aggressive. Their language alone helped make them excellent soldiers.

"Raus! Raus! Get up!"

When Reavis glanced up, a ring of Germans stood over him with their rifles pointed down like a circle of spades digging a grave he was already in. They dragged him out. His uniform hung in rags. Two men pushed him with their gun butts to move him faster, but they were fairly decent, considering the circumstances.

I'd been fighting the bastards all night, and half the day, and now — captured. The word stuck like a knot in my gut. Nothing prepares you, and my emotions turned completely around. My dauber sank to the bottom of the sea, lower than whale shit, as we used to say. I haven't been as low in my life. Disgusted and upset and disappointed and dejected and depressed because I lost the battle.

The Germans rounded up his few remaining men and herded them down to their side of the hill where the First German Parachute Division encamped. When they arrived, the men led Reavis over by a splintered tree, and four of them aimed their guns at him from about fifteen feet away.

I didn't give a damn. My shirt hung off me, covered with blood and dirt. Crazy, but I pulled it out all the way out and whipped it back so my chest was bare. It was not bravado. I just didn't want the bullets going through my dirty shirt first. It made little sense, but I did it anyway.

Reavis's mind went blank.

"Halt. Nicht schießen, (Don't shoot)" a German voice rang out from behind.

The Countess & The P.O.W.

The head of the firing squad turned, motioning for his men to lower their guns. The order came from their commanding officer.

One man came over and grabbed Isham's right forearm and yanked it up, trying to take his wristwatch. Reavis bought the Swiss timepiece in June for $50. No way would he surrender it easily.

I hit him as hard as I could. Knocked him down and split his lip. He jumped back up and hit me back with the butt of his rifle, a very uneven exchange. Then he took my watch.

Reavis's jaw throbbed as they led him to the German officer who had Isham empty his pockets. They confiscated a Parker pen and pencil set and $28.10 in currency. To his left lay a neat row of bodies, seven in all.

"You did this," said the German officer in his accented English. The tone of his voice sounded to Isham like a father chastising his son after he had broken the kitchen window with a baseball.

"Jawohl."

"Why?"

"C'est la guerre."

Without answering, the German officer turned and led Isham back to his field headquarters.

Inside the dark, timbered bunker, the German offered Isham a cigarette. He also picked up a bottle from a small wooden table, wiped the top with a handkerchief, and handed it to Reavis.

Isham took two long slugs and handed the bottle back. The German took two swallows as well. Then he called out to one of his men who took Reavis outside, where he found five or six young German soldiers lying on stretchers. Their color was purple and brown. Two had been shot in the head, two others in the throat. All were dying.

We killed a lot of men that day.

From a great distance, the big American Howitzers started firing again as the 346th was back on the job. Though they were now firing in Isham's direction, it pleased him.

*

The same day of Isham's capture, September 16, 1944, Roosevelt and Churchill completed a meeting in Quebec, Canada. There they signed off on the Morgenthau Plan, outlining how the allies would treat Germany after the war. In response, Reich Minister of Propaganda,

Dr. Joseph Goebbels, exhorted all Germans to resist with the utmost fanaticism.

The Germans grouped Reavis with several other prisoners and marched them north. During the last assault on Hill 840, one of Isham's boys had his left arm shot off. Reavis half dragged, half carried him for about ten miles (16 km).

Isham's energy remained manic, charged from the adrenaline of battle and lack of sleep. He and others were beyond fatigue, into a realm he couldn't analyze until its corrosive burn had eaten through another day or so. Only then could Reavis think about sleeping, after his nerves lost their current.

The Germans gave him another shirt to wear, but it soon stained red from the blood coming from the boy Isham carried. Hours passed. In time, they ran into some other American prisoners. The first night out, they stopped at a yellow farmhouse. There, the Germans separated Isham from the enlisted men and placed him in a barn. The doors to the place were open and two German soldiers with their rifles at port arms stood guard.

When Isham walked in, he noticed two men and a young woman, all civilians. He took them to be Italians. A pile of hay sloped against the far corner, matted into a curve from top to bottom.

Across the barn, in another corner, stood an immense barrel some six feet (1.83m) high. A German soldier pointed with his rifle, asking Isham if he wanted some wine from the barrel. Isham nodded yes. When the soldier turned the spigot, nothing came out. The German apologized.

Strange how certain courtesies transcended their circumstances.

I'm sure if he had stopped and thought about it, he never would have said anything. It was a reflex to apologize. Just as it would be to shoot me if I ran.

The older of the two Italian men - he appeared to be around 40 years of age - sat to the left on the slope of hay. He wore a bright red shirt opened to the waist. To his right stood a teen-aged girl wearing a blouse over a long, red skirt. The third civilian leaned against the supporting post beside the hay, a handsome young man in his early twenties with a pile of black hair.

The older one kept his head down and his arms crossed as Isham moved to a place on the hay and fell into a deep sleep.

Reavis awoke the next morning still lying on his right side like when he first laid down. Outside, beyond the open doors, the day dawned muted gray as the damp smell of hay filled the air. Soon, the sound of a column of marching men approached and eight Germans, four and four, arrived. A flat area of ground maybe 30 feet (9.14 m) across fronted the barn before the land fell away, leaving only the forests in the distance.

The German soldiers marched toward the fall-off and slowly sank from view. Only the sounds of their boots remained as evidence of their presence. Soon after, an officer walked up to the barn door.

"Kommen," he said to the three Italians, motioning curtly with his hand. The three rose silently and trudged toward the door. They didn't look at Reavis, and none of them said a word. But as the older man reached the door, he dug into his shirt, pulled out a piece of bread, and tossed it back to Reavis without a single shift in his features.

The German officer led them over to the flat area in front of the barn. Soon, like the soldiers before them, they slid from view down the path. Isham tore off a chunk of the bread with his teeth. The crust was hard and stale. Yet he welcomed the nourishment.

As he took a second bite, a volley of shots rang out. Small curls of smoke rose over the fall-off. The three Italians must have been members of the resistance. Isham spent their last night on earth with them. All the while, they knew what awaited them in the morning. Their last act had been to toss him a piece of bread.

On his third day out, September 19th, the Germans gave Reavis a form with the heading Transit Camp of Prisoners.

"I have been taken prisoner by the Germans, but I am well," Isham wrote to his mother. *"In the next days, I will be transported to another camp whose address I shall write you. Only there may I receive a post and answer. Many greetings."*

The Germans marched Isham a short distance, where he met up with a group of other Americans. That night outside Bologna, he and the other captives stopped in another barn. Again, they had no food, but the men got used to the hunger. They would go days without eating. But the Germans had nothing to eat, either.

Inside the barn, the Americans settled onto a line of cots. Overhead, the ladder effect of explosions followed the drone of warplanes as American bombers dropped their payloads.

Isham rolled off his cot as the explosions stepped closer and closer. "What's that going to do?"

That was Isham's introduction to Second Lieutenant Billy Ferencz, a man he would come to count on in the months ahead.

Isham rubbed his chin while trying to recover some of his self-esteem.

"Don't worry," Billy said from his adjoining cot. "You'll get accustomed to it."

"Hope the bastards miss us is all."

Billy leaned back, clasping his hands behind his head and crossing his feet at the ankles.

"They probably will."

Billy was an iron foundry worker out of Monessen, Pennsylvania. He would prove to be a good man in a crisis. Stockier than Isham, Billy stood about 5'10" with sloped shoulders and a simple manner. He had dark, thinning hair and olive skin and came from a Czech background; even spoke the language a little. 27 years-old, Billy came into German hands under similar circumstances as Isham, but a month earlier, assaulting a hill in the Italian Campaign on August 14th while a member of the 338th Regiment, 85th Infantry Division.

The two men bonded quickly. Most of the other captives were of higher rank, captain, and above. Reavis and Ferencz were only lieutenants.

The next morning, the Germans loaded the prisoners into tarp-covered trucks and drove north to Stalag VII/A in Moosburg, Germany, near Munich.

Opened in 1939 to hold Polish prisoners captured during the first weeks of the war, Stalag VII/A expanded over the course of five years to become the largest P.O.W. camp in Nazi Germany. It would eventually imprison P.O.W.s from every nation at war with the Third Reich.

The camp encompassed 86 acres lying 35 kilometers northeast of Munich in Moosburg, Germany. Divided into three main compounds, each subdivided into small stockades. Seven guard towers and a double barbed wire fence formed the camp's perimeter.

The Countess & The P.O.W.

Isham spent his first two days at Stalag VII/A in the Nordlager compound where new P.O.W.s underwent a medical examination and delousing. Afterward, they assigned him to a barracks in the Hauptlager compound, which held American, French, Polish, Yugoslav (Serbs), and British P.O.W.s. The Suedlager compound housed only Russians.

The P.O.W.s called themselves kriegies, short for *Kriegsgefangener*, German for prisoner of war. They slept on triple-deck wooden bunks with gunny sack mattresses filled with excelsior. Because materials were in short supply, each man received a single blanket and a spoon. Anything else they might need would have to come from a prisoner's own initiative. Isham found an old milk can and some tin. He wrapped the strip of tin around the can to form a handle to use as a cup. Each day around 4 P.M., the men received their ration of soup.

Isham's Stalag VII/A identification

Enlisted men made up the vast majority of the nearly 50,000 prisoners held at Stalag VII/A in the summer of 1944, as Germans segregated P.O.W.s by rank. The idea was to strip away the leadership and break the chain of command the men relied upon. They held officers in separate camps called oflags. But because of its size, Stalag VII/A also served as a transit camp, which is why Lieutenants Reavis and Ferencz spent their initial time as prisoners there.

One morning during Isham's first week at the camp, a German officer walked into his barracks bringing writing paper and pencils. He passed them out to all the new arrivals.

"You will write a letter to your homes now," he said. "And you will limit yourself to 25 words. If you use more, we will not send the message. Understand? I will return in one hour to collect."

The paper they provided resembled the newsprint found in Big Chief tablet notebooks used in American grammar schools, rough with widely spaced lines.

Toni Reavis

"*Dearest,*" Isham wrote to his mother. "*I'm wintering in Bavaria. Treatment is kind and courteous. Send chocolate and cigarettes. Do not worry. Red Cross can answer all your questions. Love, Isham.*"

The Germans picked up on Isham's "treated well and courteous" phrase and selected his letter among 50 they broadcasted to show how well they treated their prisoners.

Over the three months he spent at Stalag VII/A, Isham never stopped planning for escape. One time, he volunteered to take a copper wire out to the barbed wire fence behind the barracks to use as an antenna for a crystal radio receiver the men rigged up.

It would be a dangerous job. The Germans patrolled the camp with dogs every night, and sentries and searchlights scanned the grounds. But Isham said he would chance it and take the wire over.

After lights-out, Isham dropped from a window as the searchlight swept past. He rubbed dirt all over his face to avoid reflecting even the moonlight. He kept his face down along the ground, never looking up. Someone stationed at the barracks window directed him in a hard whisper.

By timing his movements to the sweep of the searchlights, Reavis got the copper line out on the barbed wire. Notwithstanding his efforts, the men never could pick up a signal. Despite the lack of success, such efforts maintained the prisoners' morale, given their circumstances.

Back home, Isham's mother found it difficult to write in her diary after receiving word of her son's status as "missing in action". She was on a visit to her other boy, Burton, in New York City, when the telegram came on October 20th. Burton tried to calm his mother's fear by telling her that no news from Isham was better than bad news. But she couldn't help but worry.

I was so glad I was with one of my children when that news came to me. There is nothing you can do when that telegram comes, but wait. The waiting and uncertainty are so hard.

She returned to St. Louis on October 26th. She cleaned the apartment just to keep busy while friends of Isham's and family members called to express their sympathy in every way.

The best news she received came one month later, on November 20th, when the International Red Cross listed Lieutenant Isham Reavis as a prisoner of war. Lena called her daughter Mary in Omaha and her son Burton in New York City with the news.

We were all so happy and excited we could hardly talk. Mary and I feel sure that Pop's spirit walked with Isham and saved him for us in this way. Being a P.O.W. isn't any too good, but certainly better than being gone altogether. We thanked God.

She couldn't help worry but about all the boys in P.O.W. camps, as the Germans were becoming desperate as the end of the war neared.

Of course, we in the U.S.A. have many German prisoners over here, and that may make them fearful to mistreat ours.

To help reduce her worries, Lena poured herself into work at the local Red Cross. All the mothers of prisoners worked diligently to bring them closer, at least in spirit, to their boys.

Isham and Billy remained at Stalag VII/A from October until the end of December 1944. In the wider war effort, fierce fighting continued in the Battle of the Bulge as Allied forces withstood the last convulsions of Nazi Germany. In the southern portion of the German attack, U.S. troops continued to hold out against repeated German attempts to take the vital road junction at Bastogne, Belgium.

During Isham's three months in Moosburg at Stalag VII/A, he wrote home several times to lessen his mother's worry.

"They're a nice lot of fellows here," he wrote on 23 October. *"We play bridge and read, play touch football, etc. I'm even practicing the piano, very lackadaisically, however... I saw an amateur production of Barretts of Wimpole St. with an all-male cast this week. It wasn't too bad, but Elizabeth B. was a bit more muscular than Browning. Don't forget to send chocolate and cigarettes. All is well here. I miss you, but you must have a little patience. All my love, Isham.*

***

15
SEARCHING FOR JAS

~ 1945 ~

While the U.S. and Great Britain continued to recognize the Polish government-in-exile in London, on January 1, 1945, the Soviet-dominated Lublin Committee declared itself the legitimate national government. It added another warning flag for Poland's coming fate. Four days later, the Soviet Union recognized the Lublin Committee as the Provisional Government. The change met with little resistance from the locals in Lublin, who were still suffering through the hardships of winter.

Bisia retrained in tank warfare 70 kilometers east of Lublin in Chelm through the last two months of 1944, 250 kilometers north of her home district. She kept her rank of lieutenant as a member of General Zygmunt Berling's Kosciuszko Division.

Then, in early 1945, Bisia received orders to report south to the front northwest of Kraków, where the fighting remained fierce. She had several weeks to join the Russian-led Polish People's Army near Kraków. Before heading south, she traveled to Lublin where she finally learned of the whereabouts of her brother, Jas, or at least his possible whereabouts.

When she still fought against the Germans in Zagórz before the Russians disbanded the Home Army, someone leaked Jas's identity as the quartermaster for their AK unit. If he stayed, he faced execution or deportation. He took off from Zagórz to Jasło, later to Rzemien, where he assumed his alternative name, Jan Kowalski. Under this name, the Soviets arrested him.

Friends of Jas asked Bisia to help because she could claim to be fighting with the Russians under General Berling. The idea was for her to go to Jasło, and try to bribe the Soviets to let him go.

Eager to assist, she carried several thousand zlotys and some gold rubles to use as a bribe as she boarded the train heading south. During the war, gold currency could be exchanged for U.S. dollars, Polish zlotys, and Russian rubles, which they called swinka (little pig).

A bed of straw covered the cattle car as she rode down to Jasło, and without realizing it, Bisia became infested with lice. By the time she reached Jasło, she itched horribly.

Arriving in Jasło, Bisia contacted a friend, Roma Werszctein, whose father had been the last government-appointed district overseer of Lesko. Bisia and Roma had been childhood friends. She and her younger brother, Tadzio, spent many happy hours with Bisia and Zosia. Their family had immigrated to Poland from Germany many generations before and had become thoroughly Polanaised.

"You have to rub lamp oil on it," Roma instructed after Bisia arrived at her home, complaining about the lice. Roma took Bisia to the bathroom, where she helped scrub her.

It burned like hell, but the lice hadn't had time to multiply, and so we got them.

"I'm lucky I'm not bald," Bisia said to Roma while they sat and talked after the hard cleaning.

"We received no word from Xavier and Elka in a long time," Bisia said while drying her hair. "The last was almost a year ago. They visited Zagórz shortly after Magdalena was born in November '39, but returned to Warsaw afterward. I saw them in late '42 when I delivered a message from our AK unit to Warsaw."

Bisia told Roma of her visit to Warsaw, which took place prior to the Jewish Insurrection at the end of 1942.

"The building where I met my contact was close to the Jewish ghetto, and from a window in the apartment, the AK man pointed to the guards, and described the German patrols and how the AK tried to arm the Jews through the sewer system with Molotov cocktails and any other weapons they could sneak in."

Bisia described the fresh wave of terror created by the German police and SS springing surprise arrests.

"I visited Xavier and Elka after delivering my message and took four-year-old Magdalena for a walk. We were strolling along hand-in-hand when somebody shouted, 'Lapanka! Lapanka!' (Roundup!)

"We had no warning. Soldiers closed the streets with trucks on either end and began collecting everyone like fishes in a net. No questions asked, no excuses."

"How did you get away?"

"Luck, as much as anything. I grabbed Magdalena and jumped through an opening leading into a building courtyard.

"We must stay as quiet as we can," I told her as I kneeled beside her. We hid for 15 to 20 minutes until the raid ended.

"That is when I learned the difference between the city and the countryside. In the city, they could close the streets much easier. Out in the country, we had more space, and it gave us more leeway."

When Bisia finished with her story, Roma Werszctein asked about Zosia.

"She married in January of '43 at Zagórz. She and her husband are still there."

"Who did she marry?"

"He's a very nice guy. Maybe you know of his family, Jerzy (George) Garapich? They met at a party at his property near Lesko in the summer of '42. Six months later, they married in Zagórz. I remember him coming around Zagórz after they met, but people were coming and going constantly. At first, we didn't put the two of them together as a couple."

"Zosia never liked to discuss those kinds of things, anyway, did she?"

"She still isn't. George had been a prisoner of war, and his mother wrote a long letter to the Germans explaining how his brother died in an avalanche while skiing before the war. She said she needed Jerzy back home. Believe it or not, it worked. They released him."

"That's unbelievable."

"Complete luck. Immediately, he joined the resistance like everyone else. On his mother's side he's a distant cousin of Mama's, so a Wodzicki. Not titled, but gentry."

"Did your father approve? I remember how he could be."

"Papa liked him, but he couldn't attend the wedding ceremony. He became sick again, and the weather turned horrid."

"How is your father doing now?"

"He is not well. It was a big wedding, considering the war. But - and this is typical Zosu - after the reception at the lodge, she and Jerzy planned to go to Hoczew for their wedding night. But she wanted to stay another day with everybody else. And we all commented on how she wasn't so eager to go away alone. But what are our chances now with Jas? Have you been told where he is?"

"What we understand is he and several others are being held in a basement near to here. The Russians got them because they were working on orders from our government in London, and not the Communist regime in Lublin. I also overheard the Russians invited 16 of our AK officers to Moscow to discuss possible cooperation. But when they arrived, the Russians killed them all."

Roma introduced Bisia to some people who had the latest information about Jas's whereabouts. But when she arrived at the location, she learned the Russians had already deported him. With this dispiriting news, Bisia left Jasło and returned to Lublin, her world falling apart piece by piece.

***

16
ESCAPE

~ January 1945 ~

Isham and Billy remained at Stalag VII/A from October till after Christmas 1944. Since the Germans built Stalag VII/A as a camp for enlisted personnel, they moved Reavis and Ferencz in late December along with several other officers. Their destination was Oflag 64, an officers-only camp some 900 kilometers north in Szubin, Poland.

Isham could never figure out why the Germans would move so few men, or use up a train boxcar, or remove six of their own soldiers from active duty to keep guard on them.

They must have realized the Russian front was coming through, and we Americans would only be in the way.

At night, the Germans locked the prisoners inside their boxcar with nothing more than a wooden box filled with sand for a latrine. Mostly, the men urinated out the door. But since barbed wire secured it, they couldn't escape. Instead, they inched as close as they could and peed through the wire.

The town they headed to, Szubin, Poland, lay 280 kilometers northwest of Warsaw, up closer to the Baltic Sea. Stuffed into a boxcar with nothing more than a narrow gap in the door, Isham still found beauty in the German countryside. Peering through the barbed wire at the snow-blanketed mountains covered with pine trees, he recalled a stanza from a Robert Service poem he learned in school called "The Pines": *Pine and pines and the shadow of pines as far as the eyes could see; a steadfast legion of stalwart knights in dominant empery.*

When they finally arrived in Szubin and got off the train, Isham walked beside one of the Polish officers from another boxcar. As the guards led them through the town, local people came out. One little fellow touched his hat and smiled as the prisoners marched by. The

Polish officer beside Isham said, "Make a note of their house. It's free. They'll help you."

Isham tried to remember the house, but there was no number or sign. Besides, they all looked the same. Constantly, though, his thought was to 'get away, get away, get away'.

Oflag 64 occupied the 10-acre grounds of what had once been a boy's reform school. First opened in 1940 as Oflag 21B to house British and French airmen, the camp's designation changed to Oflag 64 after the first American airmen and paratroopers arrived in November 1943 from the North African and Italian Campaigns. From then on, the Germans only kept American P.O.W.s in the camp.

When Isham and Billy arrived on January 1, 1945, as P.O.W. numbers 138861 and 138867, they joined approximately 1500 other American prisoners. But unlike their time at Stalag VII/A, they had no time to settle into camp life in Szubin. The secret radio the Americans set up in the camp — the men called it "The Bird" — kept them abreast of the Russian advances.

At five o'clock on the afternoon of January 20th, artillery fire boomed in the distance, while a bitter cold hovered over the region. Colonel Paul "Pop" Goode, the ranking American officer at the camp, walked into Reavis's barracks.

"We are moving out tomorrow," he said. "Dispose of everything you don't want to carry. That's all I can tell you, moving west. Good luck."

The end game had begun. With the Soviet Red Army closing in quickly from the east, Oflag 64's commander, Oberst (Colonel) Fritz Schneider, received orders to evacuate his camp. Throughout the first months of 1945, the Germans moved over 300,000 Allied prisoners out of P.O.W. camps as the Russians continued to liberate Poland from the east.

At 10:30 a.m. the morning after Colonel Goode's message, German guards called the roll of 1471 American prisoners, staging them in ranks in the prelude to a forced march of some 640 kilometers (400 mi.) to Hammelburg, Germany, site of Oflag XIII/B. Only those too sick or injured to travel remained behind, plus four others who hid in an abandoned escape tunnel.

As the men stamped their feet and clapped their arms to generate warmth in the frigid conditions, Camp Commander Schneider addressed the men before they set off, asking them 'to be gentlemen and not attempt to escape'.

The winter of 1944-`45 was one of the coldest on record. Temperatures dipped to 20-below zero Fahrenheit, accompanied by heavy snow. All Isham wore was a jacket with an American flag on the right shoulder, a stocking cap, and a pair of knit gloves with holes in them.

On the first day out, the American P.O.W.s joined a ragged parade of Polish villagers with their overloaded carts and animals as they marched 25 kilometers, passing near the city of Kcynia (Exin) where the road turned south. Germans posted guards along the turn to dissuade any prisoners from attempting a run toward town. That first night, they stopped at an abandoned dairy farm. The Germans instructed the prisoners to find their own places to sleep.

Along with hundreds of other men, Reavis set off to the two-story barn. Others trudged off to the manor house. Inside the barn, on the first floor, Isham found Billy Ferencz searching for a place to settle for the night.

"No, Billy, let's stay over here by the door."

"But it will be colder over there," Billy said, as he kept working on the area he had picked out in a pile of hay.

Billy was outgoing, a complete extrovert. Even in the toughest times, he seemed happy-go-lucky. What he missed most, he said, was going out on a Friday night, getting drunk, starting a fistfight, and being taken to jail. That, to him, was quite a night out.

"Just believe me. That isn't the place you want to be. This is."

Billy walked over, shaking his head but accepting Isham's decision.

"Look at all the sheep where you want to stay." Isham nodded to Billy's chosen spot. "This is their barn. What do you think happens if someone spooks them? We're better off over here."

They slept by the door in a nook blocked off by a little fence. The wind blew, and about an hour later, somebody turned over or did something, and the sheep stampeded across all the soldiers sleeping in the area where Billy wanted to stay. The decision to move offered its own nest of warmth for the rest of the night.

The next morning, the German guards rousted the men outside. As the prisoners shuffled into ranks, the guards climbed ladders to the hayloft, where they fired sub-machine guns into the stacks of hay. Men, too sick or tired to continue, stayed behind with a medic to attend them. Once again, the Germans warned against escape attempts.

Days passed in a stupor as the march progressed to the north and west toward the Baltic. On their journey, they had passed through small Polish towns like Łobżenica and Złotów. Though a bedraggled, malnourished parade, even as prisoners, the Americans represented freedom to the defenseless Polish people. Many townspeople came out of their homes and stood along the road as they passed. Some locals invited Americans inside for a few minutes before the Germans rousted them out again.

Whenever we walked through those small towns, we would stand straight and walk tall, act like soldiers.

The snow and brutal cold, along with the shortage of food, combined to sap the men's energy. Men died. Others tried to escape into the surrounding fields. After one such attempt, Colonel Goode, again requested his men not to attempt escape.

He hoped to present us as a single group when the Russian army overtook us, rather than have us scattered throughout the region.

The subsequent arrival of a detachment of Latvian SS troops accompanied by German shepherd dogs created the opposite effect. The fearsome reputation of the SS preceded them and caused the Americans to try even harder to find a way out. Yet opportunities to escape were few. As they marched west, they found themselves in open countryside and often slept without shelter.

On their fifth day out, they walked almost 20 kilometers until they found another barn to sleep in. As Isham walked in, he almost tripped over a middle-aged Russian man in civilian clothes sitting against the wall outside. The man's shirt barely covered his bony frame. The shirt was also missing most of its buttons, and he wore no undershirt below it, either. Isham felt sorry for the man, even thought about inviting him into the barn. But he didn't.

The next morning when they shuffled outside, the Russian man who Isham saw the night before was lying on his back with his arms and legs drawn up in the fetal position, frozen solid, dead as a rock. All he needed to do was step inside the barn and he would have lived. But who knows for how long?

When Isham enlisted, he stood at 6'1 ½" (1.87 m) and weighed 150 pounds (68.04 kg). By now, he couldn't have weighed much over 120 pounds (54.43 kg.). Clothes that once fit so well now hung like sheets on his frame. Such a thing would have been unimaginable before the war, as clothes had always been a concern to Isham, ever since he was a kid. While he worked at the Gatesworth Hotel, he changed clothes two or three times a day. He must have owned 15 suits, five overcoats, and 50 shirts.

Now he would have worn whatever clothing he could find. In the state the men were in, they were susceptible to any illness, and soon enough, Isham came down with a heavy fever. He could hardly move. Fortunately, they had come to the town of Zippnow, where they found a little church on the outskirts of town.

"We have to go upstairs," Isham told Billy. "The heat will rise."

He couldn't feel his hands anymore. His legs were numb up to the thighs, his lips swollen, cracked, and tender to touch. Even speaking proved painful. So, he only spoke when necessary.

Like most nights when they slept indoors, the men removed their socks and boots, hoping to dry them out to avoid trench foot. They slept packed together, head-to-foot in rows like sardines, tucking their feet into the armpits of the men on either side for warmth. What they had not counted on was how their feet swelled through the night. Putting their boots back on in the morning became a painful chore.

Isham slept poorly that night. But in the hellish cold of the Polish winter, he dreamed, too, his mind arcing back to Falls City, Nebraska, to the summers of his youth. He dreamed of slipping bare-bottomed into a pair of bib overalls and running out to play with his brother Burt and cousins, Bill and Ed Fisher. Together, the boys waited for the area farmers to bring their wagons of wheat to the granary owned by their Uncle Dave.

Draft horses hauled those wagons, their thick necks bobbing with every stride. In the bright sunshine, the boys would wait until a wagon came along, then scramble up the back, and play in the piles of wheat. It was like skimming down a waterfall through all those silky grains. For hours, they rode back and forth between empty wagons and the next full load.

In the afternoons, they walked out to Nemaha Creek, puffs of dirt popping between their toes as they walked barefoot along the country road. When they arrived at the creek, they would drop their overalls and swim out the rest of the day, washing all the wheat from their hair and clothes, while tiring themselves out before sliding down the squishy banks into the warm, muddy water.

By nightfall, all four boys lined up like tired pups in their beds on the second-floor screened-in porch of their grandmother's house. They all but slept in the tree branches, as zoning laws allowed no window panes on sleeping porches. In the prairie's stillness, the click-clack of a passing train would project their adventures deep into the heart of those endless plains.

The next morning, when Isham awoke in the cold church in northern Poland, he felt better. His fever had broken.

About a week into the march, the prisoners of Oflag 64 found themselves in an open expanse once again. Through the course of the day, they had walked maybe seven or eight miles (11–12 km). Since leaving the prison camp, they had walked over 75 kilometers. That night Isham found Billy turning like a dog in search of a spot to lie down.

"Nobody lays down tonight, friend," Isham said. "I don't care how tired you are. If you lay down here, you will never wake up again. You'll die."

They spent the night standing up, holding one another, with their heads laid on each other's shoulders, like teenagers slow dancing at the high school prom. But their only rhythm came from the thin, rapid beat of their hearts, and wracking coughs coming from the other men nearby. They never quite slept, but they didn't die, either.

When another bleak day dawned — not even a crease along the white expanse of tundra to suggest a difference between land and sky — Isham confronted Billy.

"This is it, friend. Today we go. Let the sons of bitches shoot us if they want, but I can't put up with this any longer."

Throughout the day, they walked with a new purpose. The challenge they set energized them. As they walked, they stayed on the lookout, but the emptiness was total. Late in the day, they came to an old camp near a small village on the southern end of a lake. Billy and Isham made their way to another rundown barn, but at least it was shelter.

"I'm staying when they leave tomorrow," Isham said to Billy. "This is our chance. The guards are in poor shape, too."

"Where can we hide?"

"There's some old lumber in the corner. We can hide under that. It isn't much, but this has to be it."

Billy hesitated for only a second.

"OK, I'm with you."

Other men found places to sleep, as well as the ones who shared the three rooms in the barn with Isham and Billy. The next morning, the German guards woke the prisoners, yelling, 'Aus! Schnell!' (Out! Fast!) While the others moved out, Isham and Billy made their way to the far corner and piled the lumber they found atop each other as best they could.

After a week's march of their own, the guards were in no better shape than their charges. But with nowhere for the prisoners to go, the Germans didn't bother counting heads as the prisoners formed up. Not long after, the sound of the formation walking off faded into the distance. The two Americans lay still inside the barn. Their breathing slowed. Then, the sound of footsteps crunching through the snow toward the far end of the barn alerted them to the lingering danger.

Earlier in the march, Oberst Schneider had ordered his men to shoot into all the stacks of hay in the barns where the Americans spent the night to discourage escape attempts. Isham and Billy listened as the footsteps outside stopped. What followed was the unmistakable sound of two German grenades being activated — PAC! PAC! — prefacing the dull thuds of the grenades landing in the first room.

KABOOM! BOOM!

Their bodies shuddered. A few seconds later, the staccato of machine gun fire ripped through the first room. The footsteps moved closer. Two more grenades landed in the next room over. Again, the room blew, and machine gun fire cut through the gray cloud, roiling in the broken enclosure. Part of the adjoining wall collapsed.

Isham and Billy kept their heads down, facing away from one another as they lay flattened along the cold dirt floor. The silence following the grenades and machine gun fire in the second room seemed to mock them.

In war, you prepared yourself for this eventuality without realizing it. And the moment, in its way, was sublime. How many people actually knew the exact moment of their death? At least we understood where things stood and took comfort in having anything concrete before you, even death. At least it would be a release of our own choosing.

If they could've spoken, there wouldn't have been anything to say that would've communicated any more than their mutual understanding.

After a while, the silence made Isham angry.

"Go on," he thought. "Finish the job, you goons!"

At first, he thought the Germans were having fun at their expense, playing with their emotions to break their own desolation and fear of the Russian approach. The silence hung like a solid weight. The Americans listened intently as the hollow whistle of wind chased over the broken walls in the adjoining rooms. Everything became still.

Isham and Billy stayed down on their bellies, breathing in shallow drafts, afraid their very living would give them away. They stayed under those boards for about an hour before getting up to check their surroundings.

When they ventured outside, only smudged boot tracks wandering off into the distance broke the white expanse. The column of men from Oflag 64 and their German guards were nowhere in sight. Isham and Billy sat pondering their freedom (if freedom was the word for it). Why didn't the Germans blow up that third room? Neither man said a word. They only breathed, then breathed some more.

Nearest they could figure, Billy and Isham escaped on January 29, 1945. The following day marked the twelfth anniversary of Hitler's appointment to the office of the German Chancellor. On 30 January 1945, he would address the German people for the final time, calling for fanatical resistance by soldiers and civilians, predicting "...in this struggle for survival it will not be inner Asia that will conquer, but the people that have defended Europe for centuries against the onslaughts from the East, the German nation..."

On their first night away from the Germans, Billy and Isham listened to cannon and artillery fire off in the distance. The artillery concussions sounded like giants throwing thunder at one another. Though Isham and Billy were unaware of it, the Red Army had liberated Oflag 64 two days after they had evacuated the camp. In the morning, the explosions had grown closer as the battlefront approached. They were free. But free to do what, to go where? Life is a matter of reacting, and they were dealing with almost no givens.

"You're a first lieutenant," Billy said. "I'm a second lieutenant. You make all the decisions. One of us has to do it, and you're the senior man. I'll follow whatever you say."

The temperatures remained below zero, but at least it had stopped snowing. The two Americans began moving back east in the direction from which they came, hoping to run into a friendly force. But to avoid detection by Germans, they moved only during the early morning dawn and around dusk when the light dimmed.

On their third day out, they came to a little building off the road with smoke curling up from the chimney. They shuffled toward it, hoping they might find some food.

Inside the house, they found a group of Russian soldiers. Billy and Isham presented themselves as allies and stayed with the Russians for the next day and a half.

After a long sleep upstairs, Isham came down and sat at a table with one of the Russians, who showed him his automatic weapon, which featured a sizable round magazine of ammunition.

"How many rounds does it hold?" Isham asked, pointing and using his hands to show he meant the magazine.

The Russian held up both hands and flicked his fingers seven times.

Isham shook his head. "Nyet. No magazine carries seventy rounds."

"Da, da, da," the Russian said, holding up his hands, showing seventy once again.

"Nyet," Isham said, waving his hands and shaking his head. "No way, can't be."

"Da!"

The Russian evidently took Isham's dismissal as a challenge. And before Isham realized what was happening, the man placed the butt of the gun atop the table and fired the entire contents of the magazine right up through the ceiling.

You should have heard the racket upstairs; furniture moving, noise, shouting. "Goddamn!" "Shit!" or whatever it is in Russian.

Down the stairs rushed four Russian soldiers, screaming and raising hell. Isham needed no translation as the man tried to explain the situation to his comrades.

"Amerikanets ne poveril, chto provedeno 70 raundov."

And those other bastards turned to me and exclaimed, "Da! Da!" The entire time they kept pleading that I believe them. The only thing that disturbed them was the Amerikanski doubted their gun held 70 rounds. And back upstairs they clomped.

When Isham went up to check the damage for himself, he could tell the men had been playing cards when their man downstairs fired off those seventy rounds. The bullets flew right up through their table, all to prove the magazine held seventy rounds. Nobody got hurt, so nobody cared, and they restarted their game of cards again same as nothing happened. The Russians were crazy.

As their game of cards progressed, boom! An artillery shell blew part of the back of the building away. It was a little building, and in an instant, one wall disappeared. They returned to their seats because three walls still stood around them.

Moments later–Boom! Down goes another wall.

"No place for us, friend," Isham said to Billy. "Let's go."

As they ran out of the building, Billy headed for the nearby woods. Isham yelled out after him, "Not the woods. If they put a shell up in a tree, it'll scatter it. Stay out in the open."

Billy veered left. They were about fifty yards apart and moving. Two more shells landed between them. Isham figured it was the Germans with those 88mm Flak guns of theirs.

The German 88mm was probably the best-known artillery piece of World War II. Not only excellent as an anti-aircraft gun, but it was also an ideal tank killer because of its high muzzle velocity and efficient, heavy projectile. The only problem with the 88mm Flak series was its height and weight, which forced it to rely on its power and range rather than concealment.

The 88 was a beautiful weapon, better than a rifle. They could pick off one man alone with the 88.

Another page on the calendar turned. It was February now. The U.S. 8th Air Force carried out the heaviest attack to date against Berlin, leveling extensive areas of the German capital and killing over 25,000 civilians. For weeks, Billy and Isham received no news at all, completely cut off from the world. But the world was already preparing for the post-war era.

At the Yalta Conference in Crimea, the Big Three: Roosevelt, Churchill, and Stalin discussed the post-war division of Germany into zones of occupation, along with the question of reparations, and the future of Poland. But such geopolitical considerations were way beyond what Lieutenants Reavis and Ferencz were dealing with.

In their travels east, Isham and Billy always searched for barns because they knew straw and manure would be inside. At night, they would dig into a pile of straw, take off their shoes and socks, and place their feet into one another's armpits, just to warm their feet a little. And in that odd position, they rested, arguing the relative merits of cow dung versus horse shit as an insulator.

One day, as they retraced their way east, they ran across something strange in a forest. It was a pile was about 25-feet long and four to five feet high. They went over, only to discover two large piles of naked, frozen bodies stacked one atop the other.

They made no attempt to bury them. Most likely they were Jews from the concentration camp near Oflag 64. It made no impression on me. In a different time, it would have stopped a man cold, but this was a different time, a different world.

After more than a week following their escape, Isham and Billy found their way back to the city of Bydgoszcz, a short distance east of Szubin, where they had marched out of Oflag 64 two weeks earlier. They learned then how the Red Army had liberated the camp just days after the Germans abandoned it.

Near the local airfield, Billy and Isham stopped at a tiny house where they met an elderly couple. When the couple learned they escaped from German capture, they insisted the men take their bedroom. The couple moved to the kitchen, the only other room in the small house.

The man found an old iron stove and knocked a hole in the wall of his bedroom, where he inserted a stovepipe and set up the dilapidated, wood-burning stove for the American soldiers to have heat. Isham thought it was quite a gesture for uninvited guests.

During their short time in Bydgoszcz, Billy and Isham found their meals at a Russian mess hall at the airfield near the old couple's home. An English-speaking Russian pilot helped them get in. Whenever they finished eating, Isham would reach over and take a plate of black bread and dump it inside his shirt to bring back to their hosts to pay them back for their kindness.

While they stayed with the couple, Isham noticed how the old man would go out to the road that ran alongside the airport in front of his house every afternoon. He would stand looking to the west from late afternoon until well into the night in the icy conditions.

"Billy, why do you think he does that every day?"

Billy approached the old lady and inquired in his broken Czech. She told him the Germans had taken their only daughter three years earlier, put her in a car, and driven her away to the west. Every night since, the old man would go up and wait for his daughter to return home because it was the only thing he could do.

It was as touching as any experience I ever had.

After a few days, their Russian pilot told them he had access to a small plane and planned to fly to Moscow, and offered the Americans a ride. Isham and Billy figured they would find an American embassy in Moscow. So, they hooked up with the Russian pilot, and off they flew — to Warsaw, instead.

He got drunk and lost his bearings.

As they descended over the Polish capital, the German suppression of the previous year's Warsaw Uprising came into stark relief.

My God, nothing remained standing in the entire city, total devastation: dead horses lying in the streets, electric lines sparking on the ground. But it only registered as an abstract, like looking at a newsreel.

The Russian flier only stayed for a day amidst all the destruction. Billy and Isham wanted to go, too. They took off, hoping again to land in Moscow. Of course, the Russian drank again and only made it as far as Lublin, about 100 kilometers east of Warsaw.

Lublin was the largest Polish city east of the Vistula River. During the war, it served as a German headquarters for Operation Reinhardt, the primary German effort to exterminate the Jews in occupied Poland.

In July 1944, the Russians liberated the city, designating it as the temporary capital of the Soviet-controlled Polish Committee of National Liberation. The Poles, however, continued following orders from their government-in-exile in London.

Isham and Billy were in Lublin for a few days, and quickly realized it was a safe place. They could always make it to Moscow later. The Germans had never bombed Lublin during the war, so it kept its medieval architecture.

The Americans took up residence in what had been the German ambassador's home. It must have been a beautiful place in its day, but by the time Billy and Isham arrived, not a single piece of furniture remained. But it was shelter, and they were soldiers trying to survive.

Isham would wake up in the morning thinking only of where he was going to find something to eat.

Across the street from the house was a block-long sunken garden where two anti-aircraft guns stood pointing skyward, manned by a couple of Russian girls. Isham waved over at them on the first morning he walked outside. They waved back. Then, as a good-morning gesture, he threw them both a kiss. They smiled and promptly fired off a round each from their anti-aircraft guns. Boom! Boom! And so began a morning ritual.

During their time in Bydgoszcz, the older couple they had stayed with gave the Americans a letter with an address in Lublin to post wherever it might be possible. Since they found themselves in Lublin, Billy and Isham tracked down the address and hand-carry the letter to help repay the people who had taken care of them.

It took some time, but they finally found the right house behind the city's central plaza about one kilometer out along the edge of town along the Bystrzyca River. The couple they delivered the letter to was so thankful they invited Billy and Isham to join them for dinner and later asked them to stay at their home like their friends in Bydgoszcz had. The couple's name was Szymański.

Mr. and Mrs. Szymański were both quite thin and in their late 40s. Mr. Szymański had blondish hair, his wife dark. They lived in a traditional old wooden farmhouse with a thatched roof. The walls were thick blackened timber with a white-colored mortar between. The floors inside were nothing more than swept dirt.

What Isham enjoyed most was Mr. Szymański bringing home loaves of warm black bread, which he would toss onto the dirt floor of this old, old house, ten pounds of it at a time. And Isham and Billy would break off chunks and eat it spread with lard and dunked in milk. After the hardships at Oflag 64 and the forced march, nothing ever tasted so good.

One night after the men's arrival, Mrs. Szymański invited two women over for dinner. Later, Billy and Isham made a date to have coffee with the women the next day in the early evening. At the appointed time, they walked into town with the women from the Szymański house. The women took Billy and Isham to a cafe at the end of a narrow street about three blocks on the far side of the plaza in the Old Town section of the city.

***

17
THE ARTISTS' CAFE

~ February 1945 ~

Bisia was back in Lublin, staying in a small hotel off the city's main plaza. Another of the residents was a mother and her young teenage son. The mother carried herself like she once came from some place high. Her son, maybe fourteen or fifteen years of age, bore her a strong resemblance with dark eyes, high cheekbones, and jet-black hair. Each morning in the hotel restaurant, the two ate sparingly, drinking coffee mainly and staying to themselves. After several days, Bisia noticed their absence.

"Have you seen our dramatic mother and son?" Bisia asked the server the next morning. "I haven't seen them for a few days."

The waiter lowered his tray. Sadness shaded his face.

"They committed suicide. They took poison in their room."

These pieces of news hit you hard because you understood so well the despair.

*

Bisia spent ten days in Lublin before feeling pressure to report south for her assignment. Though the temperature dipped well below zero and heavy snow was falling, she left on Wednesday, February 14th.

Despite the deteriorating conditions, she walked to the outskirts of town around 3 p.m. and waited along the road, heading south, hoping to hitch a ride. A hard wind cut like a scythe as Bisia stood huddled alone along the road. She spent two hours alone with only the heavy snow and brutish cold as companions. As darkness fully descended, Bisia realized the senselessness of waiting any longer. So, she pulled her coat in tighter and began walking back to the city, head down, arriving a little past 5 p.m.

Toni Reavis

I knew Gusia and our friend Olga Wiktor were still in Lublin, so I headed to the Artists' Café, which was where I thought they might be.

The Artists' Cafe occupied the first-floor corner of a gray limestone building at 1 Peowiaków Street, a few blocks north of Plac Unia Lubelska, the plaza in the town named for the union of Poland and Lithuania in 1556. A group of movie and radio artists who had no work because of the war ran the cafe.

The frigid wind whipped her hair as Bisia pulled open the heavy wooden door from the street. Kicking snow from her boots and shaking it from her coat, she held aside the woolen blanket that helped insulate the inner room and entered the cafe proper. Inside, the clink and clatter of piano and conversation mingled with the cloud of cigarette smoke hanging from the ceiling.

Bisia removed her coat and waved at Gusia and Olga, who sat at a table on the right with some strange-looking men in odd-looking uniforms. Before she could join them, the piano player on the small stage to her left hailed her.

"Well, I thought you said goodbye. But here you are again. Couldn't stay away. I completely understand. So, what would you like me to sing for you?"

Bisia smiled. She was familiar with the piano player's routine of requesting suggestions from the audience that he would turn into a song. What came to her mind was one of her cousins who was in a P.O.W. camp in Germany. He was a writer, and one of his letters from this camp was a poem they put to music, called "A Letter from the Prisoner of War Camp." This was her request.

It was Valentine's Day 1945. The same day American and British planes fire-bombed the city of Dresden as the death throes of the war convulsed around Germany. Through the vagaries of fate, 23-year-old Polish Home Army Lieutenant Countess Bisia Krasicka of Lesko, Poland, and 33-year-old U.S. Army Lieutenant Isham Reavis of St. Louis, Missouri U.S.A. ended up in the Artists' Café on Peowiaków Street in Lublin, Poland on a frigid wintery night. They were about to meet for the first time.

"They're escaped American P.O.W.s looking for food and any help they can find," Gusia explained when Bisia came to the table and inquired about their company. "But I thought you were on your way south."

Gusia was living in Lublin for the moment because it was safe, and because the Soviets had reassigned Adam Winogrodzki to the Communist-controlled Polish People's Army Regional Supplementary Command–RKU.

"I tried, but there weren't any rides coming in this weather. I'll tell you, Gusia, my heart isn't it. I'm glad I didn't catch a ride. Makes me think I shouldn't even go."

"You're considering *not* reporting? Adam is in Rzeszów (175 km south of Lublin). He never talked about not following orders. You're really thinking like this? I mean, what would you do? Where would you go? You are aware of what they would do if they caught you?"

"Adam is a professional soldier, Gusia, I'm not. I'm tired. I've been through years of this and I have had enough."

My mindset surprised Gusia. Yet we all were keenly aware the Poland we fought so hard to save no longer existed. So you lived for the moment because the future no longer belonged to us anymore.

Sitting across the table from Bisia, Isham nudged Billy with his elbow.

"What are they saying?"

He nodded toward Bisia and Gusia. Billy listened intently for several seconds.

"Something about where she is traveling, I think. They are speaking too fast for me."

"Well, interrupt and ask."

"Ask what?"

"What they are talking about? Who is she? Where is she from?"

Via Billy's translation, Isham found out Bisia fought as a member of the Polish Home Army but was now assigned to a Communist-led unit with orders to report south.

"She thinks the Polish general is a traitor for siding with the Russians. She also recently learned one of her brothers got deported, too."

The Polish dislike of Russians led Isham and Billy to share their encounters with the Red Army soldiers they met after their escape. They told the story of the time some Russians couldn't get a jeep started. It was dusk and they couldn't see too well. Rather than waiting for the morning light, they tipped the jeep over on its side. Then they set the barn afire, so they had enough light to figure out what was wrong with the jeep.

Burn the barn down so they could look underneath the jeep, rather than wait till morning. This is all true. The Russians are crazy.

The more foolish they painted the Russians, the more everyone laughed. But for the three Polish women, the laughter carried a bitter edge. Olga voiced their cynicism. She, like her father, had sung at the New York City Metropolitan Opera before the war.

"You are among the first Americans we've seen in Lublin. Now, here you are, but you've come too late and much too all alone."

"We didn't plan to come at all," said Billy. "If our Russian pilot had half a brain and could find his own capital, we'd be in Moscow now."

"Have you picked up any news on your travels? The Russians have installed their own government here in Lublin."

"That is already more than we've picked up. But you Poles are famous for your faith, aren't you?"

"I wish faith was enough."

Olga's voice carried a sarcastic edge.

"We had faith in our allies in '39, but they never came. Now it is happening again. Comrade Stalin talks with Roosevelt and Churchill about peace. But the only peace he is interested in is Russia's piece of Poland."

Like before the war began, Isham had little interest in politics. His complete attention instead had turned to Bisia.

When this woman walked into the cafe, she looked like the one I always wanted. There was strength in her eyes I had never encountered in a woman before. Reflected in her eyes was Poland itself: all the pride, defiance, strength, elegance. She was the true aristocrat, and you could tell she had a job to protect Poland.

Not five minutes after meeting her, Isham said to Billy, "ask that one if she's married," nodding at Bisia.

Billy inquired.

"She said, no."

Bisia glanced at Gusia.

"What kind of strange question is this?" she wondered.

"Ask her if she's engaged?"

Bisia considered these questions wildly inappropriate. Nowhere in the world does one ask such personal questions so soon after meeting. Isham was undeterred.

"Ask her if she's going steady?"

Was this some kind of parlor game they were playing? 'Going steady'? What kind of expression was this? Bisia never heard of any such social arrangement before, and through Billy and Olga's interpretation, she eventually laughed at the absurdity of it.

Before Isham could go on, the singer called out to their table, pointing at Isham.

"He wants you to ask a question that he can turn into a song," Olga said.

Isham thought for a moment, drumming his fingers upon the table.

"Tell him to come up with a song about why he parts his hair down the middle."

The singer mulled over the suggestion before playing. He must have done a good job because once again, the whole place erupted in laughter and applause.

She has a wonderful laugh, Isham thought.

Hell, I couldn't remember the last time I asked anyone to find out something about a woman for me. If I wanted a particular woman, I would do something about it. How a young man works, I guess. Reflection had never been my strong suit, more impetuous, arrogant.

"They want to know why you are asking all these questions about her," Billy said to Isham after they applauded the singer's effort.

Isham took the stub of a pencil from the table, and on a piece of paper drew a house with a small fence and smoke curling from the top of the chimney. When he finished, he turned it around to show.

"Tell her I'm going to marry her and take her to this house in America."

And with that, Reavis sat back and waited.

Billy translated, and the idea cracked the women up again. Bisia lifted her glass in a joking toast. But Isham simply told this woman he intended to marry her and meant it.

I thought if she was married, I'd just go kill her husband, any obstacle. And the other thing I understood right then, I would marry her.

The five of them stayed at the Artists' Cafe for an hour until police hour curfew at seven. But before leaving, Olga offered to meet up with the Americans the next day.

"Why don't we meet again tomorrow? We have some money, and can buy you dinner."

The next day, they met at the Kawiarnia Cafe across from the city square.

Snow fell heavily through the night, and they had to jump from the curbs to avoid the drifts along the gutters. Isham and Billy told more stories of their escape after four months in German P.O.W. camps.

Isham took off his military I.D. bracelet and scratched "I love you" on the back with a fork and handed it to me, insisting he wanted to marry me. He was tall with a long, pleasant face, and wavy brown hair combed back off a high, prominent forehead. Still, I only thought it was a game. I can't take such a thing seriously.

Bisia glanced at Gusia with a bemused smile.

"Tell him he's frightening me a little."

I tried to hand back the bracelet, but he held up his hands as if to say, I can't take it back once I have given it.

What she first noticed about these Americans was their sense of humor. Language, of course, remained an obstacle, but the furtive looks, the off-handed remark, the uninhibited laughter, all made these two men interesting.

The police curfew hour passed again by the time they left. Only military personnel had permission to be outside legally after 7 p.m. But Bisia had the day's password, and legally escorted the Americans back to the house where they stayed with the older farmer and his wife.

The three walked through the wide plaza as a cold, gritty wind blew across the gray stones. Two uniformed Russian soldiers with rifles slung over their shoulders approached from the other side. Bisia wore her Polish officer's uniform, and the lower-ranking Russians saluted her as they approached.

"What are you doing with these men?"

"I'm showing them back to where they are staying. They are new in Lublin."

"No one is permitted out at this hour."

Less a question than an indictment, Bisia thought they might arrest her. Isham sensed her danger. He quickly brushed by Bisia and stood between her and the Russian, forcing them to deal with him. He spoke fast.

They didn't understand, but it didn't matter. He only sought to deflect attention from Bisia. Isham told them he and Billy were searching for an American military attaché and expected the Russians, being allies, would avail an American officer's needs.

Billy's translation, along with Isham's commanding demeanor, overwhelmed the Russians. The Americans asked so many questions in such quick order; the Russians called Bisia back, so they didn't have to deal with them anymore.

I found the Americans quite ingenious and humorous, even in these tense situations. It was an appealing characteristic. Again, that evening, this tall American kept insisting he wanted to marry me.

From then on, they would meet at the cafe on the plaza, but never for more than an hour or two at a time. The weather remained horrible, so Bisia spent much of her time in her hotel room trying to figure out what her next move would be. Because she still wore a uniform and received the changing passwords, she circulated without restriction. Every night she would take Isham and Billy from the cafe down past the plaza through town to Szymański's before returning to her own hotel.

The danger never disappeared completely, though, because the Russians didn't always ask for the password, but often shot first, instead, trigger-happy. Often you would walk close to a building or take a corner, and suddenly they would show up demanding the password. Their threatening presence would make remembering nerve-wracking, especially since they would shoot as easily as hear the right word.

***

18
OLD BISHOP

~ February 1945 ~

One day, while walking through the city plaza, Bisia came upon a small knot of people. A British soldier stood in the center asking for directions. Since he spoke some French, Bisia introduced herself. His name was Lane. Bisia escorted Lane to the Kawiarnia Cafe, where Gusia and Olga joined them. Billy and Isham arrived later.

The five of them sat along the balcony overlooking the cafe with its ornate brass chandelier hanging from the center of the room. At the next table sat three Polish men. One of them called Bisia from the table. He handed her a considerable sum of money.

"I can tell those are Americans who need help. Make sure they are not hungry, and they remember Poland well."

At first, Bisia refused the gift, but the man explained his success at working in the black market during the war and insisted he wanted to help. Several days earlier, Billy gave Bisia a black onyx ring with a diamond insert he kept hidden from the Germans by tucking it into his watch pocket. Because Europeans didn't sew small pockets into the waistbands of their pants, they never searched there. Billy told Bisia to pawn the ring for whatever she could get.

When she returned to their table, Isham made a flip remark about Bisia taking money from strange men. He meant it as a joke, but Lane took issue.

"Don't you understand who she is? She is a countess!"

"Oh, that's all right," Isham said, lifting his glass in salute. "I'm an American, and she's so pretty. I'll forgive her."

Lane shook his head in disgust, muttering "Americans" beneath his breath.

Throughout the week, Isham kept insisting Bisia should marry him. Bisia still considered the proposal a joke, but as time passed and his insistence grew, Bisia finally understood the seriousness of his offer.

I found him interesting, absolutely, and somewhat like me in his attitude: taking charge, free, undeterred by the thoughts of others. Here was someone who had seen and done and been where I had been. We came from different circumstances, yes, but he'd seen the same faces of deceit and evil. You met so many people in such a short time through these years, and nothing ever came of anything.

Love affairs? Certainly. Unfortunately, they were with married men, mostly. Now standing in front of me was an American officer who meant what he said, and his assertiveness released a flood of relief. Here is someone on whom to lean without fear.

Andjey Morawski had been Bisia's best male friend, but she never shared a liaison of any real consequence. She had pleasant things said to her before, but she always dismissed them as another man giving her a line. Plus, she always armed herself, tongue-in-cheek. Everyone and everything was so temporary, so fleeting. The whole of life made little sense.

I think you lived day by day. In my mind was curiosity. I was not a conformist. I felt maybe no hope was left here, though I really didn't want to leave Poland.

In time, Lieutenant Colonel James Wilmeth, the chargé d'affaires of the American mission in Moscow, came to Lublin to round up stray escapees. Isham and Billy were among those permitted to leave on the first train to Odessa.

Bisia stayed in her hotel room on Friday, preparing to go out, when someone knocked on her door. When she opened it, Isham and Billy were standing in the hallway.

"Why are you still here? Why didn't you leave?"

"We stayed because I don't think you understand. I'm not leaving until you marry me."

That is when I thought, "perhaps I should take this offer seriously and avoid this mess." This was the eighth day after our first meeting. We had never even kissed one another. But we needed some legality. There was no time to post banns, and neither of us had any documentation beyond our military IDs.

They walked out to find a notary public to notarize a note Isham wrote to seal his proposal.

To the American authorities:

The bearer of this note is Elisabeth Krasicka, to whom I am engaged to be married. Orders arriving for my departure prevented our marriage, but it is my intention to send for her immediately upon my arrival in the States. I ask for your cooperation in this matter. Do everything you can to facilitate this for us. My mother, Mrs. Lena S. Reavis, and I of 5514 Pershing Ave. St. Louis, Mo. will both be responsible for her until she and I can be married. Sincerely yours,
   Isham Reavis, 1st Lt. Inf. U.S.A. O-1319775.

One last requirement Bisia insisted upon was permission from the church. She said she knew the local bishop as a friend of her family and they should visit him. When they got to the diocese office, Bisia met with the bishop first by herself.

An elderly man with soft hands he kept folded in his lap, the bishop was aware of the Krasicki family because the name meant something historically and Poland wasn't a large country. So, this man immediately recognized Bisia wasn't anyone from anywhere. At first, after Bisia explained her situation, the bishop balked.

"How can I give my blessings when your parents wouldn't give theirs? How long have you even known each other?"

He reminded me of all the other people who told me what I could and couldn't do throughout my life. Again, another case of other people wanting to decide for me after I already decided for myself.

"Is this fiancée of yours here?"

"Yes, he is waiting outside."

"I'd like to speak to him."

Bisia got up and brought Isham back in. This time, she sat outside and waited as the bishop questioned Isham.

The bishop struck Isham as a perfect gentleman, dressed in his black cassock and white clerical collar, though the cassock was ~~worn and~~ ragged at the hem.

"Do you attend church?"

"Occasionally, I do. Yes."

"What religion do you practice?"

"I am a Protestant, Methodist."

"Would you be willing to convert to Catholicism and raise your children as Catholics?"

Isham told him he would consider converting and explained he lived in St. Louis in the U.S.A. and would send for Bisia as soon as possible.

The bishop thanked him, and they rejoined Bisia outside.

"He seems to be an honest man," the bishop told Bisia in Polish. "Though in normal times I would never sanction this marriage, in this case, I will give you my blessings."

~ Wedding Jitters ~

One of the marriage traditions in Poland was to attach a gold piece to the bride's veil for good luck. Bless his heart; Mr. Szymański gave Bisia a gold Russian ruble after they returned from gaining permission from the bishop.

"Mr. Szymański, this is a tremendous amount of money," Bisia said, not wanting to take yet another gift.

"Please, I don't want you to worry. I would love to contribute to this union. You both deserve some happiness."

Later they found a jeweler in the city and bought their wedding bands with the gold ruble. They had their names engraved along the inside of each other's rings. That night Bisia returned to the small hotel off the city plaza, alone in her little room.

Life had changed such a great deal. Nothing remained. Papa was already quite sick, and we would never return to Lesko. The Russians sat on their hands as the Germans destroyed Warsaw and we could already tell how the world would reorder itself following the war. Why didn't the Americans understand? Something would eventually force them to deal with the Russians. Why not now when the guns were already here?

The night before the wedding, the weather deteriorated again. In her small hotel room, Bisia sat on the bed. A lamp on the bedside table cast a shallow amber light against the wall. Feelings came in waves, like the wind-whipped snow swirling around the city. She never expected to live through the upheaval of the last six years. No one ever schooled her for the pressure of so many killings and bombings. Bone-tired, her life had become a pressure cooker, the danger unrelenting.

Yes, it is all very noble to fight for your country, but you would also like to live a normal life, whatever that was.

All that remained were her memories. How many people and places from her past no longer existed? How many family members and friends had been deported? How many were dead? The world they fought so hard to save ceased to exist, and a new occupation was taking form. Perhaps this was the hardest to accept. Poland still existed, but it was not the same country she grew up in — or the one she wanted to grow old in, either. Yes, the flame of youthful rebellion still burned, but it had to withstand the winds of despair more than once.

I sat on the edge of the bed with my head in my hands; confused, depressed, loneliness setting in. I didn't know what to do. "What am I getting into?" I wondered. "I made the commitment. I said I will do it. What will happen? How will I handle it?"

Her thoughts raced, but only with questions, never any answers. It might have been easier to cling to the remnants of a dream than to face the harsh reality that may lie ahead. But after six years of living on a knife's edge, afraid to say or do the wrong thing — but not knowing what is right — with no ability to plan, only react, she felt emotionally spent.

Hanging on the back of the chair at the desk, Bisia saw her pistol nesting in its holster. The wind rattled the window. After so long, she simply wanted to be, nothing more. Would it be right to marry a stranger? Her instincts were all that remained. And her instinct said, yes, go forward.

Stop thinking and worrying, I told myself. Nothing is certain. Only you can create a future for yourself.

Bisia remembered it as the longest conversation she ever had with herself. But she resolved if she were to enter this marriage, she would never use an easy annulment. It wouldn't be fair. She may not have fully understood what she was doing, but it was something serious.

I told myself, "If I decide to do it, I will make a go of it, no matter what. Besides, if he left on the first transport opportunity, this would never have happened. Yet he stayed."

The next morning dawned, Sunday, 25 February 1945. B-29 bombers flew off the U.S. Fifth Fleet carriers and struck Tokyo in a devastating raid. That same day, Bisia Krasicka married Isham Reavis in the Church of Saints Peter and Paul, one block from the Artists' Cafe, where they first met eleven days earlier.

***

19
WEDDING DAY

~ February 25, 1945 ~

The sound of their boots echoed off the stone floor in the cold nave of the empty church as they walked in. Saints Peter and Paul Church was built in the Tuscany Baroque style, featuring a triangular gable atop the facade featuring The Eye of Providence, same as on the U.S. dollar bill.

Saints Peter and Paul Church

In the center of the high altar hung a fresco of St. Antoni of Padua, the city's patron saint. Bisia said a brief prayer, asking him to keep them safe and promising if she might conceive a son by this union, she would name him Antoni.

Gusia and Olga both attended, Billy served as interpreter, and Father Stefan Sabejski performed the ceremony.

Bisia, Isham, and Billy sat in a pew set off by itself, away from the others, perpendicular to the altar. Before the ceremony began, Isham patted Bisia on her side. She touched his hand, but he motioned for her to unstrap her pistol and leave it on the pew.

"Don't want people to think this is some shotgun wedding," he said. He and Billy laughed. Bisia didn't understand the joke, but she removed her pistol and laid it aside.

She wore her uniform while Isham dressed in a combination of Czech, British, and American uniforms. Around his neck, he wore a British legging for an ascot. Billy served as best man and translator. He told Isham to say yes to all questions, meaning to say tak, which is yes in Polish, but pronounced, tock.

Throughout the ceremony, Isham sounded like a clock: tock, tock, tock.

After the ceremony, they went to the Hotel Europa off the city square for a reception. They downed a lot of vodka and caviar. A band played the American national anthem, and everyone stood and cheered. A Russian army colonel, Sasha Dmitrius, who was sitting with some comrades at a table by the window, got himself drunk and gave Bisia a box of chocolates.

"It is good that allies are getting allied," he toasted to their table. "And the Poles have something to celebrate in these bad times."

They spent their first night together back at Bisia's hotel room. Somebody gave them a hard-boiled egg as a wedding present, a rare commodity. Neither liked eggs, but they shared it with gusto.

While her son was being married in Poland, Isham's mother returned to her diary in St. Louis. She hadn't written an entry from July 25, 1944, to February 8, 1945. On February 24th, the day before Isham and Bisia married, she wrote:

"This is a beautiful sunshiny day with springtime in the air... tomorrow we are going to the picture For Whom the Bell Tolls. It has been said to be a fine picture... I do hope our P.O.W. boys in Germany will soon be liberated. I worry about Isham, God love him. It looks like the big push in Germany is on."

During their ten days together as a married couple, Bisia and Isham continued to laugh. The bout of depression Bisia experienced the night before the wedding disappeared. Beforehand, she felt torn between her allegiance to Poland and her service with the Berling Division, between her friends and her family. It made for a hard night. But the wedding reinvigorated her. No longer did 'if only I could turn back time' haunt her. Now she faced the present head-on while projecting to an unknown but expected future.

While solitude could be a friend, loneliness could be a deadly enemy. I lived so many of the war years alone. But now I focused on a new horizon, to find my way to America and be with someone who cared for me. It was something to hold on to, no matter how tenuous my situation.

~ Separation ~

While Bisia and Isham spent their first week and a half together as husband and wife, the world around them continued to fall apart. Still, they carved out a sliver of happiness. Though between them, they couldn't come up with fifty cents for a room, and neither owned anything beyond the clothes on their back, both made sure the other one ate. Whatever they found, they shared.

On March 8th, 1945, secret negotiations began in Bern, Switzerland for an early surrender of German forces in Italy. The talks were between Allen Dulles, head of the American OSS, and members of the German High Command (General Heinrich von Vietinghoff and SS General Karl Wolff). To the East, the Red Army approached the southern suburbs of Breslau.

March 10th dawned with snow piled deep on the streets. Overhead, clouds hung low, laden with more. Billy, Bisia, and Isham walked to a small coffee shop off the town square for breakfast, where they met a woman who told them about a nearby photographer's shop, as they wanted at least one picture together before separating.

When they arrived at the studio, Isham thought they were in the wrong place.

The studio was nothing more than a boarded-up shack that looked from the outside like something the neighborhood kids tossed together. The inside gave him the same impression, except for the photographs on the wall. Some of his pictures were truly masterpieces, though somewhat theatrical. But the composition, the relationship of the line between subject and background, and his work with small shadows on his portraits all differed greatly from any others I had ever seen.

The man posed Bisia and Isham, gazing into the distance. Though a more serious pose than one might expect of a wedding picture, the photo turned out beautifully and captured the hope they both prayed for.

Before leaving Lublin, Isham wrote his mother, brother, and sister's addresses on a card for Bisia. Colonel Wilmeth helped by forging a

Red Cross document declaring Elżbieta Reavis to be a Belgian national released from a German concentration camp.

The forged identification paper, Isham's note, and Colonel Wilmeth's letter testifying to our marriage were the only three documents I had. We had no way of knowing whether we would ever meet one another again. I made the sign of the cross on his forehead, the Polish way, and he told me, "Go to the west. I will send for you. Just be careful."

They never spoke about an exact location for Bisia to find help, only "the West". But from the beginning, Bisia understood Nuremberg as the place.

They agreed to keep in touch as best they could, as both realized no promises were possible. Hope remained strong, though, and they worked out a small code to ensure Bisia's safety. When either wrote or sent a message to the other, they would include the words "old bishop". If Bisia heard or read the words "old bishop" in the message, she could trust its authenticity. The same rule applied to any message from her to him.

Neither of us knew what lay ahead. When the Soviets displaced Germans as our "liberators", the future for members of the aristocracy was clear. They had already deported both Xavier and Jas to Russian camps. Despite the end of the German threat, only the accent of the oppressors had changed.

The day Isham and Billy departed for Odessa, Bisia joined them at the Lublin train station.

"You've done fairly well so far," Colonel Wilmeth told Isham as he walked to the train. "I don't have any cigarettes to give you. All I can leave you with is this can of Spam. I count nine of you here and you may pick up others along the way. You're the ranking officer. You're in charge. I need you to take charge of them."

Before they boarded, Isham's final instruction to Bisia was to go to the Americans. Wherever she could find an American, go there.

Lublin remained cold and miserable as Isham and Billy's freight train pulled away. The last thing Isham watched disappear was her face. He carried her image in his mind. It would need to suffice until she arrived in America.

A day or two later, Bisia left Lublin for Zagórz, sending a cable to her parents to tell them she was returning as Mrs. Isham Reavis.

Billy and Isham took their leave from Lublin's Moorish-styled train station situated three miles (5 km) from town.

"I don't have any cigarettes," Colonel Wilmeth told them as the men prepared to board. "All I have is this can of Spam. There are nine of you now and, I believe, nine others coming. Reavis, you're the officer. You take care of them."

Isham cut the can of Spam in half and shared it with his men. The other half he saved for any other evacuees who might join them in the next days.

"Listen up," Isham said as the train pulled out. "We're going into Russia. If you want to escape, that's fine with me. I won't try to stop you. But I want you to count the number of trucks on the highway on our first day out, because that will be your only ride. Citizens don't own cars. Only officers drive, and they won't stop for you."

Of course, no trucks or cars passed that day, so everybody stayed.

It would take the train two weeks to go the 1000 kilometers to Odessa. The Spam would not last the entire trip, so whenever they halted at a village, Billy and Isham would head into town in search of food.

"Let's find the town major's office," Isham said as they walked into one such small town. "I want you to tell them I'm an American colonel and I'm upset."

"You're upset? Why are you upset?"

"Because we don't have any food. Why do you think?"

"Oh, right. But if you are a colonel, what am I?"

"You're the translator."

"But you get to be a colonel. Don't I rank, too?"

"What do you want to be?"

"Major?"

"That's too high. Captain is the best I can offer."

"Why can't I be a major?"

"Because a major wouldn't be a translator for a colonel. A captain would."

"Well, it's a start."

Eventually, they would find the village official's office.

"The colonel here is upset because his men haven't eaten in several days," Billy would begin.

"Now tell him he's our ally and the Geneva Convention says he has to give us food if we make an official request."

Billy turned back to the official.

"He says we are allies, and you must give us food if we ask because the Geneva Convention says so."

As Billy translated, Isham would stare at the man hard and mean. Then he would lean over and pounded his fist on the man's desk, all the while saying: "Mary, Mary, quite contrary, how does your garden GROW! With silver bells and cockle shells all in a long straight ROW!"

Ridiculous, really, but it worked three or four times on our journey.

The town official would shrink and give them a small bag of barley or oatmeal, whatever he had on hand. But to protect himself, he made Isham sign a receipt.

I'd take his pen or pencil and as majestically sign: Colonel Abraham Lincoln. Then I underlined it for effect. The official smiled. We smiled. Everybody smiled. Then we headed back to the train where we'd find someone with vodka and trade the food for booze.

"Can't we get into trouble for this?" one man asked when they'd return with their stock.

"What are they going to do, take us as prisoners?" Isham said.

They had long since lost any fear of retribution or death. If someone shot at them, they would pick up a rock and throw it at him. "You son of a bitch, why don't you pay attention where you're shooting?"

After one of their subsequent town visits, Billy and Isham returned as their train began pulling away under a barrage of artillery fire. They dropped what carried and ran to catch it. As Isham jumped aboard, he banged his shin and tore his leg open. Of course, they were all filthy by this time, and in a few days, infection set in.

Isham's leg swelled until even the baggy army trousers he was wearing needed to be torn along the seam to relieve the pressure on his leg. Every morning, he would yank the makeshift bandage off, which would tear the wound open again. After the puss drained, he re-wrapped it with the same bandage because he had nothing else.

After another stop, one of the enlisted men came up to Isham.

"Lieutenant, there are five Russian girls a couple of cars up ahead of us, but they won't do anything unless I marry her. What about it?"

"Billy, my leg is bad. Go up there and marry him."

"How am I supposed to marry anybody?"

"Put your hands together and say 'it is a nice day in North Dakota', or where ever."

Later, the men returned, all but their one friend. He came back a few hours later.

As their destination neared, a vast body of water came into view behind the city. Isham assumed it signaled their arrival in Odessa.

"I guess this is our place. Must be the Black Sea. Billy, I'm tired of this freight car. It hasn't been very comfortable accommodations."

"Couldn't agree with you more."

"Let's say we burn the son-of-a-bitch, should we?"

They gathered up all the oily rags the Russians used to lubricate the wheels on the train, knocked off some loose lumber, and set the boxcar on fire.

We rode into the station in the Odessa train yard with this freight car blazing away like mad.

They jumped off and came walking into the yard as the train came to a stop engulfed in flames.

All these Russians came running out going crazy. One of them caught up with us and asked what to do to put it out.

"Tell them to piss on it," Isham said to Billy as he kept walking.

Billy then asked this same man where he could find a bathroom, half squatting to pantomime going to the toilet.

"Da, da," the Russian said, nodding vigorously while reaching out and removing Billy's hat. He then handed it back bottom-up and walked away. We laughed our asses off. We told him to piss on his train, and he told us to shit in our hat.

***

20
ANOTHER DAMN FOOL THING

~ March 1945 ~

"Before the war, I would at least be able to call the embassy in Warsaw or Washington and find out who this person is, who his family is."

Count Krasicki shook his head as he spoke, responding to Bisia's news of her marriage in Lublin.

"Now what can I do? Nothing. I can't protect you at all. I can't tell who this man is. He might be a thief, God knows, anything. You can't be sure of him either. This is so irresponsible."

"He's an army officer like you," Bisia said, put off by the severity of her father's reaction to her news. "Can't you be happy for me? Why would you assume thief? Have so little faith in me?"

"Tell me how in ten days you might possibly learn about another person? Tell me."

What to say? I was still this little girl who needed to be told the right things to do.

"No, you always do things your own way. Who is he? What is he doing? Marriage is not a light thing to consider."

"Who said I was considering anything lightly? Alright, we spent little time together. Gusia met him, though, and the bishop, too. Anyway, what's done is done, and I will live by my decision. For once, can't you try to be accepting? This is my life, not yours."

Down deep, Bisia realized her father expressed more worry than anger.

Later, Zosia told Bisia of the visit they received from the German general Bisia spoke with at Andrzej Morawski's place before the skirmish with the retreating German forces.

"He asked Papa to speak with his daughter to make sure she was well. And Papa presented me. 'Here is my daughter'. But the general meant the other daughter, the one who came asking for directions."

"What did Papa tell him?"

"That 'my other daughter is in Besko, as far as I know'. When Papa mentioned Besko, the general's attitude changed in a heartbeat. He realized you duped him for information. Papa wasn't lying and handled him well, but the general turned threatening. Luckily, things went no further."

That night, the cook gave Bisia more hell than the family.

"What a thing to do to your friends. I might have held a reception for you, as I did for your sister. Now you go off and marry some nobody from nowhere? Why would you do this to me? You might have at least brought him here."

They all worried. And the questions kept coming.

"What does he do for a living?" her mother wanted to know at dinner.

"I didn't find out, exactly. His father is dead, and he mentioned something about a hotel, but I can't say if he is an owner of a hotel or works at one. He is an officer who escaped from a German Oflag."

She told them his name was Isham Reavis, which made them think he might be Jewish.

I didn't pronounce his name well, because I didn't call him by his last name. The problem wasn't even one of social class as a complete lack of knowledge about him.

Gusia met Isham in Lublin and liked him, too. Rather than backing Bisia, she offered a piece of cynical advice.

"You can always file for divorce in America if things don't work out."

Bisia shot the idea down in an instant. "I didn't marry so I could get a divorce out of convenience."

The discussion ended abruptly, though they settled nothing. Instead, the matter lay between them as an open, unspoken wound.

*

Seven kilometers from the Krasicki lodge, near the junction where the road split, turning right and climbing toward Lesko or staying straight to Zagórz, there was a small German camp housing Jews. As the Red Army advance continued, Germans began shooting the Jews imprisoned there.

We had no illusions about the Germans, yet some people sought to blame the Jews for their own fate.

"They decided not to fit in, not to assimilate into the larger society," was one argument Bisia heard. That is why the Germans trapped millions of Jews? That is why they marched millions into Hitler's gas chambers?

Everyone knew someone who had been murdered. Every village shared the horror. We all were aware during those years that we slept next door to an unspeakable evil while heaven remained mute.

The smaller camps were not as efficient as the big death camps in Auschwitz-Birkenau and Treblinka. At the small camp nearby, Germans took to burning the prisoners after shooting them. They built open bonfires because no large burning ovens were available. How does one rank the levels of brutality and sin?

The smoke from those fires hung so heavily, and we were acutely aware of its origin. That singular, pungent odor wafted so thickly you couldn't breathe. We held our ears because each bullet fired represented another man's or woman's death. Yet we were in no position to stop it.

The world was once beautiful, but with people being killed so heartlessly, memories became bitter and sad. This killing was beyond war. Soldiers can expect to die in battle, but to experience the sights, sounds, and smells of mass murder was tragic beyond words. I thought, this is how the world will end.

***

21
HOME

~ April 1945 ~

After repatriating with American forces in Odessa and spending a month regaining weight, getting a variety of shots, and medical attention for his infected leg, Isham boarded a British troop carrier to transport west.

The ship took him down the Black Sea through the Dardanelles, passed the Greek Isles into the Mediterranean. They sailed past Capri into Naples, the same port where Isham first landed in Europe the year before in July.

To illustrate how the war had changed him in human terms, one night two sergeants began complaining to Isham about their company commander, saying what a hard-ass prick he was and how they'd like to be free of the son-of-a-bitch.

"You want me to handle it?" Isham said.

"What do you mean?"

"Well, shoot him. Kill the bastard."

The two soldiers exchanged a worried glance.

"Listen, Lieutenant," said one. "We are only blowing off steam. We'd don't want you to do anything. And we certainly don't want you to kill anyone."

"Are you sure? It wouldn't be a problem."

This cavalier attitude toward life is only one reason leaders ought to be damned sure of what they are doing when they start these things. Men lose their humanity, and then the world just becomes a jungle.

On April 5th, Isham received movement orders from headquarters of the 7th Replacement Depot. Assigned as Group Commander for the "personnel escaped from enemy territory", he would ship out on or about 9 April 1945. By mid-April, at the latest, he would be on a troopship headed home.

His journey home began aboard a former luxury liner, the U.S.S. Wakefield, which no longer met its previous standard. They had refitted the ship as a troop carrier with bunks stacked up five and six high, faces inches from the bottom of the bunk above.

We tried to stay on deck as much as possible because the smell was so horrible down below. There were too many unwashed people. The latrine water sloshed with the roll of the ship. Men puked day and night, a real nightmare.

Isham had not put a razor blade to her face since being captured the previous September until he landed in Italy. Still, he never grew a beard.

I don't remember seeing a man in prison camp ever shave, or grow any whiskers at all. It must've been malnutrition. The saving grace of the ship was it was taking us home.

Along the crossing, they received news President Roosevelt died on April 12th from a cerebral hemorrhage in Warm Springs, Georgia. Vice-President Harry Truman of Independence, Missouri, took the oath as America's 34th president.

"*I feel sorry for his family,*" wrote Lena on news of President Roosevelt's death.

Though a lifelong Republican, Lena was a mother first.

"*I know how lonely one feels when your husband and father are taken. Of course, his family is provided for financially, but the loneliness is something no one can help. May he rest in peace.*"

After ten days at sea, the Wakefield docked in Boston Harbor on April 20, 1945. The men clamored ashore to call home, waiting in long lines at the phone booths. For many of the men, this was the first chance they had to call home. Isham called his sister in Nebraska.

The phone rang three times before the first familiar voice in what seemed like years came on the line.

"Hello?"

"Hello, Mary."

"Oh, my God! Isham. How are you? Where are you?"

"I'm in Boston, dear, and I'm fine. We arrived a short while ago."

"Have you called mother?" she asked before calling out to her husband. "Freddie, Isham is on the line, and he's home, and he's safe!"

"Not yet," Isham said. "I didn't want to shock her."

"She received a call saying you would be returning. A ham radio operator in New York listened to a German broadcast saying they had captured you. He called and shared the news. That was the first time we heard you were alive. It's so good to hear your voice. When are you getting home?"

"Should be in a few days, but they haven't said exactly when yet. But I'll call mother as soon as I find out. Oh, you can tell her I'm married."

"What are you talking about?"

"She's Polish."

"Isham, what's going on? This is crazy. Where — who is this wife of yours? Is she with you? When did this happen?"

There were many questions, naturally. But we had to keep our phone calls short.

"Gotta hang up now. I will tell you all about it soon. There's this long line behind me. Say hi to everyone and I'll be home in a few days. Love to all."

"My finest and best Mother's Day," wrote Lena in her diary after hearing from Mary. "My boy Isham returned from war and overseas. Thank God — and Pop — for bringing my boy home safe to me again. He has married a little Polish girl, and he seems to be in love with her. I hope he can bring her over soon. We are all prepared to love her, first for Isham's sake, and when we meet her, for her own sake, too. I am grateful for my blessings."

While awaiting his train ride back to St. Louis, Isham penned his first letter back to Poland on April 27th, addressing Bisia at her parent's castle in Lesko. He understood she wasn't there, but hoped the letter would somehow catch up with her wherever she was.

Hello, sweetheart. I am home after a long trip. It is nice to be here, but if only you could have been with me, I would have been absolutely happy. I love you, dear, more each minute. Of course, you know you are the most beautiful woman in the world. Yes, your husband is very much in love with his wife.

Everyone here thinks you will be over here soon. I think so, too. I have filed Form 633 U.S. Dept. of Justice for you, and will visit the State Department as well. You are to see the American Consulate when he comes to Poland. Show him your papers, and he will probably be aware of your situation, anyway. I love you and will go to the international bureau this afternoon about you, and tomorrow to the Red Cross.

I tell everyone about you. I love you. The picture is not the best, but it is of me and an old sergeant of mine. We took it in Italy early this month. Must close, Kochana. All my friends send their love, and I send you all my love and all my heart. My every prayer is of you. I love you, old bishop.

Three days later, on April 30th, Hitler committed suicide with Eva Braun, thus bringing an inglorious end to his vaunted Third Reich. Isham arrived home to St. Louis on May 1, 1945, to begin a sixty-day furlough.

***

22
KRAKÓW

~ April 1945 ~

Back in Europe, units of the Soviet 1st Belorussian Front penetrated the suburbs of Berlin on April 22, 1945. Hitler ignored the pleas of his entourage to escape for Berchtesgaden and stayed in his bunker to await the end with Eva Braun.

Bisia remained in Zagórz long enough to help Zosia organize their parents' move to Kraków, where they owned an apartment building. The count and countess couldn't return to Lesko or stay at the lodge in Zagórz anymore. The Polish communists ordered them to leave.

Money remained in short supply. Zosia made a little money by rolling cigarettes by hand and selling them on street corners while Bisia got a job at a Russian PX store off Market Square.

While the war wound down in Kraków, many young people bucked against the prevailing restrictions, eager to play after the city's liberation in January. But there were no places to meet. Bisia's parents' apartment building was near Market Square, and soon, people asked Bisia and Zosia if they might use the place to have parties. The sisters charged what the market would bear. Eventually, about twelve couples began using this place regularly, bringing their own food and drink. Each morning after, Zosia and Bisia would clean up and prepare for the next gathering.

In the spring of '45, Bisia and Zosia brought their parents by truck from Zagórz to Kraków. The 212-kilometer trip over poor roads was hard on their father, whose health continued to slip. Only a few trunks packed by their mother came along. At each move, less and less of Lesko survived.

Zosia and Bisia became decision-makers for their parents. Zosia's husband, George Garapich, remained on the western front as a member of the same Berling Division Bisia left illegally.

Isham first received news from Bisia two months after he returned home. Stationed in Hot Springs, Arkansas, he awaited permanent assignment. He wrote back, addressing his letter to the castle in Lesko, hoping the letter would find them.

Only after Bisia read Isham's letter to her parents did her father acknowledge Isham's sincerity. From then on, all their energy focused on getting Bisia to the U.S.

Bisia, Zosia, and their parents settled into the three-bedroom, second-floor apartment at 3A Sienkiewicza Street, the last of the family's five properties still held by her father. It was a lovely building at the end of a quiet side street in a prestigious area of the city, only a ten-minute walk to Market Square.

Zosia had lived in the apartment while she attended school in Kraków as a girl. The apartment provided a place to escape and experience the vitality of city life. But these were no longer normal times.

Unlike Warsaw, Kraków survived the occupation intact. Not only because the city surrendered without a fight in the first week of the invasion, but because Hitler established the city as the center of a new political territory called General Gouvernment, which would eventually become German within 15–20 years. Governed by Nazi overseer Hans Frank, the region would also serve as a supply base for agriculture and light industry. Similar to the days of partition, Germany used General Gouvernment as a vassal state, and had no reason to destroy its infrastructure. Warsaw, though, needed to be erased as the heart of the Polish nation.

Throughout their five-year occupation, the Germans systematically removed all symbols of Polish political and cultural life as they tried to envelop Poland into a Greater Germany. They even declared Kraków to be an *urdeustche Stadt* (original German city).

I flashed back to the German soldier atop the ladder in Zagórz, removing the Polish insignia from the little schoolhouse doorway. They destroyed or confiscated so many of our national artifacts, including the statue of Adam Mickiewicz in Market Square. Yet the city fared better, much better than Warsaw.

In January 1945, the Soviets replaced the Germans as occupiers.

Within the first week of their arrival, Bisia got a job as a cashier and bookkeeper in a Russian PX store on Szczepanska Street off the corner of Market Square. 150 meters away, facing the center of the square stood the Wodzicki Palace, Bisia's mother's ancestral home. Her parents met and fell in love during the carnival season in early 1902, next door at the Potocki Palace. In August 1903, they married across the square in St. Mary's Basilica.

One late afternoon, as Bisia closed the books at the PX, the door opened, and a voice called out in a broken Polish, "Well, well, look who is working as a clerk."

At the door stood a Russian she'd met in Chelm in November while training with the Berling Division.

I'm sure the blood drained from my face, but I pretended to be glad to see him. I had no way of knowing how much he knew of my situation because after getting married, I never reported to the front as ordered.

"Why don't you come down and meet me for a drink?" he said. "I'll wait downstairs until you finish your work."

His tone was friendly, and Bisia didn't want to raise suspicion by turning down his offer. So, after closing the shop, she joined him. He belonged to NKVD, the Russian secret police. He left Chelm before Bisia received her orders. She was unsure of his understanding, and it created new anxiety.

The sun hung higher in the May sky now as they walked through the square. A breeze pushed papers across the cobblestones, and pigeons chased any scrap or crumbs. The Market Square in Kraków was the largest in central Europe, running 200 meters along each side. All the important civic and trade buildings of the city lined this historic square.

Seated with the Russian NKVD officer in a small café, Bisia played things cool.

"Oh, I got married."

She dropped the information casually, like another bit of small talk.

"Married!"

"Yes, to an American."

"American." He nodded, taking another sip of his drink. "Is he here?"

"No. He had to leave. They sent him to Odessa."

Their conversation continued through two drinks: allies fighting the common enemy, all-in-this-together type attitude, the small talk of no consequence. When they said good night, he promised to check in on her again at the store.

I was anxious about returning to work the next day. I became quite guarded and stayed away, hoping they would call him away and he would forget about me.

But she still needed to make money, and took a job with a family by the name of Michalski, as a glorified babysitter. She took care of their two kids, Tanya and Rusa. Their mother graduated from the same Sacred Heart School in Tarnów Bisia. Bisia babysat for the Michalski family for six weeks until May 1945.

One day, while Bisia walked through Market Square in early May, a voice came over the loudspeakers announcing the German surrender ending the war in Europe. Next, the national anthems of England, America, and the Soviet Union played. While people removed their hats for the first two, they replaced them for the Soviet anthem and shook their fists at the speakers.

Bisia (left), Michal Sobanski, Maja Sobanska, Jas Krasicki, Henryk Sobanski, and sister Lula in a summer play

I walked through the square by myself, passing tragic faces weeping openly. The horror may have ended, but the celebrations were muted. We understood what the future held. It was not the freedom we fought so hard to secure.

Once her worries about the Russian NKVD officer subsided, Bisia began spending time again in Market Square. It was while walking through Cloth Hall one day with her two young charges, Tanya and Rusa, that she ran into her cousin Henryk Sobanski.

"Oh, Henryk. How wonderful! What are you doing here?"

They embraced. Bisia hadn't seen Henryk in years. He was the brother of Xavier's wife, Elka, and he and his sisters often visited Lesko or Stratyn in the summers. The two of them shared such happy memories as children together. Together, they dressed in native costumes and staged small plays for their shared grandparents and friends. Seeing his face brought so much to mind.

Henryk, too, had hoped for Poland's prince on a white horse. He fought for it; we all believed. But when you fight for something as hard

as we did, and things don't work out, you never quite believe in right over wrong again. And our cause had been so right. We could accept defeat, but not another betrayal. The future appeared so clear to us in Poland. We saw the coming horror. Why couldn't the West? We were so naïve about the West. Henryk was not so much bitter as pained, a broken man, a dreamer.

Henryk brought Bisia up on news of the family. He told her of Xavier and Elka's deportation to a Russian camp in January. Henryk's two other sisters and his own dear love died during the Warsaw Insurrection in late 1944, while he fought the Germans with the Kosciuszko Division. As you might expect, he was in a poor condition emotionally.

"Someone told me you married an American," he said. "When will you go abroad?"

Jokingly, Bisia responded, "Oh, tomorrow or the day after."

But these were now Stalinist times, and the Russians arrested anyone trying to leave Poland. And leaving by legal means was impossible. Like in the movie Casablanca, no exit visas existed.

Everybody feared his own shadow. And since I served in the Polish resistance under the government-in-exile in London, therefore anti-communist, I came under increased scrutiny.

At the onset of the war, the only allied opposition in Poland came from the Home Army. But when the Germans attacked the Russians in 1941, the situation changed, and communist party members started taking part in the resistance. Yet Stalin subjugated so many of his own people, killed so many, and was so paranoid, he extended his control at every opportunity. Since Poland and Russia were historic adversaries, what Winston Churchill later called the Iron Curtain was already being experienced in Poland.

But Henryk took Bisia's thoughts of leaving seriously.

"If you're leaving tomorrow, I will go with you. We must try. There is nothing left for us here."

"Henryk, I'm not really thinking of leaving tomorrow."

"If not now, when? The longer we wait, the harder it will be. Things are still unsettled. This will be our best chance before the borders harden. Come on, Bisia, let's not get stuck. You and me, we have to try."

Henryk's other sister, Maja Sobanska, settled in Argentina, and he wanted to join her there. Bisia would try to find an American mission like she and Isham spoke about when they separated in Lublin.

"Remember, we need to travel light. You can only bring things you can carry. But Bisia, this is our chance. Pray hard tonight, and I'll meet you at your parent's place before first light."

The wheel began spinning faster now. Bisia did not have time to evaluate her decision in every detail, or carefully decide what to take along. She waited until after dinner before she broached the subject with her parents, beginning with her mother.

"I met Henryk Sobanski in the Square today."

"I didn't know he was in Kraków."

"Neither did I; I just ran into him. But he said he wants to join Maja in Argentina. Before I realized it, I agreed we would try to cross the green frontier tomorrow."

The "green frontier" was what they called an illegal exit. Her parents exchanged apprehensive looks. They understood the danger.

Her mother folded her napkin.

"What can we say? No matter how old, a mother's instinct is to protect her cubs. Twenty years ago, I could still do it. Now there is nothing I can do. Besides, you have always made your own choices."

Bisia next turned to her father, hoping he, too, would understand.

"All we can say is we love you and pray for your safety. There's no advice I can give. This decision arrived a long time ago. You're only acting on it now. It's up to you to make a life for yourself, no matter how far away you must go."

"Saint Antoni will guide you," said her mother as she stroked her child's face.

Later, on what would be her last night in Poland, Bisia visited her father in his room.

Bisia tapped on the door frame.

"Papa?"

"Yes, dear."

The shell of him sat in an armchair by a set of French doors opening to a quiet, tree-lined street. She came and kneeled by his side, leaning against the rolled arm of the chair. The sound of birds filtered in through the open doors.

Now 71, and in failing health, Count Krasicki lived to see the rebirth of his country in 1919 and its subsequent re-subjugation in 1939. This time it was not the country alone he was losing. His ancestral home and family were both in remove, too. Now, his youngest was saying goodbye, and the finality of it aged him even more.

Hair turned white and thin, hands veined and sunken, he was a man whose world had passed. Bisia wondered about their relationship. Most often their encounters had been brief communications or recriminations. Not all fathers and daughters were like this. He and Zosia weren't.

Yet, she also remembered the great pleasure of visiting farms around Lesko with her father as a young girl. They would go by a small, horse-drawn buggy with her sister Zosia and brother Jas, the three youngest.

There was always a big commotion, because all of us wanted to drive. Finally, Jas and Zosia ended up holding one reign each, and I was handed the whip. We would see herds of cows, horses, and folds of sheep. We would ford the River San on our way home. And when Jas was sent to school, only Zosia and I would ride with Papa. Then the rides ended, and it marked the end of my childhood.

"Lisia, how old are you now?"

"Almost 24."

Lisia was the special name meaning baby he called Bisia as a young child. Father and daughter had shared precious little for many years. Age alone created distance. Only in the last years of service did the two form a bond of sorts, as he fought for their homeland during both World War I and the Polish-Russo War of 1920.

One of the French doors opened a bit more from a gust of wind. Bisia pushed it back.

"Bisia, I never want you to doubt our love. Your service made me very proud. But I don't even have five zlotys to give you, because we have nothing."

He took her hands.

It was all very hard because I was aware this was the last time I would ever be with my father, yet I didn't want to cry. I wanted us to part as soldiers because that was our tie. Yet inside, I felt total emptiness.

With his thumb, he made the sign of the cross on her forehead. Then he took her face and cradled it in his hands and kissed both her cheeks with a tenderness that would have to last a lifetime.

"Let us know if you make it."

***

23
"GEE WHIZ" DOESN'T WORK ANYMORE

~ April 1945 ~

On his first morning back in St. Louis, Isham was taking a shower in the apartment on Pershing when the bathroom door swung open. Isham stuck his head out of the shower curtain to find his old army pal Jimmy Reilly standing in the doorway.

Jimmy walked in to shake Isham's soapy hand.

"Somebody told me the army shipped you home."

"Hold on for a second," Isham replied, a little nonplussed. "Let me dry off. I'll be right out."

But when I came out wrapped in my towel, Jimmy had gone.

Isham slipped on a pair of khakis and a shirt and ran downstairs. When he got to the door of the building, Jimmy was pushing some sort of cart up the street.

I didn't know what to say, or why he came, or why he'd left so suddenly. But it was the last time I ever saw him.

After OCS at Fort Benning, Jimmy transferred with 14 other men to the air force where he wanted to train to be a pilot. But they found out his eyes were bad, and couldn't handle high altitude flying.

We had been together since our induction back at Jefferson Barracks in 1942, all the way through to OCS. And here I had been around the world and through no fault of his own, he failed to make the grade, and it hurt him.

After the strange episode with Jimmy Reilly, Isham gathered up his golf clubs and headed for the Forest Park golf course, where the starter slotted Isham into a threesome of local teachers, a man and two women in their twenties.

Golf had always been a haven for Isham, and with a club in his hands and the green grass beckoning, there was nowhere he would rather be. It had been a long time since Isham walked on a fairway.

The Countess & The P.O.W.

Even the name struck him as ironic after the mud and ice and snow and splintered trees of Europe, all the erupted land. The manicured lawns of Forest Park with their close-cut greens and full canopies of sycamore trees lining the fairways might as well have been a new Eden.

While his drives invariably sliced into the rough, it didn't matter. The place was all. The scores would come later. He was home.

The course was crowded, and they had to wait on each tee for the fairway to open. When they arrived at the par-four seventh, the two women sat down on a small bench behind the tee box. Their male friend came over to where Isham was taking a few practice swings several yards away.

"You are a soldier, right?"

"I am."

"Been in combat, too?"

"Yes."

His playing partner asked these questions, like going through a checklist. Isham paid little attention as he kept working on his takeaway.

"How long have you been back?"

"I arrived yesterday. That might explain why I'm playing so damn poorly."

Isham focused on his grip as he spoke while trying to regain the feeling of clubs he had not held in over a year.

"Well, glad you got back safely."

The man clapped him on the arm before walking back to the two women.

Isham didn't give the questions any mind, figuring the man was simply curious. But as they waited for the fairway to clear, Isham overheard the man speaking to his lady friends. The three of them sat upwind from where Isham stood, so their words carried farther than they realized.

"It's because he only returned yesterday. That's why he's cursing."

173

Isham thought for a second. Without meaning to, he kept saying things like, "That fucking son-of-a-bitch. Why didn't that putt go in?" He simply wasn't conscious of what he was saying.

On a sixty-day furlough to help adjust to life back in the States, Isham realized out on the Forest Park golf course any return to normalcy would take time, a long, long time.

When I returned to St. Louis, I was a different person, utterly profane. The harder you live, the more profane you become. "Gee whiz" doesn't work anymore, and it came through in my general conversation. I wouldn't yell or anything. But I would be at a friend's house, and they'd begin looking at me strangely.

I didn't even realize I was doing it. But that is how I broke myself of the habit, by concentrating on what came out of my mouth. You actually edited yourself as you spoke.

Besides profane language, Isham brought home a certain disdain for civilians, too. People who had not experienced what he had, seen the death and destruction, the fear and the hunger, the loss. They no longer warranted his regard.

Most of his old friends had gone, too, either in the army or navy or Red Cross. When he visited the Gatesworth Hotel, none of the old gang still worked there. The owner, Delmar Gates, was still recovering from a severe stroke and couldn't run the business anymore. His children didn't want to run it. So, they sold the place not long after.

This sort of thing didn't matter to Isham anymore like it once would. Besides, in the army, the camaraderie was born of high purpose. Civilian life now seemed trivial to him, full of individual greed. He couldn't accept it, or even overlook it, not when men he served with were dead or wounded. That might have worked before the war, but now Isham didn't have the sense of belonging. And he kept being reminded of difference wherever he went.

Life back home required adjustments, too. Isham's mother had been alone since her husband's death 13 years earlier. But to him, she appeared content on her own. She cooked, made the beds, kept the apartment, played cards with her friends: had her own life.

Every morning, she would begin her day by rolling out the piecrust for that evening's dessert. Like a ritual, they had cherry pie every night. When the family stilled lived in Nebraska, sister Mary made jello once and asked their dad how he liked it. "Very nice," he said. "But what's for dessert?"

Twice a week, Tuesdays and Thursdays, Lena would attend movie matinees downtown with Uncle Will, the brother of her sister Clara's husband. Will's chauffeur would come to collect her in his Pierce-Arrow automobile.

Even though Will had suffered a stroke, which impaired his speech and left one side paralyzed, he was a gentle soul, and very helpful to mother. Their family was quite wealthy, having made its money in mining in Illinois. Back in the nineteen-teens, they had a weekly payroll of $25,000, in the days when $5-$6 per week was a living wage.

After staying out most of the night, by 10 A.M. Isham could smell bacon and eggs cooking in the kitchen.

"You were out drinking last night," his mother said, walking into the room wiping her hands on her apron.

"What makes you think so?"

Isham propped up on one elbow in bed.

She stood by the armchair, folding his pants. Alongside, atop the table, sat what remained of a bottle of gin.

During his furlough, he returned to his ways of night owling like when we worked at the Gatesworth Hotel before the war. He developed a routine, out late, up late.

St. Louis in '45 was one big-ass party. The town didn't close, ever.

Isham met a friend one evening at a neighborhood bar. Isham wore his uniform, his friend a suit. The two of them stood leaning against the bar, drinking a beer.

"Tell me, how was it in Europe?" his friend inquired.

"You know, war."

Isham had always been a private person, not given to expressing his emotions, but his friend's question touched him. Maybe it was because he had only been back for such a short time. How was it over there? His mind drifted back to Hill 840 in Italy.

"Many things happened I find difficult to talk about. I would say the hardest was when I had to send two young men through German lines to bring reinforcements when we got isolated on a hill in Italy."

He wrapped his whole soul up in the story about those two nineteen-year-old boys, and without meaning to, he revealed the depth of his anguish to his friend as they stood at the cozy bar in St. Louis with its peaceful air, and paneled warmth, and the beer going down cold and smooth.

"We were playing the biggest game in the world," he explained, while staring at his glass for a second with all its tiny bubbles rising in the amber liquid. "Anyone could kill you, and you could kill them, like gladiators, really. And I sent these two fuzzy-cheeked kids right into it."

It was the most he ever opened himself up to anyone in his life, naked to the soul. He put it all out on the bar to his friend. He spoke of the need to do it, how the men volunteered, and what the machine gun fire down below felt like as those two boys risked their lives, so he might live. When Isham finished, his friend shook his head, scanning the crowd.

"You want another beer?" he asked, turning to the bartender.

Another beer? That is what the entire story meant to him, another stupid-ass beer? I never told the story again to anybody. How can you tell them anything? They wouldn't understand it. How could they?

The army realized the veterans returned unbalanced. They had lived through things contrary to everything they learned their entire lives, and it changed them completely.

The army sent Isham all his back pay from his deployment in Europe, including his time as a P.O.W. and through his escape. He now had almost a full year's pay, money to raise hell with. His mother kept out of his life when Isham returned, allowed him to do whatever he wanted, with no recriminations.

The army had listed him as missing-in-action for six weeks after his capture. His mother had been distraught, thinking her son had been killed. Now she was happy to have him home and alive. But Isham returned much wilder than when he left, and she was afraid of him.

Nobody said a word to me or touched me. I took crap from no one about anything.

News arrived May 1st, Joseph Goebbels, Reich Minister of Propaganda of Nazi Germany, had committed suicide in the Führerbunker after poisoning his wife and their six children.

One week later, at 2:41 A.M. on May 7th, General Alfred Jodl signed the instrument of unconditional surrender of all German forces in a schoolroom in Rheims, France. The surrender would be effective at noon the following day. Celebrations encircled the globe.

As news spread that the war in Europe was over, crowds spilled out of buildings and homes everywhere. That evening Isham took the streetcar downtown, but by midnight, he headed back home. But the crowds still swarmed in the streets. By the time Isham's streetcar got to Grand Avenue, it couldn't go cross.

Isham stepped off the trolley into a sea of humanity. He couldn't turn around, much less wade through. Factory shifts ran around the clock, and bars and movie houses stayed open to accommodate them. Nothing closed. It could be nine in the morning or midnight, and the place would still be jumping. The town never slept.

Because of war rationing, people had nothing to spend their money on except entertainment. No new clothes or automobiles or tires were for sale. The government still geared the economy toward the war effort, so people went out all the time. Hotels rented beds from noon to midnight, before someone else would take over at 12:30 A.M. same bed, new sheets.

Returning from Europe, Isham's face was dark brown and leathery from snow burn. He didn't look like other men. Plus, he brought back an attitude, as well. When he walked into a bar and ordered a beer, women would approach before the bartender returned with the bottle.

"Hi, buy me a drink to celebrate?" one woman would ask.

"Sure, why not?"

"What's your name?"

"Does it matter?"

He didn't need to search for girls. They found him.

He was still in the army, but he was a casualty of the war, all the same.

Isham left St. Louis in August to complete a training cycle at Camp Fannin. Next, he reported to Fort Benning, Georgia, where he attended Officer Candidate School in early 1943. There, he learned from the regimental adjutant they had recommended him for promotion to the rank of captain. That meant a boost in his pay of $50.00 a month. He would also begin drawing what they called longevity pay, a 5% increase in base pay after completing three years in the service. Isham would now pull down about $350 per month.

August 14, 1945, was V-J Day, the day the Second World War came to its climactic end after the atomic bombings in Hiroshima and

Nagasaki the week before. Though the terrible weapons may have saved hundreds of thousands of Allied lives, which would no longer need to be sacrificed invading the Japanese islands — and many tens of thousands of Japanese, too, who would have fought to the last man — who knew the true cost of setting the atomic genie free from his bottle?

Isham was on his way to Fort Benning, Georgia, when he got the news, holed up in a Methodist Club for servicemen in Brinkley, Arkansas. His mother in St. Louis, as mothers the world over, was ecstatic.

Thank you, God. So many young men gave their lives. We were more fortunate than many.

When Isham arrived at Fort Benning, none of his old friends were still around. Plus, with the end of the war at hand, he wanted out of the army.

"I can't see how I am serving any purpose now," he wrote home. The one purpose remaining was getting Bisia home.

***

24
THE GREEN FRONTIER

~ Spring 1945 ~

Mama and Papa were still asleep when Henryk and I left at four the next morning. I didn't wake them, but peeked in before I left. It was the last I would ever be with either of them. The dislocation that began with the wagon ride toward Stratyn in September of '39 was now complete.

The front door to her parent's apartment closed behind her. She took a deep breath and looked up through the trees to the balcony outside her father's room. Another space opened inside of her and she already felt like a sieve.

As Bisia and Henryk walked down the street, she hoped the magic of summer would renew her spirit. Her experiences in the underground taught her how to survive. Over time, she developed the instinct of a chased animal. Now she would test her instinct to its limit.

They walked to the rail station, where they climbed a fence and made their way to a freight train Henryk's man had told him was heading to Cieszyn, the Czechoslovakian border town Poland appropriated as part of the Munich Agreement of 1938 when Hitler chewed off the Sudetenland.

After checking, they climbed atop a boxcar where they remained flat and quiet. An armed Russian guard walked by, inspecting each car for illegal passengers, but not on top. The sun rose before the train moved. Bisia took in the new day as the sun spilled out over the beautiful old city, glazing the spires of St. Mary's Basilica. As the thousand-year-old city filled her eyes, she wondered if she would ever see it again.

It was a horrible feeling of loss. The only things I brought were my rucksack with my French-English dictionary, a crucifix, and a picture Adam Winogrodzki had given me when we met by happenstance around the university one day. Atop the picture he wrote, "My friend, do not forget." He signed it, "a fellow partisan."

Cieszyn lay along the southern Polish border, 140 kilometers from Kraków on the east bank of the Olza River. It was a charming place, featuring a 'Little Vienna' Old Town Central Square. After Germany's surrender, the border returned to the one established in 1920, re-splitting the town between Poland and Czechoslovakia.

Following liberation, they divided Czechoslovakia into Russian and American occupation zones, with Prague under Russian control.

After Henryk and Bisia left the train yard, they walked around, trying to figure out how to cross to the other side into Czechoslovakia. As they entered a square, a voice called out from a window in an apartment building.

"Countess, what are you doing in Cieszyn?"

A man leaned out a third-floor window and waved. Bisia turned to check if someone else answered.

"Do you recognize him?" Henryk asked.

"No."

I never visited Cieszyn before and only told my parents where I was going. Now someone recognized me 10 minutes after my arrival?

"Wait right where you are," the man said.

What choice did they have?

"What are you doing here?" he said when he arrived, still breathing hard but offering a genuine smile.

Bisia still couldn't place him, which the man picked up on.

"You don't recognize me, do you?"

He took a step back and placed his hands on his hips.

"You must remember. I owned a record shop in Jasło near Lubla. You came by several times with your brother Jas to buy records?"

That lit the lamp.

"Oh, yes, yes, I remember. How are you? What a relief."

Bisia reached out and shook his hand.

"Stefan, right?"

"Yes."

"This is my cousin Henryk Sobanski. But why are you here? What happened to you?"

"They destroyed everything in Jasło. So I came to Cieszyn to start over. I have an apartment with my wife. Come, I'll fix you something to eat."

As they walked, he asked Bisia if they were trying to leave Poland? She glanced at Henryk. He nodded.

"Yes, I got married to an American."

"Well, congratulations, but we can't be careless trying to take you across. It is not as easy as 1-2-3. They catch people all the time. But I work on the other side, so I carry a pass."

The relationship between Poland and Czechoslovakia was old and complicated. Though neighbors, the two nations were also natural rivals. Each also expressed different national characteristics. While the Poles always carried themselves with a sense of national greatness, which no number of partitions or lost wars with larger neighbors could displace, the Czechs projected a more humble character.

While Poland kept its class of nobility through the long third partition from 1795 to 1919, in Czechoslovakia, the vast majority of nobles went into exile in the aftermath of the Thirty Years' War in 1620. Polish aristocrats viewed the Czechs as a nation of peasants. When Hitler butchered the rump of the Sudetenland in '38, the Poles took their own knife to the city of Cieszyn.

As Stefan informed them, people who lived on the Polish side also worked on the Czech side. To do so, they carried a certificate allowing them to cross.

"Do they search or ask for documents every time?"

"No. We will have to take a risk on that."

They spent four days with Stefan and his wife before they tried crossing. It was the morning of the 28th of June, the feast of St. Peter and St. Paul. Since only workers had papers to cross legally, the three of them split up, mixing in with the other daily workers. The day was glorious, with the summer sun dancing off the Olza River below.

"Since I have the documents, I will take your rucksack and Henryk's too," Stefan said. "You two just walk along like people going to work carrying nothing in your hands."

Bisia tried to show no emotion. She even took the arm of an elderly woman, hoping the gesture wouldn't startle her and draw attention to them. As they approached the crossing, her heart raced like when she approached the German checkpoint with her hidden machine gun years before.

But no one asked anything, and their little act worked. Though the Russian guards checked their friend Stefan because of his rucksacks, his documents got him through without a problem.

Once across, Stefan bought them train tickets to Prague, where Bisia had an address not too far from Wenceslas Square given to her by the underground. Each progressive step carried uncertainty and hope.

They wished Stefan much happiness, and with great thanks for his help, boarded the train.

After arriving in Prague, Bisia and Henryk searched for the address, hoping they might find it in a city neither one ever visited before. Through underground channels, Henryk learned of a man and his wife who helped people escape.

Though Czech writing resembled ours, we quickly discovered the buildings had no markings, which made finding any address difficult.

They spoke in French whenever they asked directions. Bisia still held documents from the Red Cross falsified in Russian, French, German, and English, saying she was a Belgian national returning home from Auschwitz. Henryk carried similar papers.

After a frustrating search, they found their address, a six-story apartment building. They walked up to the fourth floor and rang the bell.

Henryk rubbed his chin. Bisia fidgeted.

They rang again.

Nothing.

We remained completely at a loss. Were these people still around or long gone? They were our only contacts.

While Bisia and Henryk considered what to do next, footsteps announced another arrival coming from below.

Panic. What to do now?

Fortunately, the man turned out to be the janitor. He asked about who they were looking for? But, of course, being Czech, the man would instantly realize they weren't.

Again, no way to decipher if he is a foe or a friend, so this moment is very touchy.

With calculated innocence, Bisia inquired about the people, and the man said to follow him.

Henryk and Bisia couldn't read his intentions. But with no other options, they followed along.

When they arrived at his apartment, he served them bowls of potato soup and some black bread.

"They will be back tonight," he informed them, speaking of the missing couple on the fourth floor. "They went for provisions in the country. Don't worry, I won't report you."

When the people from the fourth floor returned, the janitor took us up to meet them. We stayed for ten days. Henryk and I did a lot of sightseeing, as Prague was too beautiful to miss. While we explored, we also tried to figure out how to leave.

One day they stopped in a park to watch people playing tennis. Some other people nearby became interested in them after they overheard Bisia and Henryk speaking in French. In the strange world in which they existed, overly friendly people proved as dangerous as openly hostile ones.

They discussed several ideas on how to get out, but any choice would be difficult to put into action. Czechoslovakia was a long country, and Prague sat near the center. The American zone centered on Pilsen in the south, closer to Germany. But Bisia learned through their contacts America had a mission in Prague.

Since I had the paper from Colonel Wilmeth testifying to my marriage to an American, I tried to contact them. But the difficulty was getting in. Russians walked guards out in front of the mission, and you couldn't simply waltz in.

Bisia and Henryk went to investigate. The American mission was inside an apartment building converted into offices.

They studied the timing of the guard as he marched back and forth in front. Only one guard was on duty. Bisia bided her time on the far side of the building, sharing a smoke with Henryk. The next time the guard pivoted, presenting his back to her, Bisia dashed inside. Once in, she explained her situation to the man heading the mission. She knew she would only have one chance to tell her story right.

"Look, I am here illegally, okay. But I have these documents and they are legitimate."

She handed the man the letter from Colonel Wilmeth certifying her marriage to Isham, and the one from Isham asking any authorities to assist her in reaching the United States.

And that stupid idiot told me, "Oh, my dear, we cannot do anything for you."

"Haven't you read what they have written here? The note says to please help her."

"Russians are our allies," he said, handing back the paper. "I can't do anything for you here. But across the hallway is a military mission. Maybe you can talk with them."

Bisia crossed the corridor, where she spoke with an American colonel.

He listened from behind his desk.

"My friend from across the hall is right. I can't do anything legally. But I will give you something because we want to help. This certificate is totally illegal, but at least it's something. Don't show it unless you are in a real pinch."

Written in English, Russian, and German on American Military Mission letterhead, the document stated the American mission recognized Bisia Reavis, who may cross the border between the Russian and American occupation zones.

With this in hand, Bisia snuck out of the building the same way she got in, watching until the Russian guard marched past and running out after he turned in the other direction.

Belgians also had a presence in Prague, so Bisia checked with them as well. Since Belgium was not in eastern Europe, the Russians did not post guards at their mission. More relaxed after her meeting with the Americans, Bisia spoke straight with the Belgians. She acknowledged carrying false papers, but since they identified her as a Belgian national, she asked for their help. They said cars drove to Belgium regularly, though train service was still down amidst the devastation.

Though it wouldn't be legal, they told Bisia they wouldn't ask questions if she and Henry got into the car going to Sušice, a village in the south on the border separating the Russian and American zones.

But they also told us not to blame them if the Russians arrested us.

A couple of days later, Henryk and Bisia hitched a ride in one of those diplomatic cars. And, thank God, the guards waved the car through the checkpoint with no questions. The car was going all the way to Brussels, but Bisia and Henryk only went as far as Sušice.

They said they wouldn't risk taking us across any farther, but we could walk on our own if we wanted.

They stopped on the outskirts of town at a small marketplace. After asking around, they met a farmer who provided them with lodging and told them the Americans were right across the frontier. He also informed them that while they shouldn't have any difficulty in crossing, they needed to act nonchalantly and not draw attention to themselves. It was the same advice they received crossing from Poland into Czechoslovakia.

Early the next afternoon, they made their attempt. How many escapes had she made now? True, each previous attempt had been successful, but how much longer would her luck hold? Rather than walking through the village by checkpoints, Bisia and Henryk crossed through open fields. And, as the farmer said, nobody bothered them.

Bisia reported to American intelligence, G2, to Lieutenant Anton Viditz-Ward of the 94th Infantry Division. She explained their predicament and showed the papers Isham and Colonel Wilmeth gave her.

"I don't know if my husband survived evacuation. I have received no word from him yet."

Viditz-Ward was like a godsend.

"We will check through military channels as well. We will do all we can."

Bisia went over the plan she and Isham agreed upon for her to head toward Nuremberg. She wanted to make sure this intelligence officer thought it was still a viable option. He agreed.

"That won't be a problem, either. We have cars going back and forth regularly. We can definitely get you there."

The wheels of America's bureaucracy began turning in Bisia's direction.

~ Nuremberg ~

Before her crossing, the only Americans Bisia had ever met had been Isham and Billy. Despite their circumstances, they both laughed so much and were so genuine, more concerned with people than with protocols. She wondered if this was the way most Americans acted.

Now I found this was the great charm of Americans: how open, how eager to help even a total stranger and to do it with a smile and a glad hand.

While Lieutenant Viditz-Ward wrote to Isham, Bisia remained in Sušice long enough to have an infected tooth extracted and to receive a physical.

Oh, God, that tooth was painful. They gave me a shot of bourbon and had me sit in a straight-back chair and yanked it out. Afterward, the doctor gave me some oranges. I hadn't tasted oranges in years.

With the help of Lieutenant Viditz-Ward, Bisia and Henryk made their way to Nuremberg. But they arrived, the American Military Police rounded them up before they could find the American authorities in charge. Instead, they found themselves dispatched to a displaced persons camp.

Through underground channels, Bisia learned the name of the officer in charge of the troops in Nuremberg. He was a colonel, the nephew of General Lucius D. Clay. A single night in the displaced persons camp and Bisia told herself, this is not for me.

People were dying, delivering babies. I went to the commanding officer of the camp and said I wanted a pass.

"I don't belong here. I am not displaced. My uncle is the ambassador to England, and I know exactly where I'm going."

Count Edward Raczynski, her mother's cousin, was the Polish ambassador to England during the war. Plus, her brother was serving with the British army.

A little overwhelmed by her name dropping, he gave her a day pass, but told her, "If you don't return, we will come looking for you."

Bisia left Henryk and went straight to the headquarters of Colonel Clay. By a miracle, she got herself in front of him and explained her situation. Again, her luck held. Colonel Clay received a copy of Isham's letter asking for help from any American representatives. As Bisia explained about her cousin Henryk, who remained in the displaced persons camp, the telephone rang.

"Hello?" the colonel answered. "Yes, we do, Major. Yes. That's right. Yes. Oh, by the way, do you need somebody in your office? There is a young lady who just escaped from Poland and she tells me she speaks several languages. And your office always needs people with language skills." He listened for a moment. "OK. That will be fine. Sure, I will send her over."

Bisia returned to the camp, got Henryk out, and took her first job in the office of the Town Major with Major George Lopez, who handled the billeting for all the American troops in Nuremberg. He had his offices in a villa in the suburbs they confiscated from the Gestapo. It even had a maid. How quickly the circumstances changed. Bisia was now working for the American Third Army, commanded by General George Patton. Major Lopez could not accommodate Henryk, but placed him with a nice German family.

The Countess & The P.O.W.

It was now July 1945, the time of the Potsdam Conference outside Berlin. Roosevelt had died in April and Harry Truman of Independence, Missouri, became the new American president. The world knew nothing of him, but with the betrayal of Poland at Yalta in February, Bisia and many Poles weren't sorry to see Roosevelt go.

At Potsdam, the West recognized the Russian-imposed government in Poland after Stalin agreed to include some members of the exiled government from London. But his promise was not worth the ink he used to sign the agreement. With Potsdam, the last breath of a free Poland expired.

General Patton himself must not have believed in the agreement, either, because when he came to decorate some troops from the 3rd Army one afternoon.

"These decorations you have received today are for the war we just ended. But the medals I will decorate you with in the future will be much more important."

If only the rest of American leadership was of a similar mind. Of course, we believed in Patton's way of thinking. He wanted to go across the Polish frontier to the border of the Soviet Union and talk from that vantage point, not stop in the middle of nowhere. But they quickly silenced him.

***

25
NUREMBERG

~ Summer 1945 ~

Across the garden in the villa where Bisia worked, someone cut an opening in the fence to the adjoining villa where she had rooms on the second floor. A day or two later, as Bisia worked at her desk in this beautiful German villa, the front door opened. In walked a big, burly man with his hair parted down the middle. He greeted Sophie and Germaine with a kiss on both cheeks. Major Lopez emerged from his office.

"Colonel, you must meet our newest employee. She just escaped from Poland. Bisia is a former Countess. She married an American lieutenant."

"Not former, I am still very much alive."

The colonel took both of her hands in his.

"My dear, what size of underwear do you wear?"

Bisia blushed and turned her head to Major Lopez.

"Oh, no," the colonel said, picking up on her discomfort. "They said you recently escaped. I assume you must need things? Since I'm in charge of all enemy property, I can equip you with anything, including underwear."

His name was Colonel Pat Crowell, a man who would become another lifesaver for Bisia. Over a brief span as she got settled, Bisia came to enjoy both her work and her companions a great deal.

I gave Isham's military ID number to Lieutenant Vidiz-Ward, the intelligence officer I first reported to after crossing into the American zone. He told me he would call me as soon as he established contact with the U.S.

Two weeks after she began working at the villa outside Nuremberg, bless his heart, Vidiz-Ward came to visit with good news.

"I wrote to your husband and received a reply. He said he can't wait for your arrival and that I should give you any money you need."

Bisia told him she no longer needed any money because she had a job. But she welcomed the news that Isham had made it home safely and awaited her arrival.

Nuremberg had been the center of Nazi party politics throughout the rise of Hitler in the 1930s. Massive Nuremberg Rallies became infamous through the films of Leni Riefenstahl, *Triumph of the Will*, and *The Victory of Faith*. The city's fall on April 20th proved a devastating blow to German morale. The U.S. Seventh Army helped liberate the city during the Battle of Nuremberg and established American control afterward.

When Bisia arrived three months later, the city remained in ruins, but the atmosphere in the city had already changed. In the evenings after work, Bisia and her new friends would go to a local nightclub for the floor shows and dancing. After the starvation and other privations of war, the availability of luxuries like juices and jam and toast and coffee, or entertainment, still seemed out of place. Bisia took time to adapt to her new circumstances. So, too, to the mannerisms and attitudes of the Americans that Bisia met.

The Americans were so friendly, but different, I thought, casual. But always ready to help, no matter the obstacle.

Since Major Lopez handled all billeting in Nuremberg, his office teemed with interesting people. A visiting general showed up on one occasion to inspect and evaluate Major Lopez' operation.

Leaving the general in his office, Major Lopez approached Bisia's desk.

"Listen, Betty, I need your help."

He pointed back toward his office with his thumb.

"You better have that guy in my office drunk and under the table tonight. I can't, but I know you can."

Lopez wanted the general gone, and Bisia had shown during her short time with his command how Poles could drink liberally and still function when everyone else couldn't.

That evening, a group of officers collected the general and took him to the PX for dinner and drinks.

I didn't get drunk myself, but I made sure the general did. We played ping-pong after dinner, and the general chased me around the table until he was dizzy.

The next day, the general came into the office with such a hangover, he never asked about anything. He just left. Major Lopez pledged his undying thanks to Bisia for her efforts.

Colonel Pat Crowell traveled a lot in his work, too, and often went to London. Bisia suggested he visit her uncle and tell him her situation, and inquire about the whereabouts of her brother, Stas, and cousin Zygmund Michalowski.

Pat Crowell made a trip to the embassy in London, where he met Bisia's uncle. The ambassador gave him a letter informing Bisia her brother Stas served as an adjutant to General Stanisław Maczek with the British Army of the Rhine, and her cousin Zygmund as the Polish attaché in Brussels.

Despite her depression in Lublin, Bisia Reavis didn't remain depressed for long. Her outlook had always been more philosophical. She was someone who decided issues quickly, then lived by those decisions.

You cannot dwell, she told herself. The difficulty is to come to any decision. Once you decide, the circumstance eases.

While in Nuremberg, Bisia befriended several Poles, as a considerable Polish population lived in the city. These Poles found a wire-haired terrier puppy, white with brown and black accents. They brought her to Bisia one day at the office, wondering if she would like to adopt her.

Of course, I said yes. She was homeless. I was homeless. I called her Tipsy. She was so cute and had lots of personality. We shared quarters and became fast friends. I even brought her to work each day, and she curled up beneath my desk, barking at the people coming and going. And when she did her business on the floor, Major Lopez would say: "Liz, see what your dog did."

"Major, you cannot accuse an innocent dog if you haven't seen it for yourself."

"She made a mess in my office, too!"

"Sir, there must be another explanation. I do not want to point the fingers."

And we would both laugh.

Unfortunately, Tipsy contracted distemper and with no veterinary medicines available, the poor thing died after only two months. Bisia buried her in the villa's garden.

Darkness descended while she prepared the tiny grave. Rain fell through most of the day, but a moment before sundown, the sun reclaimed the last sliver of open sky across the horizon, a faint but translucent sunset the color of whiskey. The glow lingered below the rolls of clouds along the tree line behind the villa. Bisia took it as an omen.

The feelings welled within her as she covered Tipsy's grave. She cried for the innocence and her own loss, a loss added to all those coming before.

The next morning, while darkness still lingered, the early wildlife stirred without disturbing the surrounding silence. How I wished she was still with me in this peace, my little friend, homeless like me. Well-meaning people told me my grief would pass and I should simply accept and forget. It made no sense to indulge in my heartache. She was only an animal. How little they understood. How pitied they must be, never having felt the love only an innocent dog can give and evoke in us.

After Tipsy's death, Bisia's spirit rose whenever she received letters from Isham. She also continued to write from her side, but also began traveling to Antwerp to move forward with her emigration at the office for civilian affairs.

Bisia was fortunate to be working in the Town Major's office because, through the association, she not only received housing and food but traveled on U.S. military transports. One day she and Colonel Pat Crowell traveled west into Belgium by jeep in a larger convoy until they stopped at a British checkpoint.

The British officer collected their papers, saying, "Your passenger must stand out," referring to Bisia. "These documents show she is a civilian. Yet she is traveling with the American military. This is not correct."

Pat Crowell did not hesitate.

"If you stop her, the whole transport will stay right here because I am not leaving without her."

They went back and forth for a while. But when the Brit realized Crowell meant business, he gave up and waived them through.

This was the second time an American said he wouldn't leave without me: first, Isham in Lublin, now Pat Crowell. Neither one would gain anything by standing up for me. It left me with a sense of genuine hope knowing the country fostered these men of honor.

One of the first things Bisia did when she arrived in Antwerp was to check how to secure the required documents for overseas travel. Except for the statement by Colonel Wilmeth from Lublin confirming her marriage to an American officer, she still didn't hold any proper documentation.

She also learned around this same time horrible news that the British and Americans were going to transfer official recognition from the Polish government-in-exile in London to the provisional government of communists in Lublin.

This would mean my status as a relative of the Polish ambassador in England and the first cousin of the military attaché in Belgium would become meaningless, since they wouldn't have any office to supply me with any documents or help.

Hearing the news of the impending collapse of the Polish Government-in-exile in London, Bisia needed to arrange her documentation before the allies withdrew their official recognition. Time was not her ally.

She got through to Brussels, where she met her cousin Zygmund. Bisia also received a passport issued by the Polish government, which, within a week, ceased to exist. From Brussels, Bisia and Zygmund drove to Antwerp to contact the American authorities for civilian affairs to find out how to secure a visa.

The official at the American mission told her, "Your request will be difficult because priority goes to servicemen and equipment returning home." But with a letter in hand from the Nuremberg Town Major, vouching for "her diligence, strong character, high morals, and sincere in her intentions towards her husband," the civil affairs official in Antwerp issued her the visa.

"But don't count on being allowed to go," the man added as she left.

Bisia returned to Nuremberg and her job, buoyed by the small steps she and Isham were taking to help her make her way to the States.

~ Isham ~

By July 29th, Isham had returned to Camp Fannin in Texas following two weeks in the field. Though he didn't have to work too hard, he still had to conform to the awful army hours, including 5 A.M. reveille. They also gave him a company to command, though not officially, just the responsibility. But responsibility had been a constant partner in his life since his father's death in 1932. However, his primary responsibility had yet to be achieved, Bisia's travel out of Europe. And while he loved his new wife, Isham was also a realist.

"*I am of the opinion she left Poland to avoid the Russians,*" he wrote to his mother in St. Louis. "*They were nasty to the people of her class. In war, you learn to eliminate the leaders. Then the rest are easy to handle. But now, things are on their way to being straightened out.*"

Despite contact with Bisia and American officers in Nuremberg, Isham never knew where she was exactly. He hoped she might eventually move to Paris and establish herself in the French capital. As he liked to say, "*she speaks French better than the French themselves*". Such a move would also relieve his growing anxiety about the toll the war was taking.

"*This running around desolate Europe is not good,*" he confided to his brother Burton in New York City. "*I did for a while, myself, and know what one must contend with.*"

He related the facts of life in Europe to family and friends, but despite the rationing and hardships experienced in America during the war years, unless someone walked in the war itself, the utter devastation was difficult to convey.

Words alone were insufficient in describing the hopelessness, the sense of no light in the future, the stark day-to-day existence, where there was no help from any source. If you are sick, you are sick. If you die, you simply join the millions who have gone before.

He likened the situation to a man committed to a treadmill, walking endlessly, yet going nowhere, forever remaining in the same place, nothing accomplished.

It would be enough to break all but the strongest spirits.

He had experienced something similar himself. He feared the longer Bisia stayed in those conditions, the more damaged she would be.

~ Bisia ~ Old Wounds

Bisia finally contacted her brother Stas. Their uncle in London informed him of Bisia's arrival in Nuremberg. One day not much later, Stas called the Town Major's office with news of his impending visit. The two had not seen one another since 1939.

Stas drove to Bisia's place of work by jeep from his post in northern Germany along the Rhine with the British forces. Bisia waited for him outside, on the steps of the villa. A haze hung on the meadow, and she drew in the aroma of the herbs, flowers, and grass. Deep and comforting, the aroma reminded her of Lesko before the war.

She waited for Stas for several hours, returning to the office periodically to check if he called. But he never arrived or called. After work, Bisia walked back through the garden to her rooms at the neighboring villa. She didn't sleep well, worrying about Stas, wondering if something had happened to him.

Bisia realized this might have been the first time she ever worried about her older brother. When she was young, among all four boys, Stas took particular pleasure in challenging her, like when Bisia first took up the gauntlet to jump their horses together.

They went riding in the forest. Bisia felt like a fly atop the horse's broad back. Stas believed they should fix the barriers in place, "because if you only set them loose, the horses will learn they can bump and throw the bar." He screwed the barriers into position.

Bisia rode behind when Stas reined his horse. The forest gathered on either side.

"Well, here we are," he announced as they came to the set jumps. "If you're afraid, you can go around."

And with only this subtle put-down, off he rode, the tail of his coat flapping before her like a challenge.

Kuba had been their father's last cavalry mount during World War I. Trained to take these jumps, and there was no way he would go around, nor for Bisia to make him. He was much too strong.

So, with a deep breath, and admittedly a little fear, she clucked gentle encouragement to his ear, clenched her knees against his wide flanks, and off they went. And one hup! Two hup! Three and four, hup, hup! They made all the barriers in full stride. She pulled up alongside Stas, patting Kuba's neck, her face flushed with a sense of accomplishment.

"Well done," her brother said. "I guess you'll stop being a coward now."

Her brother's remark turned her flush from one of pride to anger. When Stas set off again going through some water, Bisia followed with a set determination.

Coming onto shore, they confronted a steep grade. Across the path stretched a long, low-hanging tree branch. She tried to avoid it by ducking while maintaining her pace. But when Stas spurred his horse as he prepared for another barrier, it was one she didn't expect.

Kuba gathered himself, but Bisia's weight tilted too far back and to the right. Hopelessly off-balance as Kuba leaped, Bisia tipped backward and tumbled off like a thrown sack of potatoes. The ground rushed to meet her, and she landed with a thump! Her head whipped against the ground, sending the world into a spin.

As she lay shaken, the warm smell of earth rose close to her nostrils. Slowly, she regained orientation before rising on shaky legs.

She checked to find her right hand, arm, and leg bloodied, her riding pants torn. Kuba was nowhere to be seen, nor Stas. She stood, brushed herself off, and began limping up the path, angry and hurt. Soon after, her brother returned with Kuba's reins in hand.

"Are you alright?"

Though he asked about her well-being, his tone suggested her fall was only a bother.

"I'm fine."

Bisia kept her head lowered and eyes averted. No way would she would show him her pain. He leaned over and tossed the reins at her. Without a word, she climbed back up and they rode off.

The episode exemplified the challenges that had come from her brothers since she was a little girl. But she refused to give in or allow their trials to intimidate her.

*

The next morning, she received a telephone call from Stas. He said it would have been too late by the time he arrived last night. So he stopped overnight at a British billeting office. She told him to stay put, and she would come to him.

When she arrived, she wondered if she would even recognize him.

I wore my American uniform with a 3rd Army patch on my left shoulder and a little red Polish patch on my right. On my collar lay the single silver star of Polish lieutenant, the same insignia worn by an American brigadier general.

Bisia called upstairs from the lobby and waited among a group of British officers. Shortly, coming down the steps, she saw him wearing his British uniform. She thought, "Dear God, two Poles, neither in the uniform of their country. What happened to us?"

"The Russians captured me in '39 after leaving Gusia and the boys in Stratyn," Stas told her over lunch. He parted his hair on the right side, combed back from his much-welcomed face.

"That's why we had heard nothing of your whereabouts after the start of the war?"

"Correct."

She pressed him for every detail.

She learned they captured Stas in the first weeks of the war, but he escaped before they could organize the prisoners. Once away, he joined the 12th Regiment of the Polish Light Cavalry.

"The best time to escape is always as soon after you're captured as possible before they enter you in the system."

Stas in Stratyn before the war

"Isham said the same thing. But he waited until they evacuated the camp and escaped during a forced march."

Stas fled to Hungary, but once he arrived, they interred him again.

"What a crazy time. I realized if I didn't escape, they would send me to a German camp."

He made his way to France through Italy and, for a while, remained on the Maginot Line. After the Germans overran France, and Stas joined the thousands of allied troops evacuated to Britain from the beaches at Dunkirk.

"No one knew if we would make it off those beaches. When the flotilla of ships and boats appeared from England, it was like a miracle."

Arriving in England, they assigned him to North Africa under General Władysław Anders in the Polish II Corps, a unit of the Polish Armed Forces of the West. He ended up as an adjutant to General Maczek with the British Army of the Rhine.

His own experiences made what Bisia experienced seem less dramatic. But even in retelling their stories of war, they found a place for fun.

"But marriage?" he asked after Bisia finished telling the story of how she and Isham met and married. "Wasn't that rather... sudden?"

She shrugged.

"You never met him; you wouldn't understand. Remember, I had orders to serve under Berling. Isham was so optimistic, despite spending four months in German camps. He painted such a hopeful future. Plus, he seemed like a genuinely good man. I think you would like him. Mama and Papa would, too, though they were not happy when I first told them."

During the war, Stas' two sons, Jerzy and Andrzej, lived with the family at the lodge in Zagórz. He hadn't seen them in years.

"Do you know if Gusia is coming with the boys?"

Bisia feared he might bring up Gusia, who was now pregnant with Adam's baby.

"You will have to talk to her yourself. I don't know what her plans are."

Bisia and Stas stayed together for two days before having to return to their duties. It was the first time they were together as adults. Before departing, they reverted to the old roles that defined so much of Bisia's early years with her brothers.

"But you were like bandits," he said when their talk turned to Bisia's service with the AK.

"Are you kidding? How can you say that?"

"When you were in the underground, you hanged people. You didn't put them in camps or anything, right?"

Bisia leaned forward, her anger tilting with her. His attitude brought back with such clarity the dismissive treatment she received as a young girl.

"How dare you say that?" she began, pointing a finger straight at his face. "Your uniform gave you all the Geneva Convention privileges. We didn't have that because we fought in civilian clothes. If you got caught by the enemy, they treated you as a prisoner of war, like in '39. They shot and hanged us on the spot.

"You're right, we might have killed them, but don't forget, they were killing us equally well. Don't you think for a second we were any less patriotic than any of you who wore uniforms?"

This was, by far, their sharpest exchange. Yet the acrimony didn't linger. They were too grateful to be together to hold on to hurt feelings. It also reflected their similar natures. Each fought hard for their convictions.

Following their few days together, Bisia returned to Nuremberg to wind up her business. Stas returned to the west. The two would never see one another again.

While Bisia met with Stas, Henryk made plans to go to Paris, where he had connections. The two cousins said goodbye, and in November, Bisia set off for Brussels, where she stayed with her first cousin Zygmund Michałówski on Avenue Cortenbergh.

***

26
REUNITED

~ Fall/Winter 1945 ~

Brussels served as a hub for allied activity in late 1945. In the evenings, Bisia would sometimes go with friends to a nightspot called Le Kremlin Rouge. The musicians were all former czarist officers and aristocrats who were refugees from the Russian Revolution and World War I.

"Oh, you are just beginning," they said to the new exiles. "Decades have passed since our wars. You will find things difficult at first, but you'll adapt just as we did."

Though Bisia lived in Brussels, she traveled to Antwerp to check on ship departures as often as she could. She received a call one morning from Germaine, who used to work with Bisia in Nuremberg but transferred back to her native Brussels.

"Why don't you meet me for lunch," she said.

She told me to meet her at the office where she still worked for Americans. But when I got there, another familiar voice boomed out from behind me.

"And what are you still doing in Europe?"

"Oh, Pat, dear. This is fantastic! Why are you here? I am waiting for Germaine."

Pat Crowell, her old friend from Nuremberg, held out his arms as Bisia ran into his embrace.

"I am just coming from seeing her. She said you two were going to meet for a lunch date. But why, for heaven's sake, are you still hanging around?"

"Pat, there is no way I can get on a boat. Believe me, I've been checking. It's not so easy."

"That's crazy. You just have to know the right people, and you know me. I'll tell you what. Let's drive to Antwerp tomorrow. I'm friends with the commanding officer at the port. We'll figure something out."

The next day, when they arrived in Antwerp, Colonel Crowell marched right into the port commander's office. He presented Bisia, holding both arms from behind.

"I want this girl on the first boat going to the United States. She's gone through enough. I think she should be back in a more stable environment with her husband."

The following week, she departed.

~ Shipping News ~

Isham sent letters overseas regularly, but regulations only allowed service personnel to service personnel communications. So, he posted his letters to Lieutenant Viditz-Ward in Prague. After Bisia moved to Nuremberg, he wrote care of Major George Lopez at the Town Manager's office, hoping they would forward his letters through to Bisia. In each letter, he included small amounts of money, $10, $15, but nothing more, for fear she wouldn't receive it.

On August 25th, Isham wrote he had filed her entrance papers into the States and mentioned the government had ended gas rationing, as the post-war era slowly took form.

Next, he headed to Camp Fannin near Tyler, Texas, certain he would receive his orders to demobilize soon. He also completed all the paperwork for Bisia and mailed the last form to the American consul's office in Antwerp, though once again not knowing if the letter would catch up with Bisia in all her jumping around.

On October 17th, he received a wire from Major George Lopez from the Town Major's office in Nuremberg.

"Elisabeth hasn't heard from you. Wire me at Town Major Nuremberg without delay. Major Lopez."

Isham wired Lopez and airmailed a letter to Bisia, and sent another to Brussels to make sure. What Bisia needed most was clothing, not for fashion but for the coming season if she still found herself stuck in Europe. He mailed his mother with the list of items she should pack and send to Major Lopez in Nuremberg.

On Bisia's 24th birthday, November 4, 1945, Isham wrote from Camp Fannin, saying he received a telegram from her cousin

Zygmund in Brussels informing him officials had approved Bisia's visa and transportation was next on his list. Zygmund was the son of her mother's only sister, Aunt Maryncia, and the brother of her cousin Anna.

I was very pleased with this news, and now dearest, you are almost here. I await impatiently, old bishop. Take care of yourself and keep well for me. I love you with all my heart. My prayers are with you. All my love, now and forever, Isham.

He also sent money and clothes to her cousin Zygmund's address in Brussels, along with a food package with cigarettes, before going in the field for two weeks on bivouac.

~ November 1945 ~

Major George Lopez took on the job to Americanize Bisia while she lived in Nuremberg by calling her Betty, the American version of Bisia. She turned 24 on November 4, 1945. Ten days later, she received a letter from him:

Dear Betty,
I have been thinking about you ever so much since you left. The house is like a morgue. I am sure you made it this time, or you would have been back here by now.
Last evening, I visited the 'Club Americana'. Your very good friend Colonel Moates and Lt. Colonel Hill were with me. As you know, it was 'Kraut Evening', and the place was packed. Everything there in the way of entertainment and music reminded me of you and Germain. I could almost see you dancing on the floor to some of our familiar music. I guess I was not too good a company. No mail has been coming through. I wonder if you received some up there? Please give Germaine a big hug for me until I see you. I'm tentatively planning to come up on the 1st of December. And I will do my own hugging. My ping-pong game has slipped. Goodbye now. Hope to see you soon.
Discontented,
George

Because of the interruption in mail service, the clothes her new mother-in-law sent never arrived. But the money Isham sent through Zygmund in Brussels, did. She returned to Antwerp in early December and bought a ticket aboard the Belgian Unity for $165 plus $8 tax for the Atlantic crossing.

When she went to check the ship, its small size surprised her, though at 441-feet, like all Liberty-Class freighters, Belgian Unity proved sturdy and ocean-worthy. Up on the foredeck, they lashed some trucks to the side along with some other equipment covered with tarps.

The only other passengers with Bisia were three newspapermen, Molly Gigandet of Brussels, Nicole Rolin, also of Belgium, and Baroness Monique de Nerveau of France. Before boarding, Bisia shared a glass of Chianti with cousin Zygmund, as they wished one another well in their new lives.

Throughout the war, the port of Antwerp supplied a constant flow of ships and supplies to the Allied war effort. For its loyalty, the city suffered a high price. Before liberation by the British in September 1944, Antwerp experienced constant German attacks as they tried to destroy the city's port operations. Though London received greater public attention, Antwerp endured more V-2 rocket attacks than all other targets combined. Over 1600 V-2s rained down on the ancient city between October 1944 and March 1945. 30,000 people lost their lives to the indiscriminate drones. But though *Time Magazine* dubbed Antwerp the "City of Sudden Death," her port operations never shut down throughout the terror. Only after German V-2 crews retreated in the face of advancing Allied troops did the attacks halt in late March 1945.

At long last, Bisia sailed out of Antwerp on December 4, 1945, headed for New York City. She berthed with Monique de Nerveau, a young woman the captain introduced her to just before sailing. They spent their time aboard the ship playing bridge, telling their stories of the war, dining with the captain, and, as always, drinking and laughing a lot.

~ Isham ~

Isham returned home to St. Louis on November 27th on terminal leave until February 1, 1946. Before she departed, Bisia sent Isham a letter. Inside, she placed a copy of the picture they had taken in Lublin.

Tu es très, très charmante. Très belle. Très, très, everything. So, you like to be called kochana. Well, kochana it shall be (Polish for darling). And how do you like my French? You used to tell people I couldn't speak French. You cannot imagine how happy I am to get the picture and to hear you have made many American friends already. You will have many more very soon.

He also wrote to his mother-in-law saying her daughter was coming to a home that loved her very much and was waiting to welcome her into their hearts as their own daughter.

When news arrived from cousin Zygmund Bisia had sailed, Isham's heart lifted. He had crossed the Atlantic twice himself and understood the trip would last about ten days, given the weather. But when he stopped getting word on her ship's progress, he got worried, especially since they were in the storm season.

When I called the company that owned the ship (Lykes Brothers) asking about the arrival schedule, they said, 'we can't tell.' 'Well, where are they?' 'We don't know.' 'Why?' 'Because we can't reach them.'

Isham called his brother Burt each morning in New York City and mailed him $100 with a note. "We aren't certain where she will land, but go grab her wherever she is and send her home."

Feeling helpless, an anxiety-riddled Isham waited for word. Before Bisia sailed, he hoped she might arrive in time to spend Christmas together. Now the question was whether she would arrive at all.

~ Bisia ~

Belgian Unity was one of 2,710 Liberty Ships mass-produced between 1941 and 1945 at 18 shipyards around the U.S.A. At first, people mocked the ships as "Ugly Ducklings" because of their simple but rugged modular design. Later, the fleet came to be known as Liberty Ships, because they christened the first one SS Patrick Henry, after the American Revolutionary War hero who famously said, "Give me liberty or give me death."

President Roosevelt said, "This new class of ships would bring liberty to Europe." Bisia only hoped this one would bring her safely to America.

They loaded the ship with war materiel returning from Europe and had to distribute the weight with great care. A Liberty Ship's five holds carried over 9,000 tons of cargo, plus airplanes, tanks, and locomotives lashed to the deck.

Though it and its two companion ships had to navigate through a string of mines still littering the North Atlantic, the captain was saying in French, "Oh, those are just mines, ma cher. But do not worry, they will not bother us."

After several days at sea, a layer of ice built up, a potential danger to the weight distribution of the ship. Next, the storm hit, threatening the ship's very survival.

While the captain struggled to hold his ship in position, a massive wave dropped the ship in a harrowing descent. Though 441-feet long, the *Belgian Unity* was no match for the fury of a hurricane-swept Atlantic.

Bisia stood as she was told as the ship bucked and rolled like a wild horse. The impact of each pounding wave caused the tiny ship to shudder before it lurched forward again in a groaning spasm of release. To further complicate matters, out along the foredeck, one of the two trucks tethered in position had broken free of one of its lines. Now, like a child amidst a tantrum, it began to thrash back and forth, complicating their crisis.

"Secure that line now!" bellowed the captain into the horn, sending two men out into the fury. "If that second line breaks, we're done," he confided to Bisia.

She had never been on the ocean before and now cursed the fate that had put her on this one. What was she doing here? How had it come to pass that she found herself lost on the Atlantic in the middle of a massive storm? Yet what lay behind had proven no less dangerous, and remaining in Europe held even fewer promises than the unknown toward which she now headed.

With safety lines attached to their waists, the two merchant seamen struggled forward, legs splayed, heads down, as they inched toward the stricken truck. The crest of each breaking wave tore off as it battered the ship, transforming into a lashing swarm like some biblical pestilence.

Turning to Bisia, the captain tried to calm her with a wink. Then, with his hands hard against the wheel, he returned his gaze to the two beams of light knifing into the blackened night.

There was no let-up in the storm throughout the night as the ship heaved through the mountainous seas. It labored as it pitched and rolled; solid walls of water pounded the deck, sounding like a big bass drum every time one struck.

During his tense vigil on December 20th, Isham received official notification from the War Department Adjutant General's office they had awarded him the Silver Star medal for his action on Hill 840 in Italy in September the year before. The *St. Louis Post-Dispatch* printed news of Isham's decoration as far back as August, but four months passed as the army corroborated the facts. The citation read: *For gallantry in action on 16 September 1944, near Mt. Calvi, Italy: Lieutenant Reavis was commanding a rifle platoon in an attack on a strongly fortified enemy hill. Courageously leading his men through intense artillery, mortar, and small arms fire, he took the hill against fanatical enemy resistance. He personally knocked out one machine gun, killing one officer and two men and capturing two prisoners. The enemy immediately launched a vicious counterattack in such force that reinforcements were necessary to hold his position. Lieutenant Reavis had no communication and did not receive this message. Small arms fire, heard for some time after, indicated he did everything in his power to avoid an inevitable annihilation or capture by a very superior enemy force. Lieutenant Reavis' gallantry, determination, and devotion to duty reflect great honor on himself and country.*

The Silver Star brought Isham's service in line with Bisia's two Polish citations for bravery: The Gold Cross of Merit with Swords, and the Cross of Valor. But with so much occupying his mind — Bisia so close, yet lost at sea — he didn't dwell on news of his award. His concentration was unwavering.

Belgian Unity never docked in New York City, as it was off-course and lost for days. Finally, on Wednesday, January 2, 1946, Bisia received a radio telegram out of Chatham, Massachusetts from Isham's brother Burton in New York City.

"I will meet you in Boston when you arrive on Friday. Welcome to America."

It was the most welcome message I may have ever received. And it brought me closer to Isham, to have a brother as kind as this.

As the New Year of 1946 turned, Isham's mother Lena Reavis returned to her diary, summing up what many, many millions of people were thinking.

The old year is over. It has brought sorrow and happiness to me and everyone. But, all in all, it has been a good year for the world as a whole, for it saw the ending of the war for all of us. There is much unrest, strikes, etc., but I am hoping that this is only a temporary thing, and everybody, the people of the whole world, will work together now for the good of humanity everywhere.

Isham's little wife is expected to arrive on January 4th. I hope her health has improved, for the child has had so much to endure these war years that it is surprising she has stood up as well as she has so far. Burton is scheduled to meet her and put her on the train for St. Louis. We are praying she will like us as much as we are prepared to love and protect her in her new country and home.

~ Bisia ~

Belgian Unity finally entered Boston Harbor on January 4, 1946.

And, bless his heart, Isham's brother Burton was there to fish me out.

The first place Burton took her was to an Irish bar for a drink before heading to South Station and the train to New York City.

He was so nice. After meeting Monique de Nerveau, he wanted to marry her. I stayed with a married couple who lived in the same building as Burton. The next morning, I told him I needed some cosmetics, so he took me to Elizabeth Arden on Fifth Avenue.

She walked into the plush Fifth Avenue shop dressed in a captured German flier's coat with a fur collar. She surprised the women in the store because, though she presented as a refugee, as Isham previously noted, she spoke French with a perfect accent as she inquired about her purchases.

Bisia stayed in New York City for a day and a half to organize herself, after which Burton escorted her to Grand Central Station on 42nd and Park Street to catch New York Central Railroad's No. 11 Southwestern Limited train to St. Louis. She carried two bags now, one more than when she docked.

"A friend of Isham's is a conductor on this train," Burton said. "He will look out after you. His name is Harold."

"This is Elisabeth, Isham's new wife from Poland," Burton said as the conductor approached.

"Well, hello, Elisabeth," Harold said, offering his hand.

His manners shocked me. Not only was he a conductor — what class of people had friends as train conductors? But he also called me by my first name. No one cack home would do such a thing. It takes years to reach this level of intimacy. It all scared me a great deal.

The No. 11 Southwestern Limited left Grand Central at 7:30 p.m., emerging into the dark, snow-covered country beyond. It traveled west along the Hudson River, bound for Albany, arriving at 10:21 p.m. As Bisia slept in her Pullman compartment, the train passed through Syracuse and Buffalo heading for Cleveland's Union Depot, scheduled to arrive at 6:20 the next morning.

Throughout the night, beneath the gentle sway of the train, memories turned like a broken wheel in Bisia's dreams. Clunk! Clunk! Clunk! Lesko! Stratyn! Żagórz! Her heart bled for what she and her country had lost, "the shining and tragic goal of noble effort", as Joseph Conrad wrote in his note to the first edition of his 1915 novel, *Victory*.

Yet if she stayed, happiness would surely have proven elusive, as well. And the frustrations she felt as a girl in Poland would remain, too, as they were as much a part of her being as the high spirits of her friendships. To everyone and anyone she would ever meet, she would have to explain why or who she was, because her accent labeled her as different.

Like New York City itself, the sheer vastness of America struck Bisia as a first impression. When she awoke and looked out on the open stretches of America's Midwest between Cleveland and Indianapolis, hope, fear, and optimism all mingled in her mind. Not much showed through the windows of the train, only the stark contrast between the reds, grays, and blacks of the majestic stations in the cities and the whiteness of the snow and barren browns of the landscape in between.

"What am I doing on this train out in the middle of nowhere?" she asked herself more than once. It was the same question she asked while riding atop the boxcar, escaping from Kraków with her cousin Henryk.

Yet over the next sixty-three years, America would show its welcome to Bisia without reservation, and life would grace her with many blessings. Still, an implacable sadness would attend her days, too, as she would always struggle to recapture some lost something, even if she couldn't identify exactly what the something was, or if it even existed beyond her imagination.

The train entered Indianapolis's Union station (opened in 1888) at 10:35 A.M., then continued on to Terre Haute, Indiana before crossing Illinois bound for St. Louis.

Isham dressed in a new, dark gray suit before walking two blocks up Pershing Avenue to check his reservation at the Branscome Hotel. Afterward, he hopped aboard a streetcar heading downtown, arriving at Union Station on 20th & Market Street around 3 P.M., one hour before Bisia's scheduled arrival at 3:55.

The crowds were so thick you weren't able to bend down to pick up your handkerchief if you dropped it.

At the time of its completion in 1894, Union Station in St. Louis was the largest train station in the world, fitting for a city at the geographic center of a continental-sized nation. During the war years, Union Station streamed 100,000 people through its doors each day.

While waiting for his bride, Isham considered the improbability of their story. He and Bisia spent only ten days together before marrying, another eleven days before having to separate. Now, after all the paperwork, missed letters, her escape and frightful ocean crossing, she was on her way.

Some 20 hours after leaving New York City, Bisia crossed the Mississippi River over historic Eads Bridge, and arrived in St. Louis around 4 P.M. on January 7, 1946. As her train clanged into Union Station, the anxiety hidden below her anticipation surfaced like a bubble released to the boil. The thought, "what world is this?" rushed through her mind.

How will I manage the language, the customs, and with no place to live except with a mother-in-law I have never met...? There was nobody I could call to say, 'meet me tomorrow, so we can talk'. Everything was internal.

As he waited on the platform, Isham kept telling himself, 'I'll recognize her, I'll recognize her.' He kept repeating it. Bisia also worried whether she would recognize Isham. He had been so thin the last time she saw him. But when the train came to a stop, and the passengers began filing off, both knew the other immediately.

As Bisia stepped off the train, Isham pushed through the crowd to greet her. They embraced for the first time since he departed Lublin in March the year before. Amidst the echoing sounds of the crowd and the trains, their world settled, if only for a short while, in the warmth of the other's arms. Isham took her bags and led her, arm-in-arm, through the throng.

Seeing him, to land some place, was such a relief.

Isham would arrange new clothing for her in the days ahead: whatever she needed, whatever she wanted. Her English was better than Isham remembered, but still not fluent. He realized she would be in for an adventure because there was so little from which to draw in this new life in America.

As they walked out of Union Station onto Market Street in search of a cab on a cold winter's day, with the weak winter sun setting off to the west, Isham realized the world he chose so quickly in Lublin, Poland, would now center on Bisia in St. Louis, as best he could manage it. He wouldn't go back to work in the hotel business. Hotel work required crazy hours, and it wouldn't be right.

Freedom, the dream they both fought and almost died for, would expand in the coming decades, at least in America.

"Because of the tremendous number of us in the army and other services, the army will run this country after the war," Isham wrote to his brother. *"We won't be subject to the same raw deal the men caught after the last war. If we band together — and it gives all indications of such, as soldiers talk of it now and again — 10,000,000 men and the votes they will command in their own families will be a tremendous power."*

Isham had made a week-long reservation at the Branscome Hotel near the apartment on Pershing. He wanted to give Bisia as easy a transition as possible. Though they were husband and wife, Bisia and Isham essentially remained strangers, refugees thrown together in the crucible of war.

As they walked, Bisia took in the strange new city with its wide roads, large buildings, and bundled-up bodies pushing their way along the cold pavement. They were bodies belonging to people whose histories she could never share or even imagine. The clothing they wore, the words and accents emerging from their faces, both black and white, was so different. Even the sounds of traffic whirred by at a new pitch.

What could I think? Where have I come? Where will I go?

She bolstered herself with the knowledge through all the apprehensive moments she had experienced over the last six years; she had come out the other end whole. Yet she could also see her beloved Poland abandoned on the rocks of political expedience by Roosevelt and Churchill in Yalta, left to suffer another long reign of occupation, though her people would never surrender.

Now, here she was alone with a husband she barely knew in a land about which she knew even less, a land where no decision she ever made would instinctively be correct, because a part of her would always linger in the land from which she had come.

Bisia arrived in a land where she could never say, "Do you remember?" to anyone. For years, the question would seem but an echo of a long-lost dream. She was now on an island, and the island was she.

> *Please, tell me, who am I?*
> *Who?*
> *A child, led by the hand*
> *In some fairy castle land?*
> *A reluctant scholar,*
> *From a long-vanished school*
> *Bucking at every conceivable rule?*
> *A soldier who battled*
> *On barricades high,*
> *For Utopia,*
> *For freedom,*
> *That never was won?*
> *Am I a wife?*
> *Will I be a mother?*
> *A friend?*
> *Who am I?*
> *Can you tell me?*
> *Do you understand?*
> *That I am*
> *Lost?*

The apprehension she felt was real. As relieved as she was by Isham's devotion, the question, "How will this work out?" stretched out before her like the barriers she had once jumped on horseback with her brother, Stas.

As she walked arm-in-arm with Isham along Market Street in St. Louis, Missouri, in the developing winter of 1946, Bisia swore she would prove to everyone she could make it. She swore it to herself, as well. The mind is stronger than the circumstance; she reminded herself. You are the master of your own fate, as Kipling would say, and now it would be up to Bisia to prove its truth once again.

END

PostScript

Throughout their 63 years together in St. Louis, Mom and Pop lived both happily and not. Their union produced three children: Teresa (b. January 10, 1947), me (b. January 2, 1948), and Marek(b. June 18, 1951). In time, their family expanded to seven grandchildren and nine great-grandchildren.

After Marek entered kindergarten in 1955, Mom began teaching French at the City House Sacred Heart Academy in St. Louis. When told of her daughter's new position, Bisia's mother in Poland said, "And what would you know enough to teach?" Once again, the respect Mom fought so hard to attain as a girl remained elusive, even as an adult with children of her own.

Teresa, Mom, and me, 1950

Despite her own mother's doubts, Bisia taught two generations of young women over a forty-year career, first at City House through 1968. Then, after City House closed, she went to Villa Duchesne in the suburbs until her retirement in 1994.

These all-girls academies were sister schools to the Zbylitowska Gora Sacre Cœur boarding school Bisia attended as a girl in Poland.

Pop didn't return to the hotel business after the war. The indeterminate schedules of hotel work wouldn't have been fair to Bisia as she managed a new life in a new country. Instead, Pop spent his professional career as a gemologist at Mermod, Jaccard, and King Jewelers until his retirement in 1987. He also maintained his commission in the U.S. Army

Teresa, Pop, Marek & me, 1954

Reserves, rising to the rank of Lt. Colonel, before retiring on October 11, 1971, his 60th birthday.

On April 20, 2009, Bisia died as she lived, fighting, passing from lung and stomach cancer at age 87.

Pop outlived Mom by 13 months, passing from a stroke on May 17, 2010, at age 98. His ashes were interred with military honors alongside Mom's at the Jefferson Barracks National Cemetery in St. Louis, Missouri, U.S.A.

***

Toni Reavis

Lie Down to Your Rest, Dear Soldiers

Bisia & Isham: Christmas Day 2008

Lie down to your rest, dear soldiers,
Be at ease, for the battles have been won.
Take pride in your service, well given,
Take measure of the peace that's begun.

The days of campaigning are over,
Long nights of worry now through,
From those who remain at your station,
A salute, for our heroes were you.

'twas honor we witnessed in your service,
And dignity in the manner as done,
An example to carry now forward,
A legacy for daughter and sons.

Responsibility was your generation's true calling,
Through challenges of Depression then war.
Yet through all the deprivations and hardships,
The vicissitudes you steadfastly bore.

It's that spirit of dedication that reminds us,
As we look back to honor you anew,

The Countess & The P.O.W.

How any could have asked for others,
As constant and steadfast as you.

And we who loved you most dearly,
We who now stand in your stead,
Accept your legacy well knowing,
Soon comes our time to pass it ahead.

Thus, if rewards are apportioned in like spirit,
And judgment remains constant and true,
Then your honors stand at full measure,
While ours remain to accrue.

So, lie down to rest, dear soldiers,
In our hearts, there will always remain,
Service to family and country,
As your loving, everlasting refrain.

END

Jefferson Barracks National Cemetery, St. Louis, MO.

~Author's Note~

This book took many years to complete. Fallow stretches followed periods of fact gathering and writing. Yet even when the material sat unattended, giving way to the necessities of career and family, I always returned to the task, often at the insistence of friends who encouraged me throughout the long process.

Mostly, I gathered the material through the blind of telephone conversations from my home in Boston, Massachusetts, to my hometown of St. Louis, Missouri, where, in the comfort of their own environment, Mom and Pop could reminisce at their ease. I also spoke candidly with many relatives on both sides of the family, all of whom offered invaluable help and good humor.

Whenever I returned home for holidays, I would sort through letters and family photos to gain greater detail and supporting information. Fortunately, my paternal grandmother, Lena Stites Reavis (21 Sept. 1868-4 Feb. 1968), kept all the letters Pop wrote home during his time in the army from 1942 to 1945. These letters proved a wealth of primary documentation. Grandma also kept her own war diary, affording me another contemporaneous glimpse of life on the home-front.

Perhaps most rewarding were my trips to Poland in the company of my mother to visit her family, all of whom were of immeasurable aid in reconstructing life before and during the war.

Our first trip came in March 1987, when the World Cross Country Championships were contested in Warsaw. I attended as a reporter, but also to avail myself of the opportunity to interview family members and search family archives. During that first trip, I didn't have the chance to travel beyond Warsaw to see the countryside where Mom was born, reared, and fought. Nor could I visit Lublin, where Mom and Pop met and married.

That opportunity came in the summer of 1993 after the dissolution of the Soviet Union in 1989. With the fall of the Iron Curtain, visas were no longer required to visit Poland.

Again, with Mom in tow, I landed in Warsaw where the blossoms of freedom were now in full bloom. From Warsaw, we drove 350 kilometers to Kraków, then another 300 kilometers to Lesko, the ancestral home of the Krasicki family. There, the land remained much the same as it has over the centuries. The primary exception was the family's 16th-century castle, which the communist government turned into a pensioner's hotel.

Next, we journeyed to Lublin, 250 kilometers north, to visit the Artists' Cafe where Mom and Pop first met, Saints Peter and Paul Church where they married, and the Europa Hotel where they held their small reception.

Special thanks to my sister Teresa and brother Marek for their tireless advice and support throughout the long journey. Thanks, too, to our late cousins Ignacy Krasicki in Warsaw, the son of Mom's oldest brother Antos, and Jerzy (George) Krasicki in Melbourne, Australia, the son of second-born brother Stas, both of whom helped flesh out details for the Polish side of the story.

My appreciation also extends to the many friends who encouraged me to finish the book, notably Bob Wood of Salt Lake City, Utah, who assisted in the development of the final draft. But it is to the lasting memory and love of Mom and Pop I truly dedicate this book.

October 11, 2022

(Pop's 111th birthday)

~Selected Bibliography~

Conrad, Joseph, *Victory*, The Modern Library 1915
Davies, Norman, *Heart of Europe–A Short History of Poland*, Oxford University Press 1984
Dando-Collins, Stephen, *The Big Break: The Greatest American WWII P.O.W. Escape Story*, St. Martin's Press 2017
Eisenhower, Dwight, *Crusade in Europe*, Doubleday 1948
Garliński, Józef, *The Survival of Love, Memoirs of a Resistance Officer*, Basil Blackwell Ltd. 1991
Irwin, Will, *Abundance of Valor–Resistance, Survival, and Liberation*, Presidio Press - March 2010
Kilzer, Louis, *Hitler's Traitor: Martin Bormann and the Defeat of the Reich*, Presidio Press 2000
Kridl, Manfred, *A Survey of Polish Literature and Culture*, Columbia University Press 1956
MacMillan, Margaret, *Six Months That Changed the World*, Random House Trade 2003
Ostrowski, Jan K., *Kraków*, Wydawnictwa Artystyczne I Filmowe 1992
Paul, Allen, *Katyn, the Untold Story of Stalin's Polish Massacre*, Scribners 1991
Polonsky, Antony, *Politics in Independent Poland, 1921-1939, The Crisis of Constitutional Government, 1972*
Poteranski, Waclaw, *The Warsaw Ghetto*, Interpress Publishers 1968
Rings, Werner, *Life With the Enemy, Collaboration and Resistance in Hitler's Europe 1939-1945*, Doubleday 1982
Schlesinger, Arthur, *The Cycles of American History*, Houghton Mifflin Co. 1986
Sharp, Samuel L, *Poland–White Eagle on a Red Field*, Harvard University Press 1953
Smith, Gene, *The Dark Summer: An Intimate History of the Events That Led to World War II*, Collier Books 1989
The Story of the Powder River 91st Infantry Division, August 1917–January 1945
War Department Field Manual FM 7-20 1944–*Infantry Battalion*
Zamoyski, Adam, *The Polish Way*, Hippocrene Books 1987
World War II Axis Military History Day-by-Day
Bourneuf, Jr., Gus, *Workhorse of the Fleet, A History of the Liberty Ships*, American Bureau of Shipping 1990
Prisoners of War Bulletin, Vol. 2, NO. 9 Sept. 1944
War letters of Isham Reavis, 1942-1945
War diary of Lena Stites Reavis, 1939-1945
Toni Reavis journals and taped telephone interviews, 1985–2009

~ Chronology ~

June 1939 - Bisia completes Sacred Heart boarding school
Sept. 1, 1939 - German invasion of Poland begins WWII
Sept. 10, 1939 - Bisia travels east to Stratyn
Sept. 17, 1939 - Russian invasion of Poland from the east
Oct. 3, 1939 – Krasicki family moves west from Lesko to Zagórz
Spring 1940 – Russians massacre Polish officers in Katyn Forest
June 21, 1941 - Germany attacks Russia
Aug. 1941 - Bisia moves to Nowy Sącz
Dec. 7, 1941 - Japanese attack Pearl Harbor
Feb. 1942 - Armia Krajowa, the Polish Home Army founded
March 1942 - Isham signs up for service in St. Louis
July 17, 1942 - Feb. 2, 1943 - Siege of Stalingrad
Jan. 12, 1943 - Zosia's wedding in Zagórz to George Garapich
Feb. 20, 1943 - Isham enters OCS, Ft. Benning, Ga.
March 1943–Bisia sworn into Armia Krajowa
April 1943 - Stalin breaks w/ Polish government-in-exile over Katyn Massacre accusations
April 19, 1943 - Jewish ghetto Insurrection begins in Warsaw
May 16, 1943 - Jewish Insurrection brutally suppressed
May 29, 1943 - Isham graduates OCS as 2nd lieutenant
June 6, 1944 - D-Day, Allied forces invade Europe
July 1, 1944 - Isham sails for Europe
Aug. 1, 1944 - Warsaw Insurrection begins
Aug. 7, 1944 - Soviet army reaches Vistula River
Sep. 1944 - Eastern front moves west through Lesko
          - Bisia's AK unit in skirmish with Germans
Sep.16, 1944 - Isham captured in Po Valley in northern Italy
Sep.19, 1944 - Russians disband Poland's Armia Krajowa unit OP-23
Oct. 2, 1944 - Warsaw insurrection crushed the city destroyed
Oct. 1944 - Isham imprisoned in Stalag VII/A outside Munich
Nov. 1944 - Bisia to Chelm Lubelski to join Berling Division
Dec.28, 1944 - Isham moved from Stalag VII/A to Oflag 64

Jan. 17, 1945 - Kraków liberated by Russians, Warsaw, too
Jan. 21, 1945–1400 American officers evacuated from Oflag 64
Jan. 28, 1945 - Isham and Billy Ferencz escape from German forces
Feb. 4, 1945 - Yalta Conference begins
Feb.14, 1945 - Bisia and Isham meet in Lublin, Poland
Feb.25, 1945 - Bisia and Isham marry in Lublin
Mar. 6, 1945 - Isham evacuated from Odessa, Russia
May 2, 1945 - Fall of Berlin
May 7, 1945 - War in Europe ends with Germany's surrender
May   1945 - Bisia moves her parents to Kraków from Zagórz
June   1945 - Bisia begins her escape from Poland
Jul. 9, 1945 - Isham hears from U.S. authorities in Czechoslovakia
Jul.17, 1945 - Potsdam Conference begins
Aug.6, 1945 - Atomic bomb dropped on Hiroshima
Aug.15, 1945 - V.J. Day ends World War II
Dec. 4, 1945 - Bisia sails for America
Jan. 4, 1946 - Bisia lands in Boston, Massachusetts, U.S.A.
Jan. 7, 1946 - Bisia arrives by train in St. Louis, Missouri
Jan. 10, 1947 - Teresa Reavis born
Jan. 2, 1948 - Toni Reavis born
June 18, 1951 - Marek Reavis born
Oct.11, 1971–Isham retires from U.S. Army Reserves as Lt. Colonel
        1972 - Bisia becomes U.S. citizen
Apr. 20, 2009 - Bisia dies at age 87 in St. Louis
May 10, 2010 - Isham dies at age 98 in St. Louis

***

~INDEX~

91st Infantry Division, 99, *See* Powder River Division
Africa Korps, 63
American Fifth Army, 84
American Third Army, 186
Anders, General Władysław, 196
Anschluss, Austrian union with Germany, 4, 22, 45
Anti-Comintern Pact, 22
anti-war movement, 25
Antwerp, 191, 199, 200, 202
Apennine Mountains, 99
Armia Krajowa, Polish Home Army, 44, 66, 67, 68, 89, 94, 122
Arno River, 99
Artists' Cafe, 140
Auschwitz, 160
Bal estate, 36, 38
Bal, Maria, 37
Bal, Stanislaw and Maria, 33
Baltic Sea, 12, 22, 126
Baranowka, 74
Baroness Lipowska von Lipowitz. *See* Krasicka, Adija, wife of Bisia's brother Antos
Barretts of Wimpole, 121
Bastogne, Belgium, 121
Battle of Nuremberg, 189
Battle of the Bulge, 121
Bavarian theory, 37
Bay of Naples, 98
Bazanowka, 94
Beck, Colonel Józef, Polish Foreign Minister, 17
Beer Hall Putsch, 3
Belgian Unity, 1, 2, 202, 203, 205
Bełżec, death camp, 58
Berchtesgaden, 61, 165
Berlin, 135, 165, 187

Berling Division, 152, 165
Berling, General Zygmunt, 112, 122
Bern, Switzerland, 153
Besko, 74, 76, 87
Bieszczady, 55, 111
Birkenau, 160
Black Dragon Howitzers, 101
Black Sea, 157
Blitzkrieg, 36, 44
Bohemia, 4
Bór-Komorowski, General Tadeusz, 112, 113
Boston Harbor, 162, 206
Bradshaw, Preston J., 59
Branscome Hotel, 208
Braun, Eva, 164
Bretton Woods Conference, 96
British 8th Army, 84
British Army of the Rhine, 190, 196
Brownshirts, 3
Brussels, 192
Burgon, John William, 98
Bydgoszcz, 136, 138
Bystrzyca River, 138
Camp Fannin, 177, 192
Camp Livingston, 85, 100
Camp Wolters, 62
Casablanca, 82
Chamberlain, Neville, 22, 30
Chelm, 122
Chopin, Frédéric, 47
Churchill, Winston, 30, 63, 96, 115, 135, 142, 169
Cieszyn, 22, 179, 180, 181
City House, 212
Clark, General Mark, 96
Clay, General Lucius D., 186
Cloth Hall, 168
Communist Russia, 37
Conrad, Joseph, 207

Crosby, Bing, 97
Cross of Valor, Polish medal, 93, 205
Crowell, Colonel Pat, 188, 190, 191, 199
Czechoslovakia, 22, 180, 181
Czulnia, 55
Danzig
    Free city on the Baltic Sea, 12
Dardanelles, 161
D-Day, 96
Deluge, 54
Dewey, Thomas, 99
DiMaggio, Joe, 82
Dmitrius, Colonel Sasha, 152
Dresden, Germany, 140
Dukla Pass, 16
Dulles, Allen. *See* head of American OSS
Dunkirk, 196
Dzianott, Jan, called Kanty, 66, 67, 87
Eads Bridge, 208
Édouard Daladier, French Prime Minister, 23
Eisenhower, General Dwight D., 63
El Alamein campaign, 63
Emperor Ferdinand II, 18
Falls City, 26, 29, 30, 106, 130
Fascist Germany, 37
FDR. *See* Roosevelt, Franklin D.
Ferdinand Maximilian, Austrian Archduke, 42
Ferencz, Billy, 118, 128
Forest Park, 30, 59, 172, 174
Fort Benning, 81, 177
Fort Leonard Wood, 61
France, 4, 23, 99, 202
Frank, Hans - overseer, General Gouvernment, 166
Futa Pass, 99, 101
Garapich, George, 111, 124, 165
Garapich, Zosia
    Bisia's sister, 53
    Bisia's sister, 5, 7, 9, 11, 32, 41
    Bisia's sister, 57
    Bisia's sister, 69
    Bisia's sister, 74
    Bisia's sister, 124
    Bisia's sister, 158
    Bisia's sister, 165
Gates, Delmar, 62, 174
Gatesworth Hotel, 25, 30, 59, 62
General Gouvernment, 89, 166
Geneva Convention, 155, 156, 197

George Washington's farewell address to Congress, 25
German Chancellor, 61
Germany's Fourth Paratroop Division, 101
Gestapo, 45, 47, 49, 50, 56, 69, 70, 73, 76, 78
Gigandet, Molly, 202
Gleiwitz, Poland, 23
Goebbels, Joseph, 37, 116, 176
Goering, Hermann, 37
Going My Way, movie, 97
Gold Cross of Merit with Swords, Polish medal, 205
Goode, Colonel Paul, 127
Gothic Line, 99, 101
Government of the Republic of Poland in exile, 33
government-in-exile, 33, 44, 45, 66, 88, 94, 111, 122, 192
Grand Central Station, 206
Grant, Ulysses S., 28
Great Depression, 25, 26
Gruszka, 55
Gubrynowicz, Baron Adam, 42
Gusia. *See* Bisia's sister-in-law. Stas' wife
Hammelburg, Germany, 128
Hemingway, Ernest, 31
Hess, Rudolf, 37
Hill 840, 101, 175, 205
Hindenburg, Paul von, German President, 4
Historical Institute of the Polish Academy of Sciences, 88
Hitler, Adolph, 3, 22, 23, 37, 61, 69, 84, 99, 113, 165, 179
Hoczew, 55
Holy Roman Empire, 20
Hot Springs, Arkansas, 166
Hotel Europa, 152
Huzele, 41, 53
International Monetary Fund, 96
Iron Curtain, 169, 216
Isham, Mary, 28
Isle of Capri, 98
Jasło, 67
Jefferson Barracks National Cemetery, 213, 215
Jewish Insurrection, 123
Jewish-Bolshevism, 37
Jews, 16, 37, 44, 57, 136, 137, 159
Jodl, General Alfred, 176
Katyn Forest, 88
Kawiarnia Cafe, 144

Kcynia, 128, *See* Exin
Keller, Mary, Isham's sister, 27, 162
kennkarte, 91, 92
Kesselring, Field Marshal Albert, 84, 99
Kilgore, Mary, Isham's maternal grandmother, 27
Kipling, Rudyard, 211
Kluge, Field Marshal Günther von, 99
Kmita, Peter, Great Crown Marshal of Poland, 16
KMOX radio, 64
kochana, 202
Kosciuszko Division, 112, 122, 169
Kowalski, Jan. *See* Jas Krasicki, Bisia's brother
Kowalski, Jan, brother Jas's nom de guerre, 90
Kraków, 165, 166, 167
Krasicka, Adija
  wife of Bisia's brother Antos, 34
Krasicka, Elka
  wife of Bisia's brother Xavier, 11, 44, 112, 123, 168, 169
Krasicka, Gusia
  wife of Bisia's brother Stas, 5, 11, 44, 65, 69, 110, 140, 141, 142, 146, 151, 158, 196, 197
Krasicka, Izabela, Bisia's mother, 14, 65, 170
Krasicka, Magdalena
  daughter of Bisia's brother Xavier & Elka, 44, 123
Krasicki family, 16, 18, 41, 44, 45
Krasicki lodge, 44, 109
Krasicki, Andrzej
  Bisia's nephew, Jas and Gusia's son, 5, 44, 197
Krasicki, Antoni, known as Antos
  Bisia's oldest brother, 13, 23, 32, 34, 35
Krasicki, August
  Bisia's father, 8, 12, 19, 39, 40, 43, 68, 69, 74, 110, 158, 170
Krasicki, Bishop Ignacy, 47
Krasicki, Jan, known as Jas
  Bisia's brother, 8, 9, 13, 18, 44, 51, 69, 70, 90, 122, 124, 154
Krasicki, Jerzy

Bisia's nephew, Stas and Gusia's son, 5, 44, 65, 197
Krasicki, Jerzy, family ancestor, 18
Krasicki, Kazimierz 'Kasik', 17
Krasicki, Stas
  Bisia's brother, 196
  Bisia's brother, 5, 10, 13, 38, 44, 69, 190, 193
Krasicki, Xavier, 44
  Bisia's brother, 11, 44, 112, 123, 154, 168
Kriegsgefangener,, 119
Krosno, 16
Kuba, 194
La Poloma, 42, 43
Latvian SS, 129
Laval, Premier Pierre. *See* Vichy Regime
Le Kremlin Rouge, 199
League of Nations, 19
Lesko, 1, 3, 4, 16, 19, 29, 32, 38, 39, 41, 43, 76, 171
Liberty Ships, 203
Lincoln, Abraham, 29, 156
Lindbergh, Charles, 31
Łobżenica, 129
Lopez, Major George, 186, 188, 190, 200, 201
Lublin, 137, 138, 139, 140, 142, 153, 170, 209
Lublin Committee, 122
Luftwaffe, 23, 24, 51
Lwow, 39, 44, 67
Maczek, General Stanisław, 190
Maginot Line, French line of defense, 23, 196
Malczewski, Jacek, 38
Malta, 61
Market Square, 165
Maudlin, Bill, 100
Mediterranean, 96
Mermod, Jaccard, and King Jewelers, 212
Metropolitan Opera, 142
Michałówska, Anna
  Bisia's cousin, 5, 6, 8, 11, 33, 38, 42
Michałówski, Zygmund
  Bisia's cousin, 42, 190, 192, 198
Mickiewicz, Adam, poet, 19, 166
Miracle of the Vistula, 19, 24
Model, Field Marshal Walter, 99
Molotov-Ribbentrop Pact, 21, 38
Montgomery, General Bernard, 63
Moosburg, Germany, 118

Moravia, 4
Morawski, Andrzej, Bisia's friend, 51, 52, 107, 147
Morgenthau Plan, 115
Mościcki, Ignacy, Polish President, 32
Moscow, 137, 147
Mount Vesuvius, 98
Mr. Szymański, 138, 149
Mt. Calvi, 101, 205
Munich, 3, 179
Munich Agreement, 22, 179
Muny Opera, 59
Mussolini, Benito, Italian Prime Minister, 3, 61, 84, 99
Naples, 99, 161
Nazi Party, 3, 45
Nemaha Creek, 131
Nerveau, Monique de, 202
New York City, 202, 206
Niebieszczany, 51
NKVD, Soviet secret police, 89, 167
non-aggression pact, 12, 23, 37
North African Campaign, 96
Nowy Sącz, 49, 50, 51, 57, 74
Nuremberg, 185, 189, 201
Nuremberg Rallies, 189
OCS, Officer Candidate School, 63, 81
Odessa, 147, 155, 157
Oflag 21B, 127
Oflag 64, 127, 133
Oflag XIII/B, 128
Olza River, 180
Operation Overlord, 96
Operation Reinhardt, 137
Operation Storm, 111, 112
Operation Tempest, 93
Operation Weiss, 23
P.O.W. camp, 68
Paderewski, Ignacy, 19
Pan Janek, 8, 13
Pan Tadeusz, Adam Mickiewicz' epic poem, 19
Patton, General George, 186
Pearl Harbor, 58, 60
Peter Pan, 97
Picea Krasiciana, 21
Piłsudski, Józef, Polish Chief of State 1918-1922, 4, 19, 23
Piłsudski's Polish Legions, 4
Plac Unia Lubelska, 140
Polish Armed Forces of the West, 196

Polish Committee of National Liberation, 137
Polish Corridor, 12, 22
Polish Legions, 19
Polish People's Army, 122, 141
Polish-Russo War, 171
Poraz, 46
Potocki Palace, 167
Potsdam, 187
Potsdam Conference, 187
Powder River Division, 99
Poźniak, Jas, 76, 77
Praga suburb, 112
Prague, 182, 183
Prussia, 12, 22, 37
Przemyśl, 44, 68
Raczkiewicz, Marshal Władysław, 33
Raczynski, Count Edward, 186
Reavis, Annie Dorrington, 30
Reavis, Burton Isham, Isham's father, 29
Reavis, Burton, Isham's younger brother, 25, 30, 62, 205, 206
Reavis, Edward Jr., 28
Reavis, Judge Isham, 27, 28
Reavis, Lena. *See* Isham's mother
Reavis, Lena, Isham's mother, 25, 29, 121, 162, 206
Reavis, Marek, 212
Reavis-Wetzel,Teresa, 212
Red Army, 43, 94, 111, 127, 133, 153
Red Cross, 89, 120
Reichsgraf, Imperial Count, 40
Reilly, Jimmy, 63, 81, 172
Rheims, France, 177
Rhineland, 4
Riefenstahl, Leni, 189
RKU, 141
Rogala, Krasicki family crest, 33
Rolin, Nicole, 202
Romer, Rudus, 66
Rommel, General Erwin, 63
Roosevelt, Franklin D., 31, 61, 99, 115, 135, 142, 162, 187
Rotewald, Hans, 48
Russo-Polish War, 19
Sabejski, Father Stefan, 151
Saints Peter and Paul Church, 151
San River, 3, 16, 40, 41, 42, 53
Sanok, Polish city, 16, 23, 69, 76, 89
Sawyer, Tom, 97
Schmidt, Oskar, 74, 75, 76

Schneider, Oberst Fritz, Stalag VII/A Camp Commander, 127, 132
Schuschnigg, Austrian Chancellor Kurt von, 45
Second Polish Republic, 24
Selective Service Act, 31, 59
Service, Robert, 126
Sikorski, General Władysław, 33
Silver Star, 205
Sobanska, Maja, 170
Sobanski Palace, 112
Sobanski, Henryk, 168
Soldatin books, 110
Sosnkowski, General Kazimierz, 112
Soviet 1st Belorussian Front, 165
Soviet 242nd Armoured Brigade, 111
St. Antoni of Padua, 151
St. Louis, 25, 26, 62, 172, 175, 208, 212, 213
St. Louis Post-Dispatch, 205
St. Mary's Basilica, 167, 179
Stadnicki Palace, 50
Stadnickis, Krasicki cousins, 49
Stalag VII/A, 118, 119, 126
Stalin, Joseph, 22, 37, 38, 94, 96, 112, 135, 142, 169, 187
Stratyn, Krasicki property, 4, 32, 38
Stuka, 51
    German warplane, 34, 35
Sudetenland, 4, 22, 179
Suez Canal, 61
Sušice, 184
Szlaszewski, Stefan, 23
Szubin, Poland, 126, *See* Szubin
Tarnów, 49, 168
Tatra Mountains, 49
The Victory of Faith, Reifenstahl film, 189
Third Reich, 91, 164
Thirty Years' War, 181
Tokyo, 150
Treblinka, 160
Triple Entente, 21
Triumph of the Will, Reifenstahl film, 189
Truman, Harry, 162, 187
Tuligłowy, 33
U.S. 8th Air Force, 135
U.S. Army, 26, 59
U.S. Department of Labor, 26
U.S. Dept. of Justice, 164
U.S. Seventh Army, 189
U.S.S. Wakefield, 162
unconditional surrender, 176
Union Station, 208
University of Nebraska, 26
V-2, 202
Valentine's Day, 140
Versailles, 3, 19
Versailles Treaty, 22, 24
Vichy, 99
Victory. See Conrad, Joseph
Viditz-Ward, Lieutenant Anton, 185, 200
Vietinghoff, General Heinrich von, 153
Villa Duchesne, 212
Vistula River, 112, 137
V-J Day, 177
Walnut Room, 59, 60
Warsaw, 89, 126, 137
Warsaw Ghetto Uprising, 113
Warsaw Uprising, 112, 137
Wehrmacht, 24
Werszctein, Roma, 123
Wiktor, Olga, 140
Williams, Ted, 82
Willkie, Wendell, 31
Wilmeth, Colonel James, 147, 153, 183
Winken, Blinken, and Nod, 97
Winogrodzki, Adam, 67, 68, 70, 79, 108, 110, 141, 179
Wodzicki Palace, 167
Wolff, General Karl, 153
World Bank, 96
World War I, 21, 23, 25, 54
Yalta, 135, 187
Zagórz, 41, 42, 43, 44, 48, 51, 65
Zasław, 57, 58
Zbylitowska Gora, 212
Zippnow, 130
Złotów, 129
zlotys, 122, 171

***

225

~About the Author~

Toni Reavis is an award-winning broadcaster and writer in the field of athletics and marathon running. He has broadcast major events from around the world for over four decades, while writing for such publications as *Runner's World,* the *Boston Globe, Chicago Tribune, Competitor, Meter,* and *BlackBook* magazines. He has also been a columnist for the *Boston Herald, Running Times,* and *New England Runner.* In 2009, Running USA inducted him into its Hall of Champions.

A St. Louis native, Mr. Reavis currently lives in San Diego, California with his wife, Toya, where he continues to write his tonireavis.com blog, *Wandering in a Running World.* He also serves on the board of directors of the Entoto Foundation, a 501C3 charity that brings healthcare to Ethiopia.

CPSIA information can be obtained
at www.ICGtesting.com
Printed in the USA
BVHW041311210323
660846BV00005B/152